"The love and wisdom of Jesus Christ shine through in June Hunt's practical guide to handling your emotions. But make no mistake. This is no mushy "be-warmed-and-filled" collection of fuzzy anecdotes. June grounds her thoughtful analyses of emotional problems and her practical advice on the bedrock of the Bible. *How to Handle Your Emotions* will build your 'heart muscle' as it shows you how to draw emotional strength from God's Word and His Spirit. So get ready for a spiritual workout. You couldn't ask for a better coach than June Hunt."

—DR. REG GRANT
Professor, Pastoral Ministries
Director, M.A./MC
Dallas Theological Seminary

"If you think you need a counseling degree to offer Biblical help and practical hope to those in your world who are struggling with emotional wounds, think again! June has created a masterful tool that everyone with a heart to help can put to good use."

—DR. ROBERT JEFFRESS
Pastor, First Baptist Church, Dallas, TX

"June Hunt is a woman who leads with her heart—which is why she is such a tender and effective comforter for so many whose hearts are broken. In *How to Handle Your Emotions,* June reminds us that emotional health can be found in the words of the Great Comforter Himself. Thank you, June, for taking us back to where we can all find healing and hope."

—JANET PARSHALL
Host, Janet Parshall's America

"People are increasingly turning to their churches (instead of secular counselors) for help with depression, anxiety, anger, and other emotional challenges. This resource provides a practical biblical avenue for addressing these issues. It is not a collection of simple answers, but rather it honestly confronts the questions raised in these situations. This is an excellent resource for the one enduring these struggles, and for those who would desire to help."

—DR. MICHAEL R. LYLES
Board-certified psychiatrist, Lyles & Crawford Consulting

"If you need a single resource to help family and friends find practical, biblical help for handling anger, depression, fear, grief, rejection, and self-worth, you've come to the right place. June's ability to relate on a warm, sensitive level is both powerful and personal. This is a must-read book to enjoy—and apply!"

—DR. THELMA WELLS
Professor/Speaker/Author
President, A Woman of God Ministries

HOW TO
HANDLE YOUR
EMOTIONS

JUNE HUNT

HARVEST HOUSE PUBLISHERS

EUGENE, OREGON

Cover by Garborg Design Works, Savage, Minnesota

Cover photo © Lee Foster / iStockphoto

This book is not intended to and does not provide nor should be construed to provide medical advice or consultation, but rather offers information for greater understanding of the human condition, spirituality, and interpersonal relationships that may sometimes be affected by biochemical or physiological conditions or diagnoses. Consult with a qualified caregiver regarding any medical questions, diagnoses, or treatments.

HOW TO HANDLE YOUR EMOTIONS
Copyright © 2008 by Hope for the Heart, Inc.
Published by Harvest House Publishers
Eugene, Oregon 97402
www.harvesthousepublishers.com

Library of Congress Cataloging-in-Publication Data
Hunt, June.
How to handle your emotions / June Hunt.
    p. cm.
Includes bibliographical references
ISBN-13: 978-0-7369-2328-6
ISBN-10: 0-7369-2328-4
1. Emotions—Religious aspects—Christianity. I. Title.
BV4597.3.H86 2008
248.4—dc22

                                                    2008011726

This book is dedicated to my precious, loving mother who now lives in the presence of the Lord...and who will always live tenderly in my heart. Without a doubt, love is the most powerful of all emotions.

I know few people to "be completely humble and gentle... patient, bearing with one another in love" (Ephesians 4:2)—but this verse describes her perfectly...her humility of heart and sweet surrender to the Savior.

How I thank God for the way He used her compassionate heart and unconditional love in my life.

Acknowledgments

What a privilege to come to work each day without feeling pressed down by the load—not because there isn't always more to do in every 24-hour period than I can possibly accomplish, but because of the joy God has given me just writing what He leads me to write...and because of the dedicated team of co-workers He has provided for the journey. The following individuals make even the toughest tasks seem more manageable...more enjoyable...more intensely interesting. So it is with a heart full of gratitude that I acknowledge:

Angie White, for holding on to the project administratively and working long hours from start to finish to ensure its excellence;

Jill Prohaska and Barbara Spruill, whose grasp of creative ideas, research, writing, and editing enlivened every page;

Elizabeth Gaston and Jeanne Sloan, who were willing and capable of doing whatever the task required;

Rita Smith, for her excellent contributions on nutrition and depression;

Bea Garner and Laura Lyn Benoit, for poring over every page to eliminate errors and guarantee consistency;

Titus O'Bryant, who ensured the accuracy of the manuscript's content and endnotes, going the extra mile to re-search the research;

Connie Steindorf, for keying page after page of revisions...and more revisions;

Kay Deakins, for masterfully juggling the myriad administrative details of my daily workday (and night!) worlds so that I can focus on my challenging tasks;

Steve Miller, for sharing our passion for excellence and demonstrating patience time and again as we tweaked and toiled to get the manuscript "just right"!

The Lord Jesus Christ, for His miraculous transformation from a life of emotional upheaval and pain into a life of joy-filled service.

CONTENTS

THE LIFE GOD
CREATED YOU TO LIVE

Have you ever been told, "Get a handle on your emotions…get a hold of yourself…get a grip!"? Each of these phrases implores us to take control…take charge…take responsibility—and not let our emotions rule over us. That first means getting a firm grasp of the situation. And that's what this book is about: learning how to lay a strong foundation and build a victorious life.

This book—the first in the *Counseling Through the Bible Series*—contains six related topics from HOPE FOR THE HEART's 100-topic **Biblical Counseling Library**. And each topic—called "Biblical Counseling Keys"—is divided into four distinct parts: *Definitions, Characteristics, Causes,* and *Solutions.* Each topic contains both biblical principles and practical steps that will help you be all God created *you to be*…so you can do all He created you to do.

If you've ever flown off the handle with anger, been pressed down by the weight of depression, found yourself fraught with fear…if you've grappled with grief, wrestled with rejection, or struggled with self-worth, then realize this: God has a firm grasp on your situation, and has provided the necessary tools in His Word to help you know *How to Handle Your Emotions.*

Therefore…

> *"Do your best to present yourself to God as one approved,*
> *a workman who does not need to be ashamed*
> *and who correctly handles the word of truth"*
> (2 TIMOTHY 2:15).

Ultimately, this can be a life-changing book enabling you to get a handle on life—the life God created you to live.

Yours in the Lord's hope,
June Hunt

ANGER
Facing the Fire Within 11

Facing the Fire Within

The day begins like any other day, but ends like no other—for on this day, he gives full vent to his anger...and, as a result, finds himself running for his life.

He is part of a mistreated minority—grievously persecuted, not for doing something wrong, but for being perceived as a threat. Raised with privilege in the palace of a king, he had been spared the heartless treatment inflicted on his kinsmen. But watching the *injustice* day after day and year after year finally becomes too much for him to bear.

When he sees one of his own people suffering an inhumane beating at the hands of an Egyptian, Moses is filled with rage. He snaps. In an instant he kills the Egyptian and hides the body in the sand. But his angry, impetuous act is not committed in secret. When news of the murder reaches Pharaoh, Moses fears for his life and flees (see Exodus chapter 2).

When you look at the life of Moses, you can see both the power and the potential problems inherent in anger. Has anger ever clouded your judgment to the point that you acted rashly, and later regretted it? Ultimately, you have the choice to *act* wisely or to *react* foolishly. In his lifetime, Moses did both. And like him, you can learn to keep your anger under control. You can learn how to act rather than react! In doing so, you will demonstrate wisdom.

> *"A fool gives full vent to his anger, but a wise*
> *man keeps himself under control"*
> (Proverbs 29:11).

I. Definitions of Anger

Understandably, Moses felt anger over the *unjust* treatment of his Hebrew brothers, but what he did with that anger got him into trouble. Moses allowed his emotions to overpower him. He committed an impulsive crime, and a serious one at that—murder.

Although Moses was right about the *injustice,* his reaction was wrong. His hotblooded volatility revealed how unprepared he was for the task God had planned for him. Consequently, God kept Moses on the back side of a desert for the next 40 years so he would realize that rescuing his own people *in his own way* would ultimately fail.

Moses needed to learn this vital lesson well before God could turn him into the leader through whom God would accomplish His will *in His supernatural way.* In truth, Moses had tried to earn the Israelites' respect by coming to their rescue. Instead, his murderous rage earned only their scorn.

> *"Moses thought that his own people would realize that*
> *God was using him to rescue them, but they did not"*
> (Acts 7:25).

A. What Is the Meaning of Anger?

What began as a smoldering ember in the heart of Moses quickly burst into deadly flames. Perhaps no one noticed the angry sparks flying from his eyes, but his spirit was consumed with the heat of anger. What do you do when you're inflamed with angry thoughts and feelings?

Firefighters know the danger of letting a flame get out of control. They are trained to respond quickly. You must respond quickly also in order to control the flame of anger before it consumes your life and destroys your relationships. How true it is that

> *"a quick-tempered man does foolish things"*
> (Proverbs 14:17).

- **Anger** is a strong emotion of irritation or agitation that occurs when a need or expectation is not met.[1]

> *"An angry man stirs up dissension, and a hot-*
> *tempered one commits many sins"*
> (Proverbs 29:22).

- *Angry* people in the Bible are often described as hot-tempered and quick-tempered.

> *"A hot-tempered man stirs up dissension,*
> *but a patient man calms a quarrel"*
> (PROVERBS 15:18).

- *Anger,* in the Old Testament, is most frequently the Hebrew word *aph,* which literally means "nose" or "nostrils" and figuratively depicts nostrils flaring with anger. Later, *aph* came to represent the entire face as seen in two ancient Hebrew idioms:[2]

—"Long of face" (or nose) meaning "slow to anger."

> *"The LORD is gracious and compassionate,*
> *slow to anger and rich in love"*
> (PSALM 145:8).

—"Short of face" (or nose) meaning "quick to anger."

> *"Do not make friends with a hot-tempered man,*
> *do not associate with one easily angered"*
> (PROVERBS 22:24).

In the New Testament, the Greek word *orge* originally meant any "natural impulse or desire," but later came to signify "anger as the strongest of all passions." It is often translated as "wrath" because of its powerful, lasting nature.[3]

> *"For those who are self-seeking and who reject the truth*
> *and follow evil, there will be wrath and anger"*
> (ROMANS 2:8).

B. What Is the Magnitude of Anger?

Anger, like heat, can be measured in varying degrees. It ranges from mild, controlled irritations to hot, uncontrolled explosions. In fact, anger is a wide umbrella word that covers many levels of the emotion.[4]

> *"Simeon and Levi are brothers—their swords are*
> *weapons of violence. Let me not enter their council, let*

> *me not join their assembly, for they have killed men in*
> *their anger and hamstrung oxen as they pleased. Cursed*
> *be their anger, so fierce, and their fury, so cruel! I will*
> *scatter them in Jacob and disperse them in Israel"*
> (GENESIS 49:5-7).

- **Indignation** is *simmering anger* provoked by something appearing unjust or unworthy and often perceived as justified. Jesus became "indignant" when the disciples prevented parents from bringing their children to Jesus so He might touch and bless them.

  > *"When Jesus saw this, he was indignant. He said to them,*
  > *'Let the little children come to me, and do not hinder*
  > *them, for the kingdom of God belongs to such as these'"*
  > (MARK 10:14).

- **Wrath** is *burning anger* accompanied by a desire to avenge. Wrath often moves from the *emotion* of anger to the outward *expression* of anger. In Romans 1:18, God expresses His wrath as divine judgment on those who commit willful sin.

  > *"The wrath of God is being revealed from heaven*
  > *against all the godlessness and wickedness of men*
  > *who suppress the truth by their wickedness"*
  > (ROMANS 1:18).

- **Fury** is *fiery anger* so fierce that it destroys common sense. The word *fury* suggests a powerful force compelled to harm or destroy. Some members of the Sanhedrin were so angry with Peter and the other apostles for proclaiming Jesus was God that "they were furious and wanted to put them to death" (Acts 5:33). That is why the Bible says,

  > *"Anger is cruel and fury overwhelming"*
  > (PROVERBS 27:4).

- **Rage** is *blazing anger* resulting in loss of self-control, often to the extreme of violence and temporary insanity. After an outburst of rage, a cry of remorseful regret or disbelief is often expressed: "I can't believe I did that!" Yet those who continue to vent their rage toward others, including God, find themselves defeated by their own destructive decisions and ruined relationships.

> *"A man's own folly ruins his life, yet his*
> *heart rages against the* LORD*"*
> (PROVERBS 19:3).

A Father and His Fury[5]

All the feuding between them fueled his fiery vengeance... and it exploded all over their little boy.

This six-year-old was caught in a tug-of-war between his divorced parents, who continually battled over visitation rights. Marie Rothenberg had custody of young David. However, angry words, slammed phones, and smashed doors characterized the relationship with her ex-husband, Charles, as they argued over drop-off and pick-up times, and who got to spend Christmas morning with David.

Every argument stoked the inner flames of fury in Charles— until one day his anger raged wildly for all the world to see. It was February 1983. Marie reported that David had not been returned at the proper time following a visit with his father. Not until several days later did Charles contact Marie, informing her that he had taken the boy to California.

Incensed by his unauthorized actions, Marie likened the illegal trip to a kidnapping and threatened to keep Charles from ever seeing David again. Uncontrollable rage consumed Charles. All the strain and struggle, the resentment and rage, became like two sticks rubbing together, ready to ignite at any moment. And in March 1983, they did.

Charles turned his eyes to his sleeping son in the small motel room. Vengeful fury warped his reasoning. *If I can't have him, nobody's going to have him!* Propelled by rage, Charles picked up a can of kerosene and poured it over defenseless David, saturating his sheets and pajamas. Charles then struck a match, set the bed ablaze, and fled the scene.

The boy, the bed, and the motel room were all quickly engulfed in flames. Miraculously, David's life was not snuffed out that night. Due to the heroic efforts of guests in nearby rooms, David was snatched from the flames. He was alive...but heartache would forever hover over the horrific scene.

Although David survived the inferno, severe burns covered 90 percent of his body, leaving him permanently disfigured. From head to toe he would become a lasting picture of how one hot-tempered moment can change a life forever.

Among the many repercussions of burning anger are the countless lives permanently scarred with pain—the pain of devastated hope—the pain of destroyed dreams. Psalm 37:8 tells us, "Refrain from anger and turn from wrath; do not fret—it leads only to evil."

These words were certainly prophetic for Charles Rothenberg. That's precisely where his wrath led. His rage led him to be a "baby burner"—his rage ruined his life.

C. What Are Some Misconceptions about Anger?

Do you always view anger as negative and sinful? Do you seek to hide your anger from others, even from yourself? Misunderstandings about anger give this powerful emotion a less than positive reputation! If you are blind to God's purposes for anger and you are afraid of revealing your true feelings, you may be in bondage to undefined or false guilt. The Bible says,

> *"Surely you desire truth in the inner parts; you*
> *teach me wisdom in the inmost place"*
> (PSALM 51:6).

Question: "Is it a sin for me to be angry?"

Answer: No. The initial feeling of anger can be a God-given emotion. It is the way you *respond* and *express* this emotion that determines whether or not you allow your anger to become sin. The Bible says,

"In your anger do not sin"
(EPHESIANS 4:26).

Question: "How can I keep from feeling guilty when I'm angry?"[6]

Answer: Your anger is a signal *something is wrong*—like the red warning light on the dashboard of a car. The purpose of the light is *to propel you to action*—to cause you to stop, to evaluate what is wrong, and then to take appropriate action. Jesus became angry at the hypocritical religious leaders who interpreted "resting on the Sabbath" to excess—even to the extent that, in their eyes, healing the sick on the Sabbath was an offense worthy of the death penalty. In sharp contrast, Jesus intentionally fully restored a man's crippled hand on the Sabbath.

> *"He looked around at them in anger and, deeply distressed at their stubborn hearts, said to the man, 'Stretch out your hand.' He stretched it out, and his hand was completely restored"*
> (MARK 3:5).

Question: "How can a God of love be a God of wrath at the same time?"[7]

Answer: Because of God's great love for you, He directs His anger toward anyone or anything that thwarts His perfect plan for you. God's anger never operates independently of His love. He expresses anger on your behalf and for your ultimate good.

> *"His anger lasts only a moment, but his favor lasts a lifetime"*
> (PSALM 30:5).

Question: "Can people be really angry even when they don't look or sound angry?"

Answer: Yes. Many have difficulty expressing or even recognizing their emotions. Instead, they have learned to deny, ignore, or repress their anger by burying it deep within their hearts. However, the anger is not hidden from God, who sees it and understands it.

> *"The LORD said to Samuel, 'Do not consider his appearance or his height, for I have rejected him. The LORD*

does not look at the things man looks at. Man looks at the
outward appearance, but the LORD looks at the heart'"
(1 SAMUEL 16:7).

D. What Is the Misuse of Anger?

Periodically, everyone feels the heat of anger, but how you handle the heat determines whether you are misusing it. The small flame that lights a cozy campfire, if left unchecked, can quickly become a fierce forest fire. Conversely, the initial spark of anger that can be used for good, if snuffed out, can keep anger from accomplishing its designated purpose. Evaluate whether you are mishandling your anger.[8]

"Mockers stir up a city, but wise men turn away anger"
(PROVERBS 29:8).

Prolonged anger—the "simmering stew"

This kind of anger is held in for a long time. This anger results from an unforgiving heart toward some past offense and offender. Unforgiveness eventually results in resentment and deep bitterness that harms other relationships.

Example: "I'll never forgive the way he talked to me years ago."

"See to it that no one misses the grace of God and that no
bitter root grows up to cause trouble and defile many"
(HEBREWS 12:15).

Pressed down anger—the "pressure cooker"

This is denied or hidden anger. Usually resulting from a fear of facing negative emotions, this kind of anger can create a deceitful heart and lead to untruthfulness with others. Failure to honestly confront and resolve angry feelings can result in self-pity, self-contempt, and self-doubt—ultimately sabotaging most relationships.

Example: "I never get angry...maybe just a little irritated at times."

"Whoever would love life and see good days must keep
his tongue from evil and his lips from deceitful speech"
(1 PETER 3:10).

Provoked anger—the "short fuse"

This anger is quick and impatient, instantly irritated or incensed. A testy temper is often expressed with criticism or sarcasm under the guise of teasing.

Example: "I can't believe you said that! You're so childish!"

> *"Do not be quickly provoked in your spirit,*
> *for anger resides in the lap of fools"*
> (ECCLESIASTES 7:9).

Profuse anger—the "volatile volcano"

This anger is powerful, destructive, hard to control. This way of releasing anger is characterized by contempt, violence, and abuse toward others.

Example: "You stupid fool—if you ever do that again, you'll wish you'd never been born!"

Jesus gives an ominous warning toward those who demean others:

> *"I tell you that anyone who is angry with his brother*
> *will be subject to judgment...But anyone who says,*
> *'You fool!' will be in danger of the fire of hell"*
> (MATTHEW 5:22).

Holdout Harry and the Volcano[9]

He was cautioned, counseled, commanded. He was warned, and well aware of the danger. He received repeated instructions to leave as Mount St. Helens quivered and quaked. But 84-year-old Harry Truman stood his ground near the volatile volcano.

As shifts beneath the surface were regularly recorded—seismic activity logged day after day—Harry became infamous for holding out and ignoring orders to evacuate. This former rebellious bootlegger had left his life of running Canadian whiskey to California during the Prohibition years, but he wasn't about to budge from his lodge near Spirit Lake in Washington state. In 1929, he staked a 40-acre claim—and in the spring of 1980, he staked his life.

Known as a cantankerous guide—as rough and rugged as the surrounding wilderness—Harry had already withstood

100-mile-an-hour windstorms, a fire that engulfed his house, and numerous earthquakes. If lava should start pouring out of the crater, Harry expected the lava to travel slow enough for him to escape into an old mine shaft he had discovered and stocked with food and whiskey.

Ignoring the early earthquakes and avalanches of ash, Harry stubbornly refused to budge...despite ongoing steam eruptions, harmonic tremors, and even a summit explosion. Although the number of eruptions lessened through March and April, the might of their magnitude marched on.

Harry had a tenacious streak, much like his presidential namesake who quipped, "If you can't stand the heat, you better get out of the kitchen!"[10] As conditions worsened in the vicinity of the volcano, most in proximity "did get out of the kitchen"— but not ole Harry.

Amidst all the media notoriety, a national news show visited Harry via helicopter and a Portland television station did the same. Both were ready to rescue him. Harry remained unwilling to leave.

"I'm gonna stay right here...I stuck it out 54 years and I can stick it out another 54,"[11] he declared defiantly. Harry thought he could "stand the heat" and wouldn't get hurt. But on May 18, a 5.0 magnitude earthquake sent lava shooting in a searing pyroclastic blast—timed at 300 miles per hour! This powerful eruption triggered an avalanche of devastating debris—one of the largest landslides ever recorded.[12] That fateful day, 57 people lost their lives—including Harry, who was buried deep under a massive flow of ash and lava.

Like volatile volcanoes, the angry people in our lives simmer and stew beneath the surface. Those who are angry have a mounting pressure within them threatening to spew out. Eventually they release their molten rage on those standing nearby, venting volcanic wrath with its exploding heat...causing devastating harm.

> The biblical warning is understandable and unmistakable: "Do not make friends with a hot-tempered man, do not associate with one easily angered" (Proverbs 22:24). God's Word instructs us to leave the presence of a hot-tempered person— someone with volcanic anger. Otherwise like Harry, we will be hurt, we will be harmed, we will be burned! Proverbs 27:4 says "Anger is cruel and fury overwhelming."
>
> Only because Harry ignored the warning of the volatile rumblings did he experience destruction and death and he did so needlessly. Harry thought he could escape unharmed—he was dead wrong.

II. CHARACTERISTICS OF ANGER

Betrayal by any person is bruising, but betrayal by a friend cuts especially deep, wounding the soul. Everyone expects opposition from those on the outside, but what do you do when opposition comes from within—from among your own circle, your closest confidants, your trusted few?

One national leader knew the hurt of such betrayal. He had led wisely, demonstrated courage, and won the confidence of his people. He was there for them—and they knew it.

However, a leader under him—an enemy in the camp—undermined the chief leader's authority. He created such dissension that this man stole the loyalty of 250 of his other leaders. Those whom he had trusted throughout the years—those who knew him the best, those who should have been most loyal to him—turned against him. In response, however, Moses did not express his anger by taking personal revenge, but rather appealed to the Lord to act on his behalf.

> *"Moses became very angry and said to the LORD, 'Do not accept their offering. I have not...wronged any of them'"*
> (NUMBERS 16:15).

Although justifiably angry, Moses had learned how to *act* rather than *react*. He restrained his rage, poured out his heart, and pleaded with the Lord to deal with His offenders. In turn, God took up Moses' cause, destroyed his betrayers, and defended his honor. Moses refused to take revenge, but rather allowed the Lord to be his avenger because God had given this promise:

"It is mine to avenge; I will repay"
(DEUTERONOMY 32:35).

A. What Are Your Anger Cues?

The human body has a physical reaction when it experiences anger. These "anger cues" can alert you when you are beginning to feel angry. Discerning your anger cues can help you avoid trouble. Likewise, being aware of the signs of anger in others can alert you of the need to appropriately defend yourself, if necessary.

A biblical example of an anger cue is Jonathan's loss of appetite when he was hurt and grieved over his father's unjust, shameful treatment toward his close friend David.

> *"Jonathan got up from the table in fierce anger; on that second day of the month he did not eat, because he was grieved at his father's shameful treatment of David"*
> (1 SAMUEL 20:34).

Your Anger Cues

In seeking to identify your anger cues, answer the following questions:

- Do you have a decreased appetite?

- Do you have tense muscles?

- Do you feel unusually hot or cold?

- Do you have increased perspiration?

- Do you find that you are breathing faster and harder?

- Do you practice silence (shutting down verbally)?

- Do you feel flushed?

- Do you use loud, rapid, or high-pitched speech?

- Do you clench your fists?

- Do you experience an upset or churning stomach?

- Do you feel your heart racing or pounding?

- Do you use language that is inappropriate, harsh, or coarse (sarcasm, gossip, profanity)?

- Does your mouth get dry?

- Do you clench your teeth?

- Do you twitch or exhibit anxious behaviors (tapping pencil, shaking foot)?

- Do you walk hard and fast or pace back and forth?

Once you have identified your anger cues, you will be in a position to quickly identify when you are angry. Then you can direct your energies toward producing a positive outcome.

> *"See what this godly sorrow has produced in you: what earnestness, what eagerness to clear yourselves, what indignation, what alarm, what longing, what concern, what readiness to see justice done. At every point you have proved yourselves to be innocent in this matter"*
> (2 CORINTHIANS 7:11).

B. Do You *Act* or *React* When You Are Angry?[13]

When you are angry, does reason rule your mind, or do tense emotions take control? Do you allow the mind of Christ within you to determine how you should act—a choice that leads to *appropriate action?* Or do you have a knee-jerk reaction that leads to *inappropriate reaction?*

If you have never evaluated what happens when you feel angry...if you lack insight as to how others perceive you when you are angry...seek God's wisdom and understanding.

> *"If you call out for insight and cry aloud for understanding, and if you look for it as for silver and search for it as for hidden treasure, then you will understand the fear of the LORD and find the knowledge of God. For the LORD gives wisdom, and from his mouth come knowledge and understanding"*
> (PROVERBS 2:3-6).

—An *appropriate action* is expressing your thoughts and feelings with restraint, understanding, and concern for the other person's welfare.

> *"A man of knowledge uses words with restraint,*
> *and a man of understanding is even-tempered"*
> (Proverbs 17:27).

—An *inappropriate reaction* is expressing your thoughts and feelings in such a way that stirs up anger in others and produces strife. Proverbs, the book on wisdom, paints this graphic picture:

> *"As churning the milk produces butter, and as twisting the*
> *nose produces blood, so stirring up anger produces strife"*
> (Proverbs 30:33).

To help assess whether you *act* rather than *react,* answer the following questions:

=== *Ask Yourself...* ===

Appropriate Actions	Inappropriate Reactions
• Do you use tactful, compassionate words?	• Do you use tactless, condemning words?
• Do you try to see the other person's point of view?	• Do you see only your point of view?
• Do you want to help the one who angers you?	• Do you want to punish the one who angers you?
• Do you focus first on your own faults?	• Do you focus only on the faults of others?
• Do you have realistic expectations?	• Do you have unrealistic expectations?
• Do you have a flexible and cooperative attitude?	• Do you have a rigid, uncooperative attitude?

- Do you forgive personal injustices?

- Do you have difficulty forgiving injustices?

Even though a situation may evoke anger, those who allow the Lord to be their strength will respond appropriately.

> *"As God's chosen people, holy and dearly loved,*
> *clothe yourselves with compassion, kindness,*
> *humility, gentleness and patience"*
> (COLOSSIANS 3:12).

C. What Are Symptoms of Unresolved Anger?

The emotion of anger is not a problem in itself, but anger becomes a problem when left *unresolved*. Prolonged anger fans the flame of bitterness and fuels unforgiveness. One way you can choose to harbor anger is by refusing to face your feelings in a healthy way.

Such unresolved anger not only creates a rift between you and God, but also damages your body, destroys your emotions, and demoralizes your relationships. Whether you recognize it or not, prolonged anger can cause significant physical, emotional, and spiritual problems. Jesus said,

> *"I tell you that anyone who is angry with his*
> *brother will be subject to judgment"*
> (MATTHEW 5:22).

Unresolved anger is known to produce in many people some of the following physical, emotional, and spiritual symptoms:[14]

Physical Symptoms
- high blood pressure
- heart disease
- stomach disorders
- intestinal disorders
- headaches
- blurred vision
- insomnia
- compulsive eating

Emotional Symptoms
- anxiety
- fear

- bitterness
- compulsions
- depression

- insecurity
- phobias
- hatred

Spiritual Symptoms

- Loss of *perspective*
  Allowing your emotions to distort your thinking
- Loss of *vision*
  Losing a sense of purpose for your life
- Loss of *sensitivity*
  Failing to hear the Spirit of God speaking to your heart
- Loss of *energy*
  Lacking strength for your service to God and others
- Loss of *freedom*
  Becoming a prisoner of your circumstances
- Loss of *confidence*
  Feeling insecure about your response to difficulties
- Loss of *faith*
  Failing to trust that God is working in your life
- Loss of *identity*
  Becoming like the person toward whom you are bitter

Unresolved anger produces bitterness. And the Bible links bitterness with being in bondage to sin.

> *"I see that you are full of bitterness and captive to sin"*
> (Acts 8:23).

D. Do You Have Hidden Anger?

Many people live life unaware they have hidden anger—suppressed anger that only occasionally surfaces. While this hidden anger is usually rooted in past childhood hurts, the underlying effects are always ready to surface. For example, when someone says or does something wrong, the one with suppressed anger often overreacts. When someone makes an

innocent mistake, the magnitude of anger exhibited is out of proporti.
to the mistake.

If you have hidden anger, you can find yourself at one extreme or
another—from feeling hopeless to feeling hostile—and yet be totally
unaware of why you are experiencing these feelings. The Bible makes it clear
that some of our motives and emotions are hidden from our own view.

"Who can discern his errors? Forgive my hidden faults"
(PSALM 19:12).

Clues to Finding Hidden Anger

- Do you become irritable over trifles?
- Do you smile on the outside while you hurt on the inside?
- Do you find your identity and worth in excessive work?
- Do you ever deny being impatient?
- Do you have to have the last word?
- Do those close to you say you blame others?
- Do you feel emotionally flat?
- Do you find yourself quickly fatigued?
- Do you have a loss of interest in life?
- Do you become easily frustrated?

As the Lord reveals any hidden anger that has taken root in your heart,
take action to resolve it because

"man's anger does not bring about the
righteous life that God desires"
(JAMES 1:20).

III. CAUSES OF ANGER

Imagine leading thousands of people through the desert. They look to
you for both their physical and spiritual needs. While setting up camp at
the base of a mountain, God calls you to climb up to meet with Him alone
because He plans to give you the Ten Commandments.

As you meet with God, unbeknownst to you, the people whom God has asked you to lead turn their hearts away from Him, melt their gold, mold a golden calf, and then begin their idol worship. God then interrupts your meeting to inform you that your people have turned against Him. Flushed with anger and fear, you rush down the mountain to intervene.

Exodus 32:19 describes the scene: *"When Moses approached the camp and saw the calf and the dancing, his anger burned and he threw the tablets out of his hands, breaking them to pieces at the foot of the mountain."*

Moses reacted because he was full of *fear.* He was afraid that God's righteous anger against his disobedient people would result in their destruction. He knew they needed to

"worship God acceptably with reverence and
awe, for our 'God is a consuming fire'"
(HEBREWS 12:28-29).

A. What Are the Four Sources of Anger?

Throughout the world, spontaneous fires can be started and fueled by one of four naturally occuring sources: seeping oil, seeping gas, molten lava, or coal bed methane (a flammable gas that can cause mining explosions). In a similar way, anger is typically started and fueled by one of four sources: hurt, injustice, fear, or frustration.

Probing into buried feelings from your past can be painful. Therefore, it can seem easier to stay angry than to uncover the cause, let go of your "rights," and grow in maturity.[15] Yet the Bible urges us to persevere:

"Perseverance must finish its work so that you may
be mature and complete, not lacking anything"
(JAMES 1:4).

1. *Hurt—Your Heart Is Wounded* [16]

Everyone has a God-given inner need for unconditional love.[17] When you experience rejection or emotional pain of any kind, anger can become a protective wall that keeps people, pain, and hurt away.

BIBLICAL EXAMPLE: 12 SONS OF JACOB

Joseph was the undisputed favorite of the 12 sons of Jacob. Feeling hurt and rejected by their father, the older sons became angry and vindictive toward their younger brother.

*"Israel [Jacob] loved Joseph more than any of his other sons,
because he had been born to him in his old age; and he
made a richly ornamented robe for him. When his brothers
saw that their father loved him more than any of them,
they hated him and could not speak a kind word to him"*
(GENESIS 37:3-4).

2. Injustice—Your Right Is Violated [18]

Everyone has an inner moral code that produces a sense of right and
wrong, fair and unfair, just and unjust. When you perceive that an *injustice*
has occurred against you or others (especially those whom you love), you
may feel angry. If you hold on to the offense, the unresolved anger can begin
to make a home in your heart.

BIBLICAL EXAMPLE: KING SAUL

King Saul's *unjust* treatment of David evoked Jonathan's anger. When
Jonathan, Saul's son, heard his father pronounce a death sentence on his
dear friend David, he asked,

*"'Why should he be put to death? What has he
done?' Jonathan asked his father. But Saul hurled
his spear at him to kill him [Jonathan]. Then
Jonathan knew that his father intended to kill David.
Jonathan got up from the table in fierce anger"*
(1 SAMUEL 20:32-34).

3. Fear—Your Future Is Threatened [19]

Everyone is created with a God-given inner need for *security*.[20] When
you begin to worry, feel threatened, or get angry because of a change in
circumstances, you may be responding to *fear*. A fearful heart reveals a lack
of trust in God's perfect plan for your life.

BIBLICAL EXAMPLE: KING SAUL

Saul became angry because of David's many successes on the battlefield.
He felt threatened by David's popularity and feared he would lose his kingdom (read 1 Samuel 18:5-15,28-29).

*"Saul was very angry... 'They have credited David
with tens of thousands,' he thought, 'but me with*

only thousands.'...Saul was afraid of David, because
the LORD was with David but had left Saul"
(1 SAMUEL 18:8,12).

4. *Frustration—Your Performance Is Not Accepted* [21]

Everyone has a God-given inner need for significance.[22] When your efforts are thwarted or do not meet your own personal expectations, your sense of significance can be threatened. *Frustration* over unmet expectations—your own or others'—is a major source of anger.

BIBLICAL EXAMPLE: CAIN

Both Cain and Abel brought offerings to God, but Cain's offering was clearly unacceptable. Cain had chosen to offer what he himself wanted to give rather than what God said was right and acceptable. When Cain's self-effort was rejected, his *frustration* led to anger, and his anger led him to murder his own brother.

> *"In the course of time Cain brought some of the*
> *fruits of the soil as an offering to the LORD. But Abel*
> *brought fat portions from some of the firstborn of his*
> *flock. The LORD looked with favor on Abel and his*
> *offering, but on Cain and his offering he did not look*
> *with favor. So Cain was very angry, and his face was*
> *downcast...Now Cain said to his brother Abel, 'Let's*
> *go out to the field.' And while they were in the field,*
> *Cain attacked his brother Abel and killed him"*
> (GENESIS 4:3-5,8).

Question: "What does God want me to do about my inappropriate anger?"[23]

Answer: God wants you to examine the true source of your anger. Is it hurt, injustice, fear, frustration, or a combination of these? Then evaluate whether you are using anger to try to meet your inner needs for love, for significance, or security.

- Have you been *hurt* by rejection or someone's unkind words? If so, evaluate:

Are you using anger to intimidate or coerce someone into remaining in a relationship with you?

- Have you been the victim of a real or perceived *injustice?* If so, evaluate:

 Are you using angry, accusatory words to cause someone to feel guilty and obligated to you?

- Has something occurred that causes you to have *fear?* If so, evaluate:

 Are you using anger to overpower and control someone in order to get your way?

- Do you feel a sense of *frustration* because of your unmet expectations? If so, evaluate:

 Are you using angry threats and shaming words to manipulate someone into meeting your demands?

In searching your heart, decide that you will *not* use anger to try to get your needs met. Instead, repent and enter into a deeper dependence on the Lord to meet your God-given needs.

> *"The LORD will guide you always; he will satisfy your*
> *needs in a sun-scorched land and will strengthen*
> *your frame. You will be like a well-watered*
> *garden, like a spring whose waters never fail"*
> (ISAIAH 58:11).

B. What Causes a Sudden Change of Intensity?

A person's ways of expressing anger usually change slightly over time, and rarely change dramatically. When a major change occurs, there is also a major cause.

If someone is uncharacteristically impatient, irritable, or provoked, be aware that changes in mood and behavior can result from...

- drug abuse (steroids, cocaine)
- head injury (sports, fall, car accident)
- medications (certain antidepressants)
- chemical deficiencies (hormonal imbalances)

- certain illnesses or diseases (brain tumor, brain cancer)
- physical or emotional trauma or stress (post-traumatic stress disorder)

Sudden changes of behavior warrant a close examination as to possible physical causes, especially in the brain.

> *"Every prudent man acts out of knowledge,*
> *but a fool exposes his folly"*
> (PROVERBS 13:16).

C. How Do Expectations Lead to Anger?

How easy to live under the illusion that we can determine what people *should* do or how situations *should* be decided. "My destiny should be *this;* therefore, people should do *that.*" We pray and *expect* God to do everything we ask.

The primary problem with such expectations is that it often stems from *pride.* Ask the Lord, "Do I act as though I am at the center of my world?"

> *"What causes fights and quarrels among you? Don't they*
> *come from your desires that battle within you? You want*
> *something but don't get it. You kill and covet, but you*
> *cannot have what you want. You quarrel and fight. You*
> *do not have, because you do not ask God. When you ask,*
> *you do not receive, because you ask with wrong motives,*
> *that you may spend what you get on your pleasures...'God*
> *opposes the proud, but gives grace to the humble'"*
> (JAMES 4:1-3,6).

===== *Unrealistic Expectations* =====

- *Anger toward circumstances*

  "I expected good things would always come my way, but life is clearly not what I'd expected."

- *Anger toward others*

  "I expected that you would always be here for me, to always support and love me. But now I'm left alone."

- *Anger toward yourself*

  "I expected to always excel, but now I am struggling and feel like a failure."

The more we expect people to do what we want, the angrier we become when they fail us. The more we try to control others, the more control we give them over us. The more demands we put on others, the more power we give them to anger us. Instead, we need to humble ourselves and submit to God's sovereignty over our lives and over the lives of others. The Bible says we need to leave our destiny in His hands, where it rightly resides.

> *"Find rest, O my soul, in God alone;*
> *my hope comes from him"*
> (PSALM 62:5).

Question: "How can I handle my anger over the losses in my life?"

Answer: When you experience significant loss in your life, you will go through a time of grieving.

- Admit your feelings—your hurt or sense of injustice, your fear or frustration.
- Release to God all the pain you feel, along with the situations that are beyond your control.
- Trust God to give you the grace and insight to deal constructively with each loss.
- Release your expectation that life must go your way.

Pray,

> *Lord,*
> *Thank You that You are sovereign over my life.*
> *Whatever it takes, I want to respond to You*
> *with a heart of gratitude and to accept*
> *these unchangeable circumstances in my life.*
>
> *I choose to stop making myself and*
> *those around me miserable for something*
> *none of us can change.*

Instead, I thank You for how
You are going to use everything in my life
for my good and for Christ's glory.
In His holy name I pray. Amen.

"Give thanks in all circumstances, for this
is God's will for you in Christ Jesus"
(1 Thessalonians 5:18).

D. What Is the Root Cause of Anger?

When we feel our real or perceived "rights" have been violated, we can easily respond with anger.[24] But what are our legitimate rights? One person answers, "Happiness." Another says, "Freedom to have my way."

Yet this was not the mind-set of Jesus—He yielded His rights to His heavenly Father. *We do have the right to live in the light of God's will as revealed in His Word,* but if we want to be Christlike and not be controlled by anger, we too will yield our rights to the Lord and let Him have His way in our hearts.

"Trust in the LORD with all your heart and lean not on
your own understanding; in all your ways acknowledge
him, and he will make your paths straight"
(Proverbs 3:5-6).

Wrong Belief:

"Based on what I believe is fair, I have the right to be angry about the disappointments in my life and to stay angry for as long as I feel like it. I have the right to express my anger in whatever way is natural for me."

Right Belief:

"Because the Lord is sovereign over me and I trust Him with my life, I have yielded my rights to Him. My human disappointments are now God's appointments to increase my faith and develop His character in me. I choose to not be controlled by anger, but to use anger to motivate me to do whatever God wants me to do."

"In this you greatly rejoice, though now for a little
while you may have had to suffer grief in all kinds of
trials. These have come so that your faith—of greater

worth than gold, which perishes even though refined
by fire—may be proved genuine and may result in
praise, glory and honor when Jesus Christ is revealed"
(1 PETER 1:6-7).

IV. STEPS TO SOLUTION

On that hot, dry day, Moses' frustration reached a boiling point. He had led more than a million of his people through the vast desert. But for all his efforts, they continually complained, questioning his leadership and blaming him for their plight:

"If only we had died when our brothers fell dead…! Why
did you bring us up out of Egypt to this terrible place?"
(NUMBERS 20:3-5).

Once again, the Israelites had no water. Earlier in their journey, God had miraculously provided water by instructing Moses to strike a rock with his staff. When Moses obeyed, a stream of water—enough for all Israel—poured out of the rock (see Exodus 17:1-6).

At this point, God intended to perform a similar miracle, but this time He told Moses to simply *speak* to, not strike, a rock. However, Moses was so frustrated that his anger boiled over. Rather than speaking to the rock, he struck it forcefully…*twice.* Gushing water is what God intended—gushing anger is not what God intended. As a result, God disciplined His chosen leader by not allowing him to lead His chosen people into the Promised Land (see Numbers 20:1-12).

At times, are you like Moses? Do you sometimes allow hurt, injustice, fear or frustration to make you furious? If so, what should you do when you get angry? The Bible says,

"Refrain from anger and turn from wrath;
do not fret—it leads only to evil"
(PSALM 37:8).

A. Key Verse to Memorize

"Everyone should be quick to listen, slow to speak
and slow to become angry, for man's anger does not
bring about the righteous life that God desires"
(JAMES 1:19-20).

B. Key Passage to Read and Reread

> *"'In your anger do not sin': Do not let the sun go down*
> *while you are still angry, and do not give the devil a*
> *foothold...Do not let any unwholesome talk come out*
> *of your mouths, but only what is helpful for building*
> *others up according to their needs, that it may benefit*
> *those who listen. And do not grieve the Holy Spirit*
> *of God, with whom you were sealed for the day of*
> *redemption. Get rid of all bitterness, rage and anger,*
> *brawling and slander, along with every form of malice.*
> *Be kind and compassionate to one another, forgiving*
> *each other, just as in Christ God forgave you"*
> (EPHESIANS 4:26-27,29-32).

=========== *God's Analysis of Anger* ===========

—*Anger* is appropriate at certain times . . . . verse 26

—*Anger* must be resolved, or it becomes sinful . . . . verse 26

—*Anger* can be curtailed . . . . verse 26

—*Anger,* if handled inappropriately,
  can be used by Satan . . . . verse 27

—*Anger,* if prolonged, gives ground to Satan . . . . verse 27

—*Anger* can lead to corrupt, unwholesome,
  degrading talk . . . . verse 29

—*Anger* can grieve the Holy Spirit . . . . verse 30

—*Anger* can be eliminated . . . . verse 31

—*Anger* becomes sin when it results in bitterness . . . . . . verse 31

—*Anger* must be eradicated before it turns into rage . . . . verse 31

—*Anger* must be forfeited before it leads to fighting . . . . verse 31

—*Anger* must be stopped before it becomes slander . . . . verse 31

—*Anger* must be mastered before it becomes malicious . verse 31

—*Anger* can be conquered through compassion . . . . verse 32

—*Anger* can be broken through forgiveness . . . . verse 32

C. Analyze the Amount of Your Anger

Have you seriously considered how much anger you are holding inside your heart...and holding toward others? On the next page draw pie-shaped circle. Divide the pie into segments and put a name inside each segment to represent the amount of anger you feel toward the different people in your life—past or present. (We've done a sample "anger pie" for you.)[25]

As you think about your own anger, consider what the Bible says:

> *"You must rid yourselves of all such things as these: anger,*
> *rage, malice, slander, and filthy language from your lips."*
>
> (COLOSSIANS 3:8).

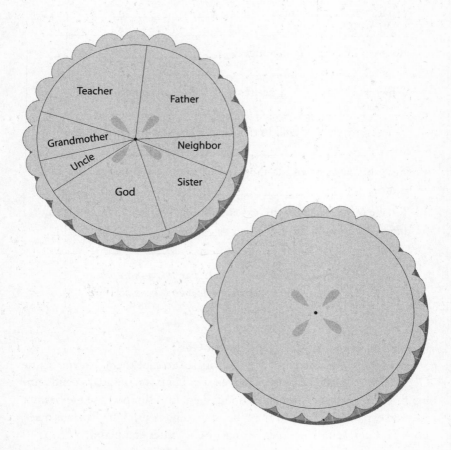

D. How to Analyze Your Anger[26]

It will prove helpful to stop and ask yourself some questions each time you experience anger. Analyzing what is going on can help move you from subjectivity to objectivity, from being controlled by your anger to benefiting from it. As you practice patience and utilize understanding, you will find yourself at a point where you can use your anger for God's purposes and prevent it from leading you into sin.

> *"A patient man has great understanding, but*
> *a quick-tempered man displays folly"*
> (PROVERBS 14:29).

What triggered my anger? _____

_____

How am I expressing my anger? _____

_____

What are the true inner desires motivating my anger? _____

_____

What is my view of God in the midst of this anger-producing situation? _____

How should I respond to God and others in the midst of this situation? _____

What can I learn from this experience that will help me handle my anger better in the future?_____

_____

> *"Better a patient man than a warrior, a man who*
> *controls his temper than one who takes a city"*
> (PROVERBS 16:32).

E. Are You Harboring Anger Toward God?

Problems, pain, and perplexities—you can't escape them. Do you blame God for the pain and heartaches in your life? Have you pointed a condemning finger at God and pronounced judgment on Him because He has not stopped evil or suffering? In the Bible, a man named Job had serious questions for God. In fact, we see the anger in his bitter complaint:

> *"Even today my complaint is bitter; his hand is heavy*
> *in spite of my groaning. If only I knew where to find*
> *him; if only I could go to his dwelling! I would state my*
> *case before him and fill my mouth with arguments"*
> (JOB 23:2-4).

Is anger toward God justifiable? God answers Job with these words:

> *"Who is this that darkens my counsel with words*
> *without knowledge?...Will the one who contends with*
> *the Almighty correct him?...Would you discredit my*
> *justice? Would you condemn me to justify yourself?"*
> (JOB 38:2; 40:2,8).

What is the answer to such intense anger against God? Can it be resolved? And if so, how?

Resolving Anger Toward God

Know God's Character
—God is just.

> *"He is the Rock, his works are perfect, and*
> *all his ways are just. A faithful God who*
> *does no wrong, upright and just is he"*
> (DEUTERONOMY 32:4).

—God's ways are just.

> *"Just and true are your ways, King of the ages"*
> (REVELATION 15:3).

—God is love.

> *"God is love"*
> (1 JOHN 4:8).

—God's love is directed toward all people.

> *"God so loved the world"*
> (JOHN 3:16).

Know God's Purposes

—God brings good out of evil.

> *"We know that in all things God works*
> *for the good of those who love him"*
> (ROMANS 8:28).

—God turns crying into dancing and sorrow into joy.

> *"You turned my wailing into dancing; you removed*
> *my sackcloth and clothed me with joy"*
> (PSALM 30:11).

—God uses sufferings to produce perseverance, character, and hope.

> *"We also rejoice in our sufferings, because we know*
> *that suffering produces perseverance; perseverance,*
> *character; and character, hope. And hope does not*
> *disappoint us, because God has poured out his love into*
> *our hearts by the Holy Spirit, whom he has given us"*
> (ROMANS 5:3-5).

—God uses our troubles to teach us compassion.

> *"Praise be to the God and Father of our Lord Jesus*
> *Christ, the Father of compassion and the God of*
> *all comfort, who comforts us in all our troubles, so*
> *that we can comfort those in any trouble with the*
> *comfort we ourselves have received from God"*
> (2 CORINTHIANS 1:3-4).

Understand God's Plan

—God offers salvation to all.

> *"God did not send his Son into the world to condemn*
> *the world, but to save the world through him"*
> (JOHN 3:17).

—God will bless those who persevere under trial.

> *"Blessed is the man who perseveres under trial"*
> (JAMES 1:12).

—God will bring His righteous judgment on those who are evil.

> *"For those who are self-seeking and who reject the truth*
> *and follow evil, there will be wrath and anger"*
> (ROMANS 2:8-9).

—God will one day make everything new for His people (authentic believers).

> *"The dwelling of God is with men, and he will live with*
> *them. They will be his people, and God himself will be*
> *with them and be their God. He will wipe every tear from*
> *their eyes. There will be no more death or mourning or*
> *crying or pain, for the old order of things has passed away"*
> (REVELATION 21:3-4).

Job, who at one time had bitterness toward God, ultimately realized his anger was misplaced. With deepest remorse, he admitted his wrong:

> *"I know that you can do all things; no plan of*
> *yours can be thwarted...My ears had heard of*
> *you but now my eyes have seen you. Therefore I*
> *despise myself and repent in dust and ashes"*
> (JOB 42:2,5-6).

Controlling Your Anger and Knowing God's Plan for Your Life

No one wants to be thought of as being out-of-control. Yet those who struggle with anger will say, "I've really tried to control my anger, but for some reason, I just can't."

If that someone is you, it could be that the Lord is saying, "I know you can't but I can. I can give you the control you need. I will give you My supernatural power. But first, give Me control of your life. Then I will change you inside out."

Do you need a real change in your life? If so, there are four truths you need to know:

1. GOD'S PURPOSE FOR YOU...IS *SALVATION*
—What was God's motive in sending Christ to earth? To express His love for you by making salvation available to you!

> *"God so loved the world, that he gave his one and only*
> *Son, that whoever believes in him shall not perish but have*
> *eternal life. For God did not send his Son into the world to*
> *condemn the world, but to save the world through him"*
> (JOHN 3:16-17).

—What was Jesus' purpose in coming to earth? To forgive your sins, empower you to have victory over sin, and enable you to live a fulfilled life!

> *"I [Jesus] have come that they may have*
> *life, and have it to the full"*
> (JOHN 10:10).

2. YOUR PROBLEM...IS *SIN*
—What exactly is sin? Sin is living *independently* of God's standard—knowing what is right, but choosing wrong.

> *"Anyone, then, who knows the good he*
> *ought to do and doesn't do it, sins"*
> (JAMES 4:17).

—What is the major consequence of sin? It is spiritual death, spiritual separation from God.

> *"The wages of sin is death, but the gift of God*
> *is eternal life in Christ Jesus our Lord"*
> (ROMANS 6:23).

3. GOD'S PROVISION FOR YOU...IS THE *SAVIOR*
—Can anything remove the penalty for sin? Yes. Jesus died on the cross to personally pay the penalty for your sins.

> *"God demonstrates his own love for us in this:*
> *While we were still sinners, Christ died for us"*
> (ROMANS 5:8).

—What is the solution to being separated from God? Belief in Jesus Christ is the only way to God the Father.

> *"Jesus answered, 'I am the way and the truth and the life. No one comes to the Father except through me'"*
> (JOHN 14:6).

4. YOUR PART...IS *SURRENDER*

—Place your faith in (rely on) Jesus Christ as your personal Lord and Savior and reject your good works as a means of gaining God's approval.

> *"It is by grace you have been saved, through faith—and this not from yourselves, it is the gift of God—not by works, so that no one can boast"*
> (EPHESIANS 2:8-9).

—Give Christ control of your life, entrusting yourself to Him.

> *"Jesus said to his disciples, 'If anyone would come after me, he must deny himself and take up his cross and follow me. For whoever wants to save his life will lose it, but whoever loses his life for me will find it. What good will it be for a man if he gains the whole world, yet forfeits his soul? Or what can a man give in exchange for his soul?'"*
> (MATTHEW 16:24-26).

If you desire to be fully forgiven by God—and to experience a changed mind, a changed heart, and a changed life—you can ask Jesus Christ to come into your life right now and give you His forgiveness, His peace, and His power.

Prayer of Salvation

God,

I admit I have had a misplaced anger toward You.
I've sinned by elevating myself,
hanging on to "my rights."
Now I repent and yield my rights to You.

Jesus, thank You for dying on the cross
for my sins to take the punishment
I should have taken.
I'm asking You now to come into my life
to be my Lord and Savior and to forgive
me of all of my sins.
I give You control of my life.

Make me the person You created me to be.
Thank You for Your mercy and Your grace.

In Your holy name I pray. Amen.

If you sincerely prayed this prayer, then the following promise from God applies to you:

"His divine power has given us everything
we need for life and godliness"
(2 PETER 1:3).

F. How to Resolve Your Past Anger[27]

Unresolved anger is a bed of hidden coals burning deep wounds into your relationship with God and with others. This powerful emotion robs your heart of peace and steals contentment from your spirit.

"When my heart was grieved and my spirit embittered, I
was senseless and ignorant; I was a brute beast before you"
(PSALM 73:21-22).

Realize *Your Burning Anger*

- Willingly admit that you have unresolved anger.
- Ask God to reveal any buried anger in your heart.
- Seek to determine the primary reason(s) for your past anger.
- Talk out your anger with God and with a friend or counselor.

"I confess my iniquity; I am troubled by my sin"
(PSALM 38:18).

Revisit *Your Root Feelings*

- Did you feel *hurt* (rejected, betrayed, unloved, ignored)?
- Did you experience *injustice* (cheated, wronged, maligned, attacked)?
- Did you feel *fearful* (threatened, insecure, out of control, powerless)?
- Did you feel *frustrated* (inadequate, inferior, hindered, controlled)?

> *"Search me, O God, and know my heart; test me and know my anxious thoughts. See if there is any offensive way in me, and lead me in the way everlasting"*
> (PSALM 139:23-24).

Release *Your Rights*

- Confess that harboring anger in your heart is sin.
- Give your desire for revenge to God.
- Refuse to hold on to your past hurts—instead, release them to God.
- Pray for God to work in the life of your offender and to change your heart toward that person.
- Release the one who hurt you into the hands of God—forgive as God forgave you.

> *"Bear with each other and forgive whatever grievances you may have against one another. Forgive as the Lord forgave you"*
> (COLOSSIANS 3:13).

Rejoice *in God's Purpose*

- Thank God for the ways He will use this trial in your life.
- Know God can use your resolved past anger for your good and for the good of those around you.
- Praise God for His commitment to use all the circumstances in your life to develop Christ's character within you, making you strong, firm, and steadfast.

> *"The God of all grace, who called you to his eternal glory in*
> *Christ, after you have suffered a little while, will himself*
> *restore you and make you strong, firm and steadfast"*
> (1 PETER 5:10).

Restore *the Relationship...When Appropriate*

At times reconciliation is not appropriate (after adultery or with an unrepentant abuser) or not possible (after a death). But when it *is* appropriate to restore the relationship you must always confess your sin of harboring anger.

- Realize when someone sins against you and you hold on to anger and refuse to be reconciled to the person, you are sinning against both God and that individual.
- Confess the anger in your heart to God and ask the person to forgive you for refusing to be reconciled.
- Write out the confession first to get the wording correct: "I realize I've been wrong in holding on to my anger against you and refusing to allow God to restore our relationship. I'm deeply sorry. Will you forgive me?"
- Be sure the encounter is free of anger and accusatory statements.

> *"You have heard that it was said to the people long ago,*
> *'Do not murder, and anyone who murders will be subject*
> *to judgment.' But I tell you that anyone who is angry with*
> *his brother will be subject to judgment...Therefore, if you*
> *are offering your gift at the altar and there remember*
> *that your brother has something against you, leave your*
> *gift there in front of the altar. First go and be reconciled*
> *to your brother; then come and offer your gift"*
> (MATTHEW 5:21-24).

Receive *God's Love*

Meditate on and memorize Scripture passages affirming God's love for you:

Jeremiah 31:3	Psalm 32:10
Lamentations 3:22-23	Psalm 89:1-2
Psalm 13:5-6	Psalm 103:17

- Read from the psalms daily for one month (if you read five psalms a day, you will go through the entire book of Psalms— 150 chapters—in one month).
- Rest in the acceptance of God, not in the acceptance of others.
- Rely on the Lord to meet your inner needs for love, significance, and security.

"He made known his ways to Moses"
(Psalm 103:7).

Reflect *Christ's Love*

Actively seek to reflect the love of God toward the person who hurt you. Pray in your heart...

- "Lord, help me to submit to Your control."
- "Lord, I want Your mind to direct my mind."
- "Lord, reflect Your attitudes in my actions."
- "Lord, guide my words to express Your love."

"A new command I give you: Love one another.
As I have loved you, so you must love one
another. By this all men will know that you
are my disciples, if you love one another"
(John 13:34-35).

G. How to Rid Yourself of Childhood Anger

Many of us assume once we reach adulthood, our pain from childhood will disappear and no longer affect us. But this disappearing act does not happen unless we identify our past pains from childhood and resolve them. While we are not the sum of our experiences, we are shaped by our *responses* to our experiences.

God does not want us to store up the bad things that happened to us by stockpiling our anger. Rather, He wants us to be like a storehouse where we get rid of the bad fruit and store up the good fruit.

> *"The good man brings good things out of the*
> *good stored up in him, and the evil man brings*
> *evil things out of the evil stored up in him"*
> (MATTHEW 12:35).

Resolving Childhood Hurts

The next time anger wells up in your heart, ask yourself...

- "Am I feeling *hurt?"*

  Example: My ideas have not been accepted.

- "Did I frequently have these same feelings when I was a *child?"*

  Example: When my father was not proud of me because I wasn't a good athlete, I felt *hurt.*

- "How did I *feel* when my father made it known that instead of wanting me, he wanted an athletic son?"

  Example: I felt a deep sense of rejection.

Face the *anger* that is still in your heart because of the *hurts* you experienced in childhood:

- Ask God to reveal buried *hurts* from your childhood.
- Ask family members and close friends to notice what situations seem to hurt you and make you angry.
- Acknowledge that your prolonged, unresolved anger over past hurts is wrong, even if you think it is justified.
- Take personal responsibility to overcome your childhood *hurts.*
- Surrender your hurtful childhood experiences and feelings to God.
- Forgive and pray for those who have hurt you.
- Ask forgiveness from those whom you have hurt or offended.

- Pray for God to purge you of your hurtful ways and fill you with His unconditional love for others.

If your heart yearns for love and acceptance, remember...

- Psalm 66:20: "Praise be to God, who has not rejected my prayer or withheld his love from me!"

- Psalm 32:10: "Many are the woes of the wicked, but the LORD's unfailing love surrounds the man who trusts in him."

- Psalm 36:7: "How priceless is your unfailing love! Both high and low among men find refuge in the shadow of your wings."

- 1 John 4:9-10: "This is how God showed his love among us: He sent his one and only Son into the world that we might live through him. This is love: not that we loved God, but that he loved us and sent his Son as an atoning sacrifice for our sins."

Resolving Childhood Injustices

The next time you feel the surge of anger over a particular situation, ask yourself:

- "Am I feeling a sense of injustice?"

  Example: My close friend was mistreated and ignored.

- "Did I ever have these same feelings in my childhood?"

  Example: When my parents favored my siblings and ignored me, I felt their treatment was unjust.

- "How did I feel when my parents treated me this way?"

  Example: I felt angry toward my parents and concluded that life is not fair.

Face your anger from the past and begin to see how your present anger is connected to the injustices you experienced in childhood:

- Ask God to reveal all unresolved feelings over the injustices you experienced as a child.

- Ask your close family members and friends how they know when you are angry over an injustice.
- Acknowledge that your feelings of injustice may be directed at God.
- Take personal responsibility for your feelings of anger at injustice.
- Release your anger over past injustices to God and replace the anger with God's peace.
- Ask forgiveness from anyone you have treated unjustly.
- Forgive and pray for those who have been unjust toward you.
- Meditate on how God can use, for good, your awareness of injustices committed against you and others.

If your anger is rooted in unjust treatment, and you are committed to justice, remember...

- Psalm 9:16: "The LORD is known by his justice."
- Luke 18:7: "Will not God bring about justice for his chosen ones, who cry out to him day and night? Will he keep putting them off?"
- 2 Thessalonians 1:6-7: "God is just: He will pay back trouble to those who trouble you and give relief to you who are troubled, and to us as well."
- Psalm 37:6: "He will make your righteousness shine like the dawn, the justice of your cause like the noonday sun."

Resolving Childhood Fears

The next time you feel threatened or get angry over an unwanted, uncomfortable change in circumstances, ask yourself:

- "Am I feeling fear about my future?"

  Example: I've lost my job, and I don't know how I will support my family.

- "Did I have these same feelings in my childhood?"

  Example: When my parents died and I was sent to be raised by my grandmother, I felt fear.

- "How did I feel about not being raised by my parents?"

  Example: I felt angry because everybody else had a mother and father to protect them and to provide for their future.

Face your anger at God for taking your parents and leaving you with the *fear* of an uncertain future, and any other fears you experienced in childhood:

- If you have difficulty recalling your childhood feelings of fear, ask God to bring those memories to your mind.

- Ask your current family and good friends what they notice when you express distress or feelings of insecurity as a result of fear.

- Be completely honest with yourself and ask God to reveal where your fears and securities lie:

  —Is it in your financial situation?

  —Is it in your close family ties?

  —Is it in your education?

  —Is it in your accomplishments?

  —Is it in what others say about you?

- Acknowledge that placing your trust in anything other than God produces anger at Him when your security idols fail and you experience fear.

- Ask God's forgiveness for your failure to trust Him.

- Learn to place your trust in the Lord alone for your security.

- Memorize scriptures that reassure you of God's faithfulness.

- Begin developing a grateful heart for all that the Lord has provided, and thank Him daily for His generous gifts.

If your heart yearns for security, and you desire to rid yourself of fear, remember...

- Psalm 112:7-8: "He will have no fear of bad news; his heart is steadfast, trusting in the LORD. His heart is secure, he will have no fear; in the end he will look in triumph on his foes."

- Isaiah 41:10: "Do not fear, for I am with you; do not be

dismayed, for I am your God. I will strengthen you and help you; I will uphold you with my righteous hand."

- Proverbs 3:26: "The LORD will be your confidence and will keep your foot from being snared."

- Romans 8:15: "You did not receive a spirit that makes you a slave again to fear, but you received the Spirit of sonship."

Resolving Childhood Frustration

The next time you feel anger when your personal efforts are stymied or not accepted by others, ask yourself...

- "Am I feeling frustrated?"

  Example: My associate made negative remarks about my speech at our business luncheon.

- "Did I ever have these same feelings in my childhood?"

  Example: When my parents expected me to behave perfectly and not express my true feelings, I felt frustrated.

- "How did I *feel* when my parents had these expectations?"

  Example: I felt that I was not accepted by my parents because my performance was not always acceptable.

Face your past frustrations from childhood and realize that not measuring up to your own or someone else's standards indicates performance-based acceptance and can be a major source of anger.

- Ask God to reveal the buried anger you have toward your parents or others in your past who frustrated you by accepting you solely on the basis of your performance.

- Ask yourself:

  —Do I set unrealistic standards for myself?

  —Do I tend to stuff my anger?

  —Do I need to control people and circumstances?

  —Am I a caretaker?

  —Am I a perfectionist?

  —Am I a procrastinator?

—Am I a people pleaser?

—Am I a workaholic?

- Ask your family and close friends how they know when you are frustrated.
- Understand frustration is only a nice-sounding word for the anger that deeply damages your self-worth and sense of significance.
- Understand it takes concentrated commitment and great effort to uncover deeply buried frustrations and root them out of your life.
- Realize you can never earn God's love, but that He loves you unconditionally.
- Allow yourself to feel your anger at being frustrated and ask God for courage to express your anger in acceptable ways.
- Forgive those who frustrated you in the past and release your anger to God and claim the sufficiency of His love to affirm your value.

If you feel a sense of *frustration* with life and long to feel accepted and significant, remember...

- Proverbs 21:3: "To do what is right and just is more acceptable to the LORD than sacrifice."
- Galatians 1:10: "Am I now trying to win the approval of men, or of God? Or am I trying to please men? If I were still trying to please men, I would not be a servant of Christ."
- Psalm 139:23-24: "Search me, O God, and know my heart; test me and know my anxious thoughts. See if there is any offensive way in me, and lead me in the way everlasting."
- Lamentations 3:22-23: "Because of the LORD's great love we are not consumed, for his compassions never fail. They are new every morning; great is your faithfulness."

H. Know the Quick Answer to Anger

The possibility that you will feel angry remains ever present. A spark of irritation can be ignited intentionally by hurtful people or unintentionally by those who love you. God intends that you seek His answer for anger quickly, before it singes your heart and burns the bridges of your relationships.

> *"Be self-controlled and alert. Your enemy the devil prowls*
> *around like a roaring lion looking for someone to devour"*
> (1 PETER 5:8).

Ask, "Can I change this situation?"

- If you can, change it. (If the door squeaks, oil it!)
- If you can't, release it. (Give it to the Lord.)

═══════════════════ *Pray...* ═══════════════════

Lord,

You are sovereign over my life.
Because You know everything,
You know I feel a strong sense of
(hurt, injustice, fear, or frustration)
about
(name the person or the situation).
I release this situation into Your hands.
I thank You that You will use it
to further conform me to the character of Christ.

I trust You with my future and with me.

In Christ's name I pray. Amen.

> *"Let the morning bring me word of your unfailing*
> *love, for I have put my trust in you. Show me the*
> *way I should go, for to you I lift up my soul"*
> (PSALM 143:8).

I. How to Alleviate Your Present Anger

"Anger is one letter short of *danger."* This saying is more than a catchy phrase; these words reflect a painful truth. When a tongue has not been

tamed, conversations can easily escalate out of control and people and relationships can be damaged.

Acknowledge Your Anger

- Be willing to admit you are angry.
- Be aware of when you feel anger.
- Become aware of suppressing or repressing your anger because of fear.
- Be willing to take responsibility for any inappropriate anger.

> *"He who conceals his sins does not prosper, but*
> *whoever confesses and renounces them finds mercy"*
> (PROVERBS 28:13).

Ascertain Your Style

- How frequently do you feel angry? (Often? Sometimes? Never?)
- How do you know when you are angry?
- How do others know when you are angry?
- How do you release your anger? Do you explode? Do you become teary-eyed? Do you joke or tease? Do you become sarcastic? Do you criticize? Do you become defensive?

> *"Test me, O Lord, and try me, examine*
> *my heart and my mind"*
> (PSALM 26:2).

Assess the Source

- *Hurt:* Is the source of your anger hurt feelings from the words or actions of others?
- *Injustice:* Is the source of your anger an emotional response to the unjust actions of someone toward another person?
- *Fear:* Is the source of your anger a feeling of loss or fear?
- *Frustration:* Is the source of your anger frustration because something didn't go as you planned?

"I know, my God, that you test the heart
and are pleased with integrity"
(1 Chronicles 29:17).

Appraise Your Thinking

- Are you expecting others to meet your standards?
  — "She *should* take better care of her children."
  — "He *ought* to notice what I do for him."
  — "He *must* be here before 7:00 p.m."
  — "She had *better not* call during dinner!"

- Are you guilty of distorted thinking?
  — *Exaggerating* the situation
  — *Assuming* the worst
  — *Labeling* one action based on other actions
  — *Generalizing* by saying, "you never" or "you always"

"A wicked man puts up a bold front, but an
upright man gives thought to his ways"
(Proverbs 21:29).

Admit Your Needs

Anger is often used as a tactic to get inner needs met.

- Do you use anger as a manipulative ploy to demand certain "musts" in an attempt to *feel loved?*
- Do you use explosive anger to get your way in an attempt to *feel significant?*
- Do you use controlling anger, insisting on certain conditions in order to *feel secure?*
- Do you know only Christ can ultimately meet all your inner needs for *love, significance,* and *security?*

"My God will meet all your needs according
to his glorious riches in Christ Jesus"
(Philippians 4:19).

Abandon Your Demands

Instead of demanding that others meet your inner needs for *love, significance,* and *security,* learn to look to the Lord to meet your needs.

- "Lord, though I would like to feel more *love* from others, I know You love me unconditionally."

> *"I have loved you with an everlasting love; I
> have drawn you with loving-kindness"*
> (JEREMIAH 31:3).

- "Lord, though I would like to feel more *significant* to those around me, I know I am significant in Your eyes."

> *"'For I know the plans I have for you,' declares
> the LORD, 'plans to prosper you and not to harm
> you, plans to give you hope and a future'"*
> (JEREMIAH 29:11).

- "Lord, though I wish I felt more *secure* in my relationships, I know I am secure in my relationship with You."

> *"The LORD is with me; I will not be
> afraid. What can man do to me?"*
> (PSALM 118:6).

- "Lord, though I wish others would be more responsive to my needs, I know You have promised to meet all my needs."

> *"His divine power has given us everything we need
> for life and godliness through our knowledge of him
> who called us by his own glory and goodness"*
> (2 PETER 1:3).

Alter Your Attitudes

Take the steps listed below as outlined in Philippians 2:2-8:

> *"Make my joy complete by being like-minded, having
> the same love, being one in spirit and purpose. Do
> nothing out of selfish ambition or vain conceit, but in
> humility consider others better than yourselves. Each of*

you should look not only to your own interests, but also
to the interests of others. Your attitude should be the
same as that of Christ Jesus: Who, being in very nature
God, did not consider equality with God something to
be grasped, but made himself nothing, taking the very
nature of a servant, being made in human likeness. And
being found in appearance as a man, he humbled himself
and became obedient to death—even death on a cross!"
(PHILIPPIANS 2:2-8).

- Have the goal to be likeminded with Christ . . . .   verse 2
- Do not think of yourself first . . . .   verse 3
- Give the other person preferential treatment . . . .   verse 3
- Consider the other person's interests . . . .   verse 4
- Have the attitude of Jesus Christ . . . .   verse 5
- Do not emphasize your position or rights . . . .   verse 6
- Look for ways to serve with a servant's heart . . . .   verse 7
- Speak and act with a humble spirit . . . .   verse 8
- Obey the Word of God and submit
  your will to His will . . . .   verse 8
- Be willing to die to your own desires . . . .   verse 8

Address Your Anger

- *Determine* whether your anger is really justified.

> *"A wicked man puts up a bold front, but an*
> *upright man gives thought to his ways"*
> (PROVERBS 21:29).

- *Decide* on the appropriate response.

> *"[There is] a time to tear and a time to mend,*
> *a time to be silent and a time to speak"*
> (ECCLESIASTES 3:7).

—How important is the issue?

—Would a good purpose be served if I mention it?

—Should I acknowledge my anger only to the Lord?

- *Depend* on the Holy Spirit for guidance.

    *"When he, the Spirit of truth, comes, he will guide you into
    all truth. He will not speak on his own; he will speak only
    what he hears, and he will tell you what is yet to come"*
    (JOHN 16:13).

- *Develop* constructive dialogue when you confront.

    *"Let your conversation be always full of grace, seasoned
    with salt, so that you may know how to answer everyone"*
    (COLOSSIANS 4:6).

    —*Don't* speak from a heart of unforgiveness.

    Do think before you speak.

    —*Don't* use phrases such as "How could you?" or "Why can't you?"

    Do use personal statements such as "I feel..."

    —*Don't* bring up past grievances.

    Do stay focused on the present issue.

    —*Don't* assume that the other person is wrong.

    Do listen for feedback from another point of view.

    —*Don't* expect instant understanding.

    Do be patient and keep responding with gentleness.

    *"Through patience a ruler can be persuaded,
    and a gentle tongue can break a bone"*
    (PROVERBS 25:15).

- *Demonstrate* the grace of God, by saying to yourself...
    —"I placed my anger on the cross with Christ."
    —"I am no longer controlled by anger."
    —"I am alive with Christ living inside me."
    —"I will let Christ forgive through me."
    —"I will let Christ love through me."

—"I will let Christ reveal truth through me."

"I have been crucified with Christ and I no longer live, but Christ lives in me. The life I live in the body, I live by faith in the Son of God, who loved me and gave himself for me"
(GALATIANS 2:20).

J. How to Convey Your Anger Appropriately

When you feel anger toward someone, first take time to evaluate whether addressing your anger is needful, appropriate, or beneficial to strengthen the relationship. Some people simply do not know how to handle anger directed toward them. They either become hostile and defensive or weak and placating. Either way, nothing gets resolved.

If you want merely to vent your feelings, then pour out your heart to God and maybe to another person, but not to the person with whom you are angry. Should you decide to arrange a meeting, there are some things you will need to do in preparation.

- Examine your motivation.
- Be realistic in your expectations.
- Know what you want to accomplish.
- Assess the legitimacy of your request.
- Rehearse how you will approach the subject.
- Anticipate possible reactions from the other person.
- Think through how you might respond to those reactions.
- Decide if you are willing to live with any negative repercussions.
- If you are uncertain about what to do, talk with a wise and trusted individual.

Should you decide to go ahead and meet, here are two more things to consider:

- Select a time and place convenient for both of you that will provide an atmosphere conducive for listening and sharing.
- Meet on neutral ground so both of you are likely to feel you are on equal footing.

K. Answers to Common Questions

As you learn to act rather than react, and thereby allow God to use your anger to accomplish His purposes, you will be in a position to offer others hope for change. The questions below will help prepare you to give biblical answers to those who live in bondage to anger and who come to you for help and hope.

Question: "What should I do when I feel my anger getting out of control?"

Answer: Whenever you feel reason and self-control are giving way to irrational and unbridled behavior, put on the brakes and call a truce in order to take time out. In this way, you can keep the anger from escalating.

- Stop and take a deep breath.
- Hold up your hands to indicate that you are "surrendering" for the time being by calling a halt to what is taking place.
- State that you are getting more and more upset and unable to think clearly, or that the conversation is not going in a positive direction and does not seem to be resolving anything.
- Help yourself to calm down by walking around the block, listening to music, taking a shower, or whatever will enable you to regain your composure.
- If possible, agree on a time to resume the conversation or activity.

If you reach an impasse and agreement between the two of you is not possible, then:

- Agree to have different opinions on the subject, and don't let it become a problem in the relationship.
- Remember that if two people agree on everything all the time, their relationship runs the risk of becoming stagnant and void of growth.
- Make an effort to engage in stimulating conversations where varied opinions are expressed so you can develop your listening skills, learn from others, think through your own opinions, and practice expressing those opinions to others in a clear and concise manner void of anger.

> *"A fool finds no pleasure in understanding*
> *but delights in airing his own opinions"*
> (PROVERBS 18:2).

> *"Accept him whose faith is weak, without*
> *passing judgment on disputable matters"*
> (ROMANS 14:1).

Question: "One of my coworkers has threatened to harm me. What should I do?"

Answer: Angry people can lose control of their anger and cause property damage or personal injury. In extreme cases, some people have even murdered those with whom they work. This is why you must...[28]

- Take all threats of violence seriously
  - —Assume that if someone makes a threat, the intent to carry it out is present.
  - —Most people who commit violent acts at work have given a clear indication of their intent prior to taking action.

- Always report any threat
  - —Report the threat to your supervisor.
  - —Report the threat to a security officer.
  - —If serious enough, report the threat to the police.

- When threatened, proceed wisely and cautiously
  - —Consult your company's policy manual regarding the code of conduct at your workplace.
  - —Seek legal counsel or advice from the Human Resources department at work regarding informing the angry person of the consequences of making threats.

> *"A prudent man sees danger and takes refuge,*
> *but the simple keep going and suffer for it"*
> (PROVERBS 22:3).

Question: "I was severely wronged by someone I once trusted. People want me to forgive him. How can I possibly ignore my anger and simply let him off the hook?"

Answer: Picture a hook attached to your collarbone. Imagine attached to that hook both your offender and all the pain this person has caused you. Do you really want to carry that person and all that pain with you for the rest of your life?

The Lord wants you to take your anger and the pain this person has caused you and release them into His hands. Then take the one who offended you off your emotional hook and place your offender onto God's hook. Realize you can forgive a person without trusting that person.

Extending forgiveness is based not on your feelings, but on your *choice* to be obedient to God and to release your anger to Him. Extending trust is based on another person's ability to be trustworthy. Forgive everyone, but trust only the trustworthy. The Lord knows how to deal justly and effectively with all those who bring pain into your life:

> *"'It is mine to avenge; I will repay,' says the Lord"*
> (Romans 12:19).

Question: "How can I overcome road rage? I get so angry at other drivers!"

Answer: As drivers, we have all had someone cut in front of us, yell profanity at us, make obscene gestures toward us, or intentionally bump us. Whatever the situation, the moment you feel agitated, rehearse these truths in your mind:

- "I don't have to get angry."
- "I refuse to let someone else control my emotions."
- "I choose to be calm and coolheaded."
- "Lord, I don't know what is wrong with (person's name), but I pray that you will make your presence known in this situation."
- "Lord, (person's name) has a problem. I'm not going to let that problem be my problem."
- "I will stay calm in the strength of Christ."

> *"I can do everything through him who gives me strength"*
> (Philippians 4:13).

L. Accept God's Aim for Anger

Forest rangers who care for and protect national parks occasionally say they have to start a fire to stop a fire. At times God works for your good in much the same way. Ephesians 4:26 says, "Be angry and do not sin."

God clearly intends for you to experience the emotion of anger and to use it for some positive purpose. For example, He can use your anger to spark your awareness of a blazing spiritual problem that needs to be snuffed out. God often allows fiery trials to test your faith and to develop the perseverance necessary to sustain your faith.[29]

> *"Consider it pure joy, my brothers, whenever you*
> *face trials of many kinds, because you know that*
> *the testing of your faith develops perseverance"*
> (JAMES 1:2-3).

As you seek to allow God to direct your anger and use it for His purposes, remember...

- *Anger* can be used to bring positive change in your life.
- *Anger* can be the lens through which you gain insight into your past hurts.
- *Anger* can bring your true feelings to light.
- *Anger* can reveal your inappropriate ways of trying to meet your own needs.
- *Anger* can help you realize your need for the Lord.
- *Anger* can uncover your need to set healthy boundaries.
- *Anger* can be the foundation on which forgiveness is built.
- *Anger,* when appropriately verbalized, can be the spark that encourages honest communication in relationships.
- *Anger,* when appropriately verbalized, can be used by God to convict others of sin.
- *Anger,* when appropriately handled, can be used by God.

As you allow God to use your anger for good, you will become an example to others and bring praise to Him.

> *"Let your light shine before men, that they may see*
> *your good deeds and praise your Father in heaven"*
> (MATTHEW 5:16).

*If anger is allowed to smolder and ignite, it can transform you into
a ferocious, fire-breathing dragon—scaring, and even scarring,
those whom you love most. The only power strong enough to slay this
devastating dragon is the indwelling presence of Christ. When, as a
Christian, you allow Him to conform you to His character, then He
will permeate your heart with His peace.*

—JUNE HUNT

A Personal Note from June

Many people struggle with anger—with anger out of control, but that's really not me. Yet how well I remember *that* day.

The scene remains vivid in my mind. I opened my friend's desk drawer (something I had never done before) to get a few paper clips. Within seconds, I was staring at a piece of paper bearing these words: *We don't need any more June Hunts in this world.*

I was stunned…I was hurt…I was angry! Just an hour earlier, the writer of these words had said, "June, I'm really here for you. I want to help you; I want to support you."

Her words cut deep; I felt as if I had been stabbed in the back. Immediately, fire began rising inside me—my cheeks felt hot. And I knew if I didn't find a way to reduce the pent-up pressure, I would explode onto my "friend." So I thought, *I need to go outside and jog. Running will help release all this heat.*

Lacing my running shoes—tighter than normal—I walked out the front door ready to face my runaway rage. Then a few moments into my trek, I noticed my arms swinging higher than normal—intensely, vigorously, aggressively.

But after 20 minutes of running, I felt no relief. I had expected all my exertion to release the inner pressure—like a valve releasing the built-up steam inside a pressure cooker…but it didn't work. The valve over my heart seemed to be stuck! In fact, the longer I jogged, the greater the pressure became.

Soon I realized why there was no relief: I had been rehearsing in my mind—over and over—how much I had been wronged, deceived, betrayed. Yet the Bible clearly says in 1 Corinthians 13:5, "Love...keeps no record of wrongs." Keeps no record! I was doing the opposite. One thing was for certain—I wasn't helping to put out the fire.

I remember thinking, *My anger isn't any better—I need to do something else.* So I genuinely prayed, "Lord, teach me to act, rather than react." Over and over, I repeated those words: "Lord, teach me to act rather than react...Teach me to act rather than react..." Soon I was rhythmically praying that prayer, right in sync with my running stride.

After an hour, my pounding heart was finally at peace. I was no longer controlled by the debilitating sense of betrayal. Of course, the initial problem had not yet been resolved. But that night I released all my anger to the Lord.

I readily admit that the next day, during the discussion with my friend about the note, my anger did return. But this time I was able to control its fire rather than let the fire control me. I was no longer being consumed by its heat.

Ever since that day, when I feel a strong sense of anger, *if*—and I do mean *if*—I sincerely pray, "Lord, teach me to act rather than react," God gives me grace to carefully weigh my words and speak with self-control. And my heart is then at peace.

※

From my simple prayer—born out of anger—came a simple song:

> *When I feel disappointment with no soothing ointment,*
> *   and nothing is going my way,*
> *When my heart has been breaking and my soul is aching,*
> *   and I have no more words to say,*

> *I'm not under illusion, the only solution*
> *is die to my rights each day,*
> *Because Christ is inside me to comfort and guide me,*
> *and His life has taught me to pray:*
>
> *Lord, teach me to act rather than react,*
> *with Your Spirit in control of me.*
> *Lord, teach me to help rather than hinder,*
> *with the Lord being Lord of me.*
> *Lord, teach me to trust rather than mistrust,*
> *with Your Spirit inside my soul.*
> *Lord, teach me to act rather than react,*
> *I give You complete control.*

Anger—Answers in God's Word

Question: "Why should I be quick to listen, slow to speak, and slow to become angry?"

Answer: "Everyone should be quick to listen, slow to speak and slow to become angry, for man's anger does not bring about the righteous life that God desires" (James 1:19-20).

Question: "What is the result of being an angry person?"

Answer: "An angry man stirs up dissension, and a hot-tempered one commits many sins" (Proverbs 29:22).

Question: "What will happen if I hold on to anger?"

Answer: "'In your anger do not sin': Do not let the sun go down while you are still angry, and do not give the devil a foothold" (Ephesians 4:26-27).

Question: "A fool gives vent to his anger, but what does the wise person do?"

Answer: "A fool gives full vent to his anger, but a wise man keeps himself under control" (Proverbs 29:11).

Question: "A hot-tempered person stirs up dissension, but what does a patient person do?"

Answer: "A hot-tempered man stirs up dissension, but a patient man calms a quarrel" (Proverbs 15:18).

Question: "Why should I not be quickly provoked in my spirit?"

Answer: "Do not be quickly provoked in your spirit, for anger resides in the lap of fools" (Ecclesiastes 7:9).

Question: "A gentle answer turns away wrath, but what does a harsh word do?"

Answer: A gentle answer turns away wrath, but a harsh word stirs up anger" (Proverbs 15:1).

Question: "With what type of person should I not make friends or associate?"

Answer: "Do not make friends with a hot-tempered man, do not associate with one easily angered" (Proverbs 22:24).

Question: "God tells us to not sin in our anger. What should I do when I have anger in my heart?"

Answer: "In your anger do not sin; when you are on your beds, search your hearts and be silent" (Psalm 4:4).

Question: "Why should I not rescue a hot-tempered man?"

Answer: "A hot-tempered man must pay the penalty; if you rescue him, you will have to do it again" (Proverbs 19:19).

DEPRESSION
Walking from Darkness into the Dawn

Have dark clouds of depression poured their tears upon your soul? Are you emotionally stuck, your mind in the mud, your emotions all muddled? Do you feel isolated and alone, afraid that no one understands? If so, realize that you are far from being alone. People from all walks of life have languished under the dark clouds of depression.

Can anything bring back the blue skies of contentment? King David—no stranger to depression—discovered the answer. He learned how to exchange the darkness of despair for the light of hope.

Again and again, when David's soul was downcast, he intentionally changed his focus. He fixed his focus on the faithfulness of his Savior, his Redeemer, his God. Three times, in three different verses, David asked himself the same question, and three times he followed with the same answer:

> *"Why are you downcast, O my soul?*
> *Why so disturbed within me?*
> *Put your hope in God, for I will yet praise him,*
> *my Savior and my God"*
> (PSALM 42:5-6,11; 43:5).

I. DEFINITIONS OF DEPRESSION

You may be saying "I can't *think* straight. I can't *feel* anything. I can't even *will* myself out of the blues! What's going on?" You may be weathering the storm clouds of depression. And just as there are different kinds of clouds, there are also different types of depression.

A. What Is Depression?

If you place a heavy iron on a heart-shaped pillow filled with foam rubber, the buoyant pillow will become pressed down—"de-pressed." If you remove the iron a day later, the pillow will pop back up to its original form. However, if you wait six months to remove the iron, the pillow will not return to its original shape. Instead, the pillow will remain flat and depressed. A pillow, which can sustain temporary pressure, is not designed to hold its shape for a long time under heavy pressure.

The same is true for the human heart. When "pressed down" due to normal pressure from normal situations (*situational depression*), your heart is designed by God to rebound once the pressure is removed. However, if you live under the weight of heavy pressure for long periods of time, your heart can enter into a state of depression. Realize that Jesus cares about your heart and knows that you are especially vulnerable when you are heavyhearted. That is why He gives this word of caution:

> *"Be careful, or your hearts will be weighed down with*
> *dissipation, drunkenness and the anxieties of life, and*
> *that day will close on you unexpectedly like a trap"*
> (LUKE 21:34).

- *Depression* literally means a condition of being pressed down to a lower position (as in a footprint).[1]

- *Depression* can refer to a state of decline and reduced activity (as in an "economic depression").[2]

- *Depression* can describe an emotional heaviness that weighs down the heart. The apostle Paul used the Greek word *bareo,* which means "pressed or weighed down," to describe the immense emotional pressure and severe hardships that he and Timothy suffered at the hands of those who opposed Christ.[3]

> *"We do not want you to be uninformed, brothers,*
> *about the hardships we suffered in the province of*
> *Asia. We were under great pressure, far beyond our*
> *ability to endure, so that we despaired even of life.*
> *Indeed, in our hearts we felt the sentence of death"*
> (2 CORINTHIANS 1:8-9).

B. What Is Depression as Defined by Psychology?

Depression is considered a *mood disorder* because it has a disturbance in mood as the predominant feature.[4] In ancient writings, the earliest reference to what is meant by our word *depression* was the word *melancholia* (literally "black bile"). The assumption was that the melancholy person had an excess of black bile, which resulted in depression. In the second century A.D., the physician Aretaeus referred to his melancholy patients as "sad, dismayed, sleepless...They become thin by their agitation and loss of refreshing sleep...At a more advanced state, they complain of a thousand futilities and desire death."[5]

Even today *melancholia* is defined as "a mental condition characterized by extreme depression, bodily complaints, and often hallucinations and delusions."[6] This could be said of those who suffer during this dark night of the soul:

> *"For all of them, deep darkness is their morning;*
> *they make friends with the terrors of darkness"*
> (JOB 24:17).

- *Depression is the psychological term* that pertains to the mental, emotional, and behavioral characteristics of a depressed person. (*Psychology* is the study of the mind as it relates to thoughts, feelings, and behaviors, focusing on *why* people think, feel, and act as they do.)[7] For example, those engulfed in the dark waves of depression feel desperately alone and often blame God for their plight.

> *"You have taken my companions and loved ones*
> *from me; the darkness is my closest friend"*
> (PSALM 88:18).

- *Depression is a psychological state* that exists when the heart is pressed down and unable to experience joy. Those suffering with depression feel trapped underneath a dark, pervasive canopy of sadness, grief, guilt, and hopelessness.

> *"Darkness comes upon them in the daytime;*
> *at noon they grope as in the night"*
> (JOB 5:14).

- *Depression is a psychological condition* that impacts the whole person: body (the physical), soul (the mind, will, and emotions), and spirit (the source of our deepest inner needs for love, significance, and security…and the need for God Himself). Many who are depressed feel as though this verse describes them:

> *"All his days he eats in darkness, with great*
> *frustration, affliction and anger"*
> (ECCLESIASTES 5:17).

- *Depression is an umbrella term* that covers feelings ranging from mild discouragement to intense despair.[8] No matter what the degree of darkness, the Lord wants us to rely on Him to provide light.

> *"You, O LORD, keep my lamp burning; my*
> *God turns my darkness into light"*
> (PSALM 18:28).

C. What Are the Different Degrees of Depression?

The following four categories show an escalating intensity of depression. In general, depression could be divided into two categories: *situational* and *chemical.*

- *Situational depression* exists when a painful situation presses the heart down for a period of time.

- *Chemical depression* can occur when the body chemistry does not function properly. A person can have either type of depression or both types at the same time. During the heavy-hearted times when hope seems elusive, emotions feel flat and the heart feels sick. Solomon, the wise author of the book of Proverbs, explains that

> *"hope deferred makes the heart sick, but*
> *a longing fulfilled is a tree of life"*
> (PROVERBS 13:12).

(The four types of depression described below are not listed in this order in a diagnostic manual. The order given here is intended to show the increasingly negative impact of the different degrees of depression.)

1. *Normal Depression*
- Is sometimes called situational depression or reactive depression
- Is an involuntary sadness based on a reaction to painful life situations
  —*Normal problems* of life press down the heart for a short period of time (for example, rejection, failure, illness)
  —*Transitional stages* of life often press down the heart (for example, adolescence, empty nest, midlife crises, major moves, menopause, retirement)[9]

When severe troubles fell upon God's servant Job (the death of all his children, the destruction of all his possessions), one of Job's friends made this observation:

> *"Now trouble comes to you, and you are discouraged;*
> *it strikes you, and you are dismayed"*
> (Job 4:5).

2. *Masked Depression*
- Is hidden depression (for example, repressed memories of physical, sexual, verbal, or emotional abuse)
- Is a state of enduring sadness based on unresolved, buried conflict
  —Painful feelings are denied or covered up; therefore, recovery takes longer because of failure to work through the pain
  —Relief from emotional pain is unconsciously found in excessive busyness, activities, addictions, or other alternatives

The Bible describes how hidden hurts still result in heartache:

> *"Even in laughter the heart may ache,*
> *and joy may end in grief"*
> (Proverbs 14:13).

3. *Neurotic Depression*[10]

- Is a minor mental and emotional *depressive disorder* classified as Adjustment Disorder with Depressed Mood, meaning that the depression results from failure to adjust to a distressing situation

  —A person with neurosis has a disorder, meaning that normal activities of daily living are impaired

  —A person with any depressive disorder has "clinical depression" and needs diagnosis and treatment based on direct, ongoing observation

- Is a prolonged state of sadness lasting longer than the normal time frame expected for emotional recovery—based on "stressors" (for example, loss of a loved one, a financial or work crisis, retirement, or a biochemical condition)

  —Symptoms interfere with normal work and social functioning

  —The cause can usually be traced to an identifiable, precipitating event

The psalms reflect the pain of prolonged sorrow:

> *"How long must I wrestle with my thoughts*
> *and every day have sorrow in my heart? How*
> *long will my enemy triumph over me?"*
> (PSALM 13:2).

4. *Psychotic Depression*

- Is the most severe type of depression under the classification Major Depressive Disorder (MDD)[11]
- Is based on dissociation or a loss of contact with reality[12]

  —A psychosis is an extreme state of depression

  —A psychosis is usually accompanied by hallucinations and/or delusions, making those who are psychotic a potential danger to themselves or others

Those afflicted with a psychotic depression can identify with the terror, despair, and skewed perspective described in this Psalm:

> *"My days vanish like smoke...My heart is blighted*
> *and withered like grass; I forget to eat my food...I*

> *lie awake; I have become like a bird alone on*
> *a roof…I eat ashes as my food and mingle my*
> *drink with tears…I wither away like grass"*
> (PSALM 102:3-4,7,9,11).

D. What Are the Different Kinds of Mood Disorders?

Every year, new maladies, as well as new medicines, come on the scene. So, how "new" is depression? As far back as the fourth century B.C., the famous physician Hippocrates gave the first clinical description of melancholia, including the erratic mood swings of what is called *bipolar disorder* today. Yet over 500 years earlier, the psalmist, King David, gave this vivid description of his emotions during one of the most severe storms in his life:

> *"My thoughts trouble me and I am distraught…*
> *My heart is in anguish within me; the terrors of death*
> *assail me. Fear and trembling have beset me; horror*
> *has overwhelmed me. I said, 'Oh, that I had the wings*
> *of a dove! I would fly away and be at rest—I would*
> *flee far away and stay in the desert; I would hurry to*
> *my place of shelter, far from the tempest and storm'"*
> (PSALM 55:2,4-8).

The three divisions of mood disorders are:[13]

1. *Depressive Disorders (also called unipolar depression)*[14]

- Unipolar depression is primarily characterized by one extreme, emotionally-low state of depression.
- *Unipolar* (*uni* = "one," *polar* = "pole") refers to "one extreme end"
- Unipolar depression is the most common type of mood disorder.
- Unipolar, in the psychological community, is subdivided into three types: Major Depression Disorder (MDD), Dysthymic Disorder, and Depressive Disorder Not Otherwise Specified.

When a person is continually depressed, he or she can understandably pray,

> *"Be merciful to me, O LORD, for I am in distress; my eyes*
> *grow weak with sorrow, my soul and my body with grief"*
> (PSALM 31:9).

2. Bipolar Disorders (formerly called manic-depression)[15]

- Bipolar disorders are characterized by alternating patterns of extreme emotional highs and lows—mania and depression
- *Bipolar* (*bi* = "two," *polar* = "pole") refers to "two opposite ends"
- Bipolar episodes of *mania* (an excessively elevated mood) can appear positive and productive to outsiders; however, true mania is negative because it usually leads to destructive decision-making, such as buying sprees, impulsive decisions, reckless driving, foolish investments, and immoral behavior
- Bipolar disorder is subdivided into four types:
  —Bipolar I Disorder
  —Bipolar II Disorder
  —Cyclothymia
  —Bipolar Disorder Not Otherwise Specified

When the heart is distressed because of a bipolar disorder, it can be natural to cry out to God for help as the psalmist did:

> *"I cried out to God for help; I cried out to God to hear me. When I was in distress, I sought the Lord; at night I stretched out untiring hands and my soul refused to be comforted. I remembered you, O God, and I groaned; I mused, and my spirit grew faint. You kept my eyes from closing; I was too troubled to speak"*
> (PSALM 77:1-4).

3. Mood Disorders (based on etiology)[16]

- The word *etiology* means "cause" or "origin."[17]

MOOD DISORDER DUE TO A GENERAL MEDICAL CONDITION[18]

This means that unhealthy changes in a body, due to illness, cause psychological depression. For example, a 2007 study indicates that 27 percent of Parkinson's patients experience depression, while earlier studies contend that up to 50 percent of untreated early Parkinson's cases lead to depression.[19]

SUBSTANCE-INDUCED MOOD DISORDER[20]

This means that something entering the body causes depression. The substance could be medication, drugs, or exposure to a toxin (for example, alcohol, sedatives, birth control pills, medications to treat various diseases such as Parkinson's).

No matter what the cause, the depressed person feels like saying,

> *"I am feeble and utterly crushed; I*
> *groan in anguish of heart"*
> (PSALM 38:8).

E. Is Depression the Result of Sin?

This question cannot be answered with a simple yes or no. Although some people believe the answer is always yes, the accurate answer is sometimes yes and sometimes no.

Depression is not a result of sin when...

- your heart grieves over normal losses. The Bible says,

> *"[There is] a time to weep...a time to mourn"*
> (ECCLESIASTES 3:4).

- your body experiences natural deterioration due to the passing of years, or your body chemistry changes and becomes compromised. The Bible says,

> *"Outwardly we are wasting away, yet inwardly*
> *we are being renewed day by day"*
> (2 CORINTHIANS 4:16).

Depression can be a result of sin when...

- you are depressed over the consequences of your sinful actions, and you don't attempt to change.
- you don't take the necessary steps for healing (seeking biblical counseling, memorizing scriptures, reading Christian materials, getting medical help when appropriate).
- you hold on to self-pity, anger, or bitterness when you have been wronged instead of choosing to forgive.

*"Anyone, then, who knows the good he
ought to do and doesn't do it, sins"*
(JAMES 4:17).

- you use your depression to manipulate others.
- you continually choose to blame God and others for your unhappiness.
- you are depressed because you choose to let others control you instead of choosing to obey Christ and allow Him to be in control of you.

If you willfully choose to stay in sin while you are taking the Lord's Supper, remember that Jesus died on the cross for your sins—His body was broken for you (breaking of bread) and His blood was shed for you (drinking from the cup), and for you to remain in sin is to take the Lord's Supper in an unworthy manner. The Bible says of those who do this "that is why many of you are weak and sick" (1 Corinthians 11:30).

Depiction of Jonah's Depression

DEPRESSION AS A RESULT OF SIN

Jonah's bout with depression is an example of *situational depression* that occurs as a direct result of sin. Jonah is a man called by God. Yet he ends up angry, pouting, and in the depths of depression. How does Jonah become so deeply depressed?

Chapter 1: Disobedience

Jonah is called by the Lord to preach God's truth to the godless people of Nineveh. But Jonah rebels and boards a ship going in a different direction. When Jonah's disobedience brings repercussions on the ship's crew, he is rejected by the crew and literally thrown overboard.

Chapter 2: Dread

Recognizing that the judgment of God is upon him to the point of losing his life (inside the belly of a great fish), Jonah cries out for mercy: "He said: 'In my distress I called to the LORD, and he answered me. From the depths of the grave I called for help, and you listened to my cry'" (Jonah 2:2). The Lord extends mercy and spares Jonah's life.

Chapter 3: Declaration

Jonah resigns himself to obeying God's call. He declares God's truth, and all the godless people of Nineveh repent.

Chapter 4: Depression

Jonah becomes angry with God for extending mercy to those whom Jonah doesn't deem worthy of mercy. Ultimately, he plunges into a severe depression in which he is consumed with bitterness and despair to the extent of wanting to die. Jonah moans, "O LORD, take away my life, for it is better for me to die than to live" (Jonah 4:3).

Then, filled with seething anger and self-pity, Jonah makes this brief, poignant statement: "I am angry enough to die" (Jonah 4:9).

II. CHARACTERISTICS OF DEPRESSION

Those who struggle in the darkness of depression have difficulty seeing good in their lives...especially in themselves. They often look at life through a "black filter."

When a photographer uses a black lens and takes a picture during the daytime, the photograph appears to be a night scene. In a similar way, the depressed see through a dark lens that affects their perception of the world around them. Consequently, they feel helpless about their situations, hatred toward themselves, and hopeless over their future.

If you are walking in the darkness of depression, you need to focus on the light of the Lord and know that He profoundly cares. In the psalm below, you can see how King David chose to change his focus while in a difficult time:

> *"Look to my right and see; no one is concerned*
> *for me. I have no refuge; no one cares for my*
> *life. I cry to you, O LORD; I say, 'You are my*
> *refuge, my portion in the land of the living'"*
> (PSALM 142:4-5).

A. What Is the Dialogue of the Depressed?

Words are powerful. They can change minds, hearts, and ultimately lives. When a painful situation causes us to react with negative emotions, the thoughts that follow that reaction will determine if those *emotions* will rule us or if *truth* will rule us.

Why? There is actually a physical connection in all this, based on how God designed the human brain. When we feel emotional pain, if the language center of the brain is activated, the strength in the emotional center of the brain is automatically reduced. *This means our thoughts have power over our emotions—even to the point of overriding our emotions and bringing them into subjection.*

Because the spoken word has more power than the unspoken word, it is important to speak words of truth—words of faith—in order that truth and faith may be strengthened within you. Ultimately, *feelings follow thinking.* Therefore, what you *say* to yourself about yourself, about your situation, about your future, and even about God will determine how you *feel* about yourself, your situation, your future, and God and His relationship with you. As you line up your thinking with God's thinking, your words will bring life, not death.

> *"The tongue has the power of life and death"*
> (PROVERBS 18:21).

What do you say about yourself?

- "I can't do anything right!"
- "Why should I even try?"
- "My usefulness is over."
- "I hate myself."
- "Look at so-and-so" (by comparison).
- "I must have done something wrong!"
- "Nobody loves me!"

What the light of truth says:

> *"'Though the mountains be shaken and the hills*
> *be removed, yet my unfailing love for you will not*
> *be shaken nor my covenant of peace be removed,'*
> *says the LORD, who has compassion on you"*
> (ISAIAH 54:10).

What do you say about your situation?

- "I don't see any way out!"
- "It didn't matter anyway!"
- "This is intolerable!"
- "It's not fair!"
- "I'm helpless to change it!"
- "I can't do anything about it!"
- "I can't bear it!"

What the light of truth says:

> *You can say with the apostle Paul, "I can do everything through him who gives me strength"* (PHILIPPIANS 4:13).

What do you say about your future?

- "So what!"
- "Nothing will change…."
- "No one will ever love me!"
- "I'll be too old…."
- "That was my last chance for happiness!"
- "I have nothing to live for."
- "It's hopeless!"

What the light of truth says:

> *God says, "'I know the plans I have for you,' declares the LORD, 'plans to prosper you and not to harm you, plans to give you hope and a future'"* (JEREMIAH 29:11).

If you are walking in darkness, then cherish these words from the Lord:

> *"I will lead the blind by ways they have not known, along unfamiliar paths I will guide them; I will turn the darkness*

into light before them and make the rough places smooth.
These are the things I will do; I will not forsake them"
(Isaiah 42:16).

The Painter, the Razor, the Snuffed-out Candle[21]

His boyhood dream was to become a pastor—to follow in the footsteps of his father and grandfather.[22]

Once describing his life mission as "preaching the gospel to the poor," he immersed himself in studying the Scriptures. At age 23, the spiritually zealous assistant minister delivered his first sermon. Focusing on the theme "our life is a pilgrim's progress"…and he stated on numerous occasions that our lives should be led as an imitation of Christ's.[23]

Who was this Dutchman born in 1853—the one who hoped to carry on his family's spiritual legacy? He was the world-renowned artist Vincent van Gogh. Unfortunately, this highly emotional young man lacked self-confidence and experienced major problems during his life.

Following a brief stint as a missionary in a mining district in Belgium, van Gogh's spiritual fervor spiraled downward into depression. Just six months after his appointment, he was dismissed. Though "poor speaking" was cited as the cause, in actuality he encountered huge disagreements over how to conduct "real" ministry.

Van Gogh had a heart for the impoverished—the materially and spiritually poor to whom he had been assigned. He lived with them and like them—even sleeping on a straw mat night after night. He perceived the religious leaders of his day as distant and removed, caught up in stuffy propriety and protocol, disengaged from the grittiness of real-life ministry.

Following the time he was fired, van Gogh remained in the mining community and began sketching pictures…and the course of his life changed forever. He once said, "An artist needn't be a clergyman or a churchwarden, but he certainly must have a warm heart for his fellow men."[24]

As van Gogh became immersed in the tumultuous world of artists, his life became more tortuous. Originally fixated on the muddy-colored paintings of the poor, he moved to Paris in 1886 to live with his devoted brother, Theo, an art dealer. At one point, van Gogh advised his brother to take up pipe smoking, calling it "a remedy for the blues, which I happen to have now and then lately."[25] Theo introduced van Gogh to artists such as Gaugin, with whom he had a volatile relationship. Van Gogh delved into more vivid colors in Paris and there acquired the distinctive brushstrokes that now signify his work.

Then after moving to the south of France in 1888, van Gogh incorporated the yellows and hot reds of the Mediterranean into his paintings. This was said to represent his moods. Here he and Gaugin painted together—and argued together. Their deteriorating friendship culminated in van Gogh chasing Gaugin with a razor...but that infamous episode ended with van Gogh cutting off part of his own left ear lobe. The very next year, the unstable artist voluntarily committed himself into a mental asylum.

Diagnoses are diverse in regard to what may have caused the eccentric and unstable behavior in this post-Impressionist painter. Psychiatrists report that as an adult, van Gogh suffered two distinct episodes of reactive depression along with "bipolar aspects." And that the last two years of van Gogh's life were characterized by recurring psychotic episodes.[26]

The French physicians who attended van Gogh in the asylum diagnosed his condition as epilepsy caused by consuming absinthe—a liqueur with high alcoholic content and toxic herbs. Well over 150 physicians have since ventured diagnoses, but there is limited information upon which to draw a definitive conclusion.[27]

Van Gogh's life was a continual pattern of suffering and setbacks, and isolation and ill will from those around him. But his brother Theo gave him constant support and encouragement. One day as the two surveyed van Gogh's vast collection of painted canvasses, Theo commented, "When your heart shall cease to beat within your bosom, it will throb in your pictures."[28]

And on July 29, 1890, at the young age of 37, van Gogh's heart did cease beating. He died from a self-inflicted gunshot wound. Vincent van Gogh died having sold only one of his paintings, for about $100. (By contrast, in recent years his painting *Irises* sold for $53.9 million.)

The life of van Gogh does indeed throb in his pictures, but further tragedy rests in the fact that his focus on the Bible—so beloved to him in the first chapter of his life—weakened as he grew older…when he so desperately needed spiritual help and healing.

However, one sign of his spiritual heritage did appear in his art near the end of his life. Shortly after his father's death, and four years before his own, van Gogh painted *Still Life with Bible,* which depicts his father's Bible, atop a table, worn and opened.

However, van Gogh painted the Bible as sitting in the darkness beside a snuffed-out candle. Had he returned to his former passion—to be an imitator of Christ—and turned to his own Bible, he might have painted a brighter picture of the Lord's life-changing hope amidst the darkness of depression.

B. What Are the Symptoms of Depression and Mania?

Some clouds bring a gentle rain. Others evoke violent thunder and lightning. Still others spawn tornadoes with vast destructive power. And finally, some storms are so huge that weather forecasters give them names, such as Hugo and Katrina. By knowing the particular kind of "storm" your depression has produced, you can more fully understand your struggles.

Typical Symptoms of a Deep Depression[29]

- *Depressed persons* display a sad, discouraged, joyless disposition.

  Major depressive episodes involve five or more of the following classic symptoms nearly every day for at least two weeks:

  —Pervasive depressed moods

—Diminished pleasure in usual activities

—Significant change in appetite or weight

—Fatigue or loss of energy

—Diminished ability to think clearly, evaluate, or concentrate

—Slower or more agitated movements

—Too little or too much sleep

—Feelings of worthlessness or excessive guilt

—Suicidal thoughts/attempts

- *Depressed children* display some additional symptoms:

  —Academic or behavioral problems at school

  —Tearful or sad countenance

  —Mood swings from happy/giddy/silly to sad/angry/irritable

  —Temper tantrums which last over ten minutes

  —Aggressiveness towards peers, teachers, and/or other adults

  —Frequent illnesses to avoid school attendance

  —Regression in behavior (clinginess, wanting to sleep with parents, talking baby talk)

- *Depressed adolescents* display the following symptoms:

  —Change in friends

  —Social isolation

  —Interest in music promoting hatred of others or self-destructiveness

  —Defiance of reasonable parental rules

  —Drug experimentation

  —Promiscuous behavior or sexual experimentation

  —Inordinate focus on video games

  —Excessive surreptitious use of the Internet

Typical Symptoms of Manic Behavior[30]

- *Manic persons* display unfounded, euphoric dispositions coupled with various acts of abnormally poor judgment.

- *Manic episodes* occur when three or more of the following classic symptoms, not normal for the person, last for at least one week:
  —Inflated ego
  —Racing thoughts
  —Easily distracted
  —Excessive talk
  —Decreased need for sleep
  —Increased obsession over a goal
  —Excessive involvement in pleasures that risk negative consequences

- *Bipolar persons* display occurrences of both manic and depressive episodes.

King Saul's Mania and Depression

The extreme emotional and behavioral swings of King Saul are similar to many symptoms associated with bipolar disorder. At times, Saul appeared to have alternating episodes of mania and depression.[31]

CHARACTERISTICS OF MANIA	KING SAUL'S MANIC BEHAVIOR
Irritability	He disobeyed God because of impatience

Irritated that the prophet Samuel had not arrived to offer the designated sacrifice before battle, Saul became impatient and offered the sacrifice himself. After Samuel arrived, Saul voiced his excuse: "When I saw that the men were scattering, and that you did not come at the set time…I thought, 'Now the Philistines will come down against me'…So I felt compelled to offer the burnt offering" (1 Samuel 13:11-12). Saul's decision to offer the sacrifice himself disobeyed the clear command of God.

Poor judgment	He forbade his army to eat during battle

Saul's army was in distress because Saul had bound his troops to "an oath, saying, 'Cursed be any man who eats food before evening comes, before I have avenged myself on my enemies!' So none of the troops tasted food" (1 Samuel 14:24). And the men became weak.

Engaging in excessive pleasures	He kept excessive battle spoils

God told Saul to completely destroy the enemy as well as their possessions; however, Saul kept the forbidden battle spoils: "The best of the sheep and cattle, the fat calves and lambs—everything that was good...Then the word of the LORD came to Samuel: 'I am grieved that I have made Saul king, because he has turned away from me and has not carried out my instructions'" (1 Samuel 15:7-11).

Inflated self-esteem	He erected a statue of himself

Although Samuel went early to meet with Saul, Samuel was told, "Saul has gone to Carmel. There he has set up a monument in his own honor" (1 Samuel 15:12), clearly an act of grandiosity.

Easily distracted	He became distracted by the Israeli women's song

When Saul's men were returning from battle, rather than focusing on the victory, Saul was distracted by what the women were singing. Although the refrain was meant to honor the troops, "Saul was very angry; this refrain galled him. 'They have credited David with tens of thousands,' he thought, 'but me with only thousands. What more can he get but the kingdom?'" Saul's frequent irritability was obvious, as "from that time on Saul kept a jealous eye on David" (1 Samuel 18:8-9).

Excessive focus on a goal	He became obsessed with the goal to kill David

When David first began serving the king, "Saul liked him [David] very much." However, "When Saul realized that the LORD was with David and that his daughter Michal loved David, Saul...remained his enemy the rest of his days." Jonathan appealed to his father, Saul, "He [David]...has benefited you greatly." Saul took an oath: "As surely as the LORD lives, David will not be put to death." Yet later, "Saul sent men to David's house...to kill him." Saul made additional attempts to take David's life (1 Samuel 16:21; 18:28-29; 19:4,6,11).

Racing thoughts	He entertained thoughts to kill the son he loved

To determine whether his father was planning to kill David, Jonathan excused David from the king's presence, which made Saul furious. He demanded, "Bring him [David] to me, for he must die!" Jonathan asked, "'What has he done?'...But Saul hurled his spear at him [Jonathan, the son he loved] to kill him" (1 Samuel 20:31-33).

CHARACTERISTICS OF DEPRESSION	KING SAUL'S DEPRESSED BEHAVIOR
Unfounded, euphoric mood	He presumed he had the Lord's favor

Saul, in the midst of an elevated mood, said, "'God has handed him [David] over to me'...Saul called up all his forces for battle...to besiege David and his men" (1 Samuel 23:7-8). But Saul's presumption was dead wrong.

Discouragement, dismay, hopelessness	He lost hope in the face of fear

Although God had delivered Saul in many battles, when Saul's army was challenged by the Philistine giant Goliath, "Saul and all the Israelites were dismayed and terrified." Clearly God had anointed Saul as king, yet Saul continued to battle debilitating fear and hopelessness. Later, when Saul was again challenged by the Philistines, "He was afraid; terror filled his heart" (1 Samuel 17:11; 28:5).

Diminished pleasure in usual activities	He no longer enjoyed David's harp

Often David soothed Saul's troubled spirit by playing the harp. On one occasion, "while David was playing the harp, Saul tried to pin him to the wall with his spear, but David eluded him as Saul drove the spear into the wall" (1 Samuel 16:23; 19:9-10).

Increased irritability	He flew into angry outbursts

"He [Saul] was prophesying in his house, while David was playing the harp, as he usually did." With no provocation whatsoever, "Saul had a spear in his hand and he hurled it, saying to himself, 'I'll pin David to the wall.' But David eluded him twice" (1 Samuel 18:10-11).

Unrealistic negative evaluations	He accused his men of treason

Saul, in his attempt to find and kill David, made unjust accusations toward his son and innocent countrymen: "Will the son of Jesse [David] give all of you fields and vineyards? Will he make all of you commanders of thousands and commanders of hundreds? Is that why you have all conspired against me? No one tells me when my son makes a covenant with the son of Jesse. None of you is concerned about me or tells me that my son has incited my servant to lie in wait for me, as he does today" (1 Samuel 22:7-8).

Exaggerated frustration	He put to death one who confronted him

When Saul falsely accused a priest who innocently helped David, the priest sought to reason with Saul: "Who of all your servants is as loyal as David, the king's son-in-law, captain of your bodyguard and highly respected in your household?" But in denial, Saul said to the priest, "You will surely die...you and your father's whole family" (1 Samuel 22:14,16).

Sad, discouraged, pessimistic	He bemoaned his fate and feared David

Saul learned that David had spared his life. With periodic, overwhelming sadness, Saul expressed his dread of the future, saying, "I know that you will surely be king and that the kingdom of Israel will be established in your hands. Now swear to me by the LORD that you will not cut off my descendants or wipe out my name from my father's family" (1 Samuel 24:20-21).

Loss of appetite	He refused to eat

Saul was in such a depressed state that he said, "I will not eat" (1 Samuel 28:23).

Suicidal thoughts or attempts	He took his own life

Upon receiving a critical wound in battle and being unable to persuade his armor-bearer to kill him, "Saul took his own sword and fell on it" (1 Samuel 31:4).

Elijah's Descent into Depression

Elijah was a mighty man of God. At a supernatural showdown on Mount Carmel, he courageously stood up to 450 false prophets. The "contest" involved whose "God" could miraculously set fire to a wood sacrifice upon an altar. In the end, this act would prove to all Israel who was the one true God.

The false prophets, after a full day of pleading, could not cause their false god to bring down fire from heaven. When it was Elijah's turn, he began by thoroughly drenching the wood with water. Then Elijah called upon God, who sent the fire to consume the water-soaked sacrifice. As a result, all of Israel "fell prostrate and cried, 'The LORD—he is God! The LORD he is God!'" (1 Kings 18:39).

Angry that Elijah had upstaged her 450 false prophets, the wicked Queen Jezebel delivered a death threat against Elijah. This prophet who had been so bold suddenly melted in fear and fled into the desert. Discouraged and depressed, feeling like a failure, he wearily pleaded, "I have had enough LORD. Take my life" (1 Kings 19:4).

In spite of Elijah's despondent condition, the Lord ministered to him, met his needs, and gave him new hope for his heart.

Loss

One or more basic needs are threatened.[32]

Love   Significance   Security

Elijah's security was threatened.

"Elijah was afraid and ran for his life. When he came to Beersheba in Judah, he left his servant there"
(1 Kings 19:3).

Negative Thinking Patterns

Self-Pity   Self-condemnation   Fear   Hopelessness

Elijah thought to himself, *I have had enough,* **and asked God to take his life.**

"He himself went a day's journey into the desert. He came to a broom tree, sat down under it and prayed that he might die. 'I have had enough, Lord,' he said. 'Take my life; I am not better than my ancestors'"

(1 Kings 19:4).

Repressed Anger

Buried resentment over circumstances

Elijah was frustrated that all his efforts seemed in vain.

"He replied, 'I have been very zealous for the Lord God Almighty. The Israelites have rejected your covenant, broken down your altars, and put your prophets to death with the sword. I am the only one left, and now they are trying to kill me too'"

(1 Kings 19:10).

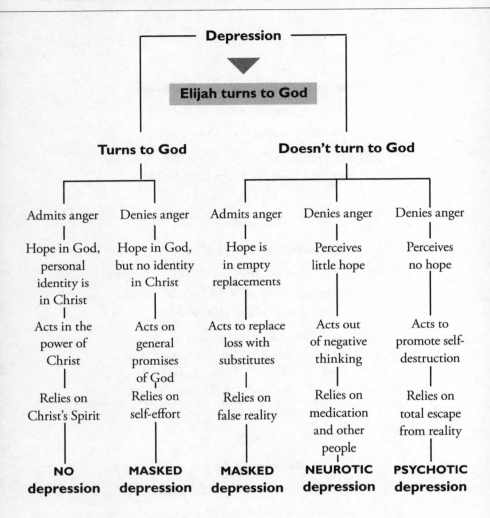

Depression

Elijah turns to God

Turns to God		Doesn't turn to God		
Admits anger	Denies anger	Admits anger	Denies anger	Denies anger
Hope in God, personal identity is in Christ	Hope in God, but no identity in Christ	Hope is in empty replacements	Perceives little hope	Perceives no hope
Acts in the power of Christ	Acts on general promises of God	Acts to replace loss with substitutes	Acts out of negative thinking	Acts to promote self-destruction
Relies on Christ's Spirit	Relies on self-effort	Relies on false reality	Relies on medication and other people	Relies on total escape from reality
NO depression	**MASKED depression**	**MASKED depression**	**NEUROTIC depression**	**PSYCHOTIC depression**

Question: "Does taking medicine for depression show a lack of faith in God?"

Answer: No. Various physical conditions can contribute to depression. For example, in bipolar and postpartum depression, a biochemical imbalance exists within the body that can be treated successfully with medication. Unfortunately, many Christians fear being labeled unspiritual if they seek medical help for their depression, yet by doing nothing, they end up suffering needlessly.

Sometimes medication is needed for a period of time to help level out mountainous swings so that those in the throes of depression can see truth and walk on level ground. Ezekiel 47:12 explains that God made "leaves for healing." Therefore, medicine is biblical.

Medicine, however, should be used not to numb pain or escape it, but to help a person process the pain. Also, medication should be the last avenue, tried only after all other steps have been taken, and always in conjunction with counseling.

III. Causes of Depression

On June 20, 2001, the nation—and the world—were stunned by a steady stream of horrific TV and radio reports about a woman named Andrea Yates, who had systematically drowned her children in a bathtub. She had done this to all five children, ranging from six months to seven years of age.[33]

In heart-wrenching disbelief, shocked people asked, "How could a mother kill her own children? How unthinkable! What could drive a mother to commit such a heinous crime…five times in a row?" In a word, the answer is depression—not just normal depression, but psychotic depression—a major depression that caused Andrea to break with reality.[34]

Couldn't someone have rescued this mother and her innocent children from this horrible tragedy? The simple answer is yes. That is why attaining an in-depth understanding of depression is vital. The Lord admonishes us all to…

> *"rescue those being led away to death; hold back those*
> *staggering toward slaughter. If you say, 'But we knew*
> *nothing about this,' does not he who weighs the heart*
> *perceive it? Does not he who guards your life know it? Will*
> *he not repay each person according to what he has done?"*
> (Proverbs 24:11-12).

A. What Are the Physical Contributors to Depression?

Andrea Yates suffered from depression following the birth of her third baby, and even more severely after the birth of her fourth child. Her doctor advised Andrea and her husband to have no more children because of the extreme hormonal changes in her body after her last delivery. When Andrea's fifth was born, the deficit of her hormones caused her to plunge headfirst into postpartum psychosis (a break with reality).[35]

Tragically, many mothers with postpartum psychosis are consumed with thoughts of death to their babies and destruction of themselves. They could have written these words:

> *"The cords of death entangled me; the torrents of*
> *destruction overwhelmed me. The cords of the grave*
> *coiled around me; the snares of death confronted me"*
> (PSALM 18:4-5).

Six Physical Contributors to Depression[36]

1. Hormonal imbalance

Can depression be caused by a chemical imbalance in the brain? This frequently asked question is answered with a definite yes! For example, hormonal changes during puberty, postpartum (after childbirth), and perimenopause (around menopause) can lead to depression.

2. Medications and drugs

Certain legal and illegal drugs can cause depression, such as analgesics, antidepressants, steroids, contraceptives, and cardiac medications.

3. Chronic illnesses

Medical problems such as a thyroid deficiency and even a bout with the flu can cause chemical imbalances in the brain, which, in turn, can cause depression.

4. Melancholy temperament

Orderly, gifted, and creative, the person with a melancholy temperament can, at the same time, be moody, overly sensitive, and self-denegrating. Because those with this temperament are analytical, critical, and hard to please, they can take everything too seriously or too personally, quickly becoming depressed over circumstances or the slightest imperfection in themselves or others.

5. Inattention to physical needs

A deficiency in the physical basics of life can contribute to a chronic sense of fatigue, lack of energy, and social withdrawal.

6. Genetic vulnerability

Based on statistical data, those with depressed family members are twice as vulnerable to depression as those with no family history of depression. Likewise, up to 50 percent of those suffering with bipolar disorder have at least one parent suffering from the same disorder.

If you are concerned about depression, then learn what you can about your family history and your treatment options. Learning as much as possible about your health issues is essential.

> *"A simple man believes anything, but a*
> *prudent man gives thought to his steps"*
> (PROVERBS 14:15).

Question: "Why do twice as many women have depression as men?"[37]

Answer: A hormone deficiency can cause severe depression, and women produce only one-half the amount of the hormone serotonin in their brains as men. However, estrogen in women multiplies the amount of serotonin to equal the level in men. For women, the greater challenge of depression occurs at three specific times—prior to a menstrual cycle, after childbirth, and around menopause—when estrogen levels drop, sometimes dramatically. If a woman's estrogen level is not sufficient to multiply serotonin, she experiences a depletion of serotonin, which can cause depression. This is one reason many women receive estrogen replacement therapy (ERT) and why other women consult their physicians for medication in order to feel healthy again.

B. Why Is Depression Often Not Diagnosed?[38]

When we see someone who feels down, we try to find logical, temporary reasons: "You're just tired...you need more sleep...you work too hard...you aren't eating right...you need alone time." While some of those observations may be true, we can also miss the real diagnosis because of a lack of awareness.

To illustrate, every mother of a newborn baby expects to feel joy and excitement over the new birth. But when she doesn't, she initially feels immense guilt and confusion. Family and friends can assume she's just tired and exhausted. Yet loved ones may not realize there are very real causes for her changes in mood and behavior. For example...

The Baby Blues

From three to five days up to two weeks after birth, approximately 70 percent of new mothers experience the following:

—Sudden mood changes

—Frequent unexplained crying

—Guilt over not bonding with her baby

—Changes in sleeping and eating

—Lack of concentration

—Irritability, anger

—A sense of loss

—Lethargy

Postpartum Depression

Experienced by up to 20 percent of birth mothers, postpartum depression is distinguished from the baby blues both by its longer duration and the debilitating indifference of the mother toward herself and her children.[39]

—Excessive concern for the baby because she senses something is wrong with her own feelings about being a mother

—Little or no feeling of love for the baby or for the rest of her family

—A lack of interest in her baby; a feeling of being trapped

—Emotional numbness, sadness, fatigue

—Withdrawal from family and friends

—Significant weight loss or gain

—Anxiety or panic attacks

—Change in appetite

Postpartum Psychosis

A life-threatening depression affecting one or two of every 1,000 birth mothers and characterized by:[40]

—Strange thoughts/making strange statements

—Feeling agitated or angry toward her baby and family

—Overly critical of her ability to be a good mother

—Thoughts of harming herself or the baby

—Paranoia, confusion, disorientation

—Delusions that the baby is demon-possessed

—Voices or visions of demons attacking her ability to be a good mother

—Hallucinations commanding her to kill the baby and her other children (infanticide)

The mother struggling with postpartum psychosis can identify with these words:

> *"The cords of death entangled me, the anguish of the grave*
> *came upon me; I was overcome by trouble and sorrow"*
> (PSALM 116:3).

C. What Role Can Medication Play in Alleviating Depression?

Were the family and friends of Andrea Yates aware of the seriousness of her depression?[41]

The court trial revealed that Andrea had been hospitalized for severe depression several times, and twice she was released prematurely. Rusty, her husband, appealed to her last doctor, stating that Andrea needed an earlier medication that had proved successful—but his plea was to no avail.

> *"The troubles of my heart have multiplied;*
> *free me from my anguish"*
> (PSALM 25:17).

Every person on earth has billions of brain cells, among them nerve cells. These nerve cells, or neurons, both send and receive "chemical messengers" called *neurotransmitters,* and without them we could neither think nor feel. These neurotransmitters are powerful chemicals that have a major impact on our happiness, sadness, anger, logic, sleep, memory, anxiety, thinking, and even facial expressions. In depression, often a deficiency of vital neurotransmitters exists—specifically low levels of serotonin, norepinephrine, dopamine, or GABA (gamma-aminobutyric acid).[42]

D. How Can Antidepressants Work to Relieve Depression?

When an electrical impulse reaches the part of a neuron where neurotransmitters are stored (called the *pre-receptor site*), these chemicals are released from the nerve cell and enter the gap between neurons (called the *synapse*). These neurotransmitters then travel across the synapse and attach to a *post-receptor site* in another neuron.

Antidepressants are nonaddicting drugs that block the reuptake (returning to the same neuron from which it left) and lessen (*degradation*) the depression-related neurotransmitters between synapses. Thus they increase the numbers of neurotransmitters and ultimately alter other chemicals within the nerve cell and nervous system. The result is a cascade of chemical reactions in the brain, which, in turn, lifts the depressed mood and alters behavior.[43]

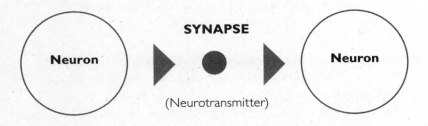

SYNAPSE

Neuron   Neuron

(Neurotransmitter)

Question: "Does any objective, medical proof exist to substantiate the need for medication in some cases of depression?"

Answer: Yes. With the aid of PET scans (positron emission tomography), physicians can see the difference between the function of a normal brain and a depressed brain. Because PET scans map how the brain functions, they also display changes in the brain after antidepressant medication has been taken. Antidepressant medication helps produce normal chemical absorption, thus increasing normal brain function and decreasing depression. How wonderful that the God of creation made the brain with the capacity to respond to appropriate medication in order to alleviate debilitating depression.[44]

> *As the Bible says, we are "fearfully and wonderfully made"*
> (PSALM 139:14).

E. What Are the Emotional Contributors of Depression?

In the Yates home, Rusty left for work every morning at 9:00. Then his mother came at 10:00 to help Andrea with the children, their homeschooling, and the housework. This meant Andrea was left alone at home with the children for only one hour each day. And during that one hour on June 20, 2001, Andrea drowned each child.

Could this tragedy have been avoided? Are there steps loved ones could have taken to help Andrea move from the darkness of despair into the light of hope? If they had been more keenly aware of the danger, they could have learned much more about Andrea's malady and been discerning about what to do.

> *"Let the wise listen and add to their learning,*
> *and let the discerning get guidance"*
> (PROVERBS 1:5).

Sometimes depression is *anger turned inward*. That is not always true, but it is true when anger is *repressed*. Repression occurs when unacceptable desires and emotions are blocked from a person's awareness and left to operate in the unconscious mind.[45] This stuffed or swallowed anger causes masked depression and keeps underlying bitterness from being exposed. Bitterness is a major cause of depression because we feel totally alone in our bitterness.

> *"Each heart knows its own bitterness,*
> *and no one else can share its joy"*
> (PROVERBS 14:10).

Do you have repressed anger over...?

—loss of a loved one	—loss of expectations
—loss of self-esteem	—loss of respect for others
—loss of control	—loss of health or abilities
—loss of possessions	—loss of personal goals

If so, the Bible says,

*"Get rid of all bitterness, rage and anger, brawling
and slander, along with every form of malice"*
(EPHESIANS 4:31).

Do you have suppressed fear of...?

—losing a job   —abandonment

—dying   —growing old

—empty nest   —being alone

—failure   —rejection

If so, the Bible says,

*"Do not fear, for I am with you; do not be dismayed,
for I am your God. I will strengthen you and help you;
I will uphold you with my righteous right hand"*
(ISAIAH 41:10).

Do you have internalized stress over...?

—work difficulties   —financial obligations

—relocation   —family responsibilities

—marital problems   —troubled child

—workload   —health issues

If so, the Bible says,

"Cast all your anxiety on him because he cares for you"
(1 PETER 5:7).

Even our deep disappointments must be resolved or else our bitterness will cause trouble, and unresolved anger and bitterness will hurt those close to us.

*"See to it that no one misses the grace of God and that no
bitter root grows up to cause trouble and defile many"*
(HEBREWS 12:15).

F. What Are the Spiritual Sources of Depression?

Due to postpartum psychosis, Andrea Yates became spiritually unbalanced as a result of having a greater focus on Satan and her sin than on God and His grace. Ultimately, she heard voices claiming that she was evil and that Satan was inside her—and the only way to be rid of him was her own execution! A *Time* magazine writer concluded, "She had to kill the children, as Satan demanded, in order to get the death penalty."[46]

Andrea said about her children, "They stumbled because I was evil. The way I was raising them they could never be saved...They were doomed to perish in the fires of hell." [47] Ultimately, after all five deaths, she hoped that her children would be in heaven. No Scripture could represent her skewed thinking more accurately than this proverb:

> *"There is a way that seems right to a man,*
> *but in the end it leads to death"*
> (PROVERBS 14:12).

Just as there are physical, emotional, and mental causes for depression, there are also spiritual causes for a despairing heart. Disobedience and guilt provide enough fertile seed to turn any white cloud into a dark storm. You can't harbor the guilt of displeasing God and still experience the full joy of His salvation. Disobedience and guilt are inseparable. And unless you apply the remedy of confession and repentance (a change of mind and a change of direction), you may find depression sweeping over your soul and spirit, and

> *"you will find no repose, no resting place for the sole*
> *of your foot. There the LORD will give you an anxious*
> *mind, eyes weary with longing, and a despairing heart"*
> (DEUTERONOMY 28:65).

G. Root Cause of Staying Stuck in Depression

Had there been clues to the seriousness of Andrea Yates's mental state? After she drowned her five young children, the media quickly learned that this rigidly religious family had been dealing with Andrea's severe depression for several years. Twice in 1999 she had attempted suicide.

The Yates tragedy is certainly not the norm, and although many people become seriously despondent, the majority of those who experience major depression will never commit acts that result in death. Unfortunately, Andrea continued to spiral downward to even lower depths with frequent thoughts of self-destruction. In the midst of paralyzing depression, she could not accept the truth that "anyone who is among the living has hope!" (Ecclesiastes 9:4).

Wrong Belief:

"I am depressed over the deep disappointments in my life. They have robbed me of all joy. There's no hope for my future, and there's nothing I can do about it."

Right Belief:

"I admit I am depressed over the circumstances in my life. But Christ lives in me, and He is my hope. I will rely on Him to renew my mind with His truth and renew my heart with His hope."

> *"In our hearts we felt the sentence of death. But this*
> *happened that we might not rely on ourselves but*
> *on God, who raises the dead...On him we have*
> *set our hope that he will continue to deliver us"*
> (2 CORINTHIANS 1:9-10).

H. How to Find Hope When Hope Seems Elusive

When you are weary...when life isn't worth living...when hope seems elusive...what do you need to know? You need to know your *Burden-Bearer*—you need to know Jesus. He wants to be the Shepherd of your soul. His compassionate comfort extends to all those who have lost all hope. He says,

> *"Come to me, all you who are weary and*
> *burdened, and I will give you rest"*
> (MATTHEW 11:28).

When you are weary, how do you receive this rest within your soul? Allow these four truths to set you free.

Hope #1—God Offers Real Solutions for Your Problems

When you don't know how to solve a problem, you will probably feel helpless because you have no direction. For example, if your wristwatch stops, you may feel helpless because you don't know how to fix it. But a skilled watchmaker can. The One who created the universe with all its intricate parts—the One who created you with all your intricate parts—knows how to fix whatever is not working, even when you don't. He will direct you in the way you should go.

> *"Trust in the LORD with all your heart and lean not on*

> *your own understanding; in all your ways acknowledge*
> *him, and he will make your paths straight"*
> (PROVERBS 3:5-6).

Hope #2—God Loves You with an Unconditional Love

God loves you with *agape* love. The Bible uses the Greek word *agape* to speak of God's commitment to seek your highest good no matter what you do or don't do. The Lord says,

> *"I have loved you with an everlasting love; I*
> *have drawn you with loving-kindness"*
> (JEREMIAH 31:3).

Hope #3—God Offers the Solution for Your Sins

The Bible says sin separates us from God. But God doesn't want you to be separated from Him. He desires to have a meaningful relationship with you. That's why He sent Jesus to take on human form, come to earth, live a sinless life, and pay the penalty for your sins by dying on the cross. When He was crucified, His blood was the purchase price to pay for the full forgiveness of your sins. Today, you can receive forgiveness when you humble your heart, confess your sins, and trust in Jesus Christ as your personal Lord and Savior.

> *"If we confess our sins, he is faithful and just and will*
> *forgive us our sins and purify us from all unrighteousness"*
> (1 JOHN 1:9).

Hope #4—God Offers You Permanent Peace

The word *Lord* means "master, ruler, owner."[48] Are you willing to entrust your life to the Lord Jesus Christ, knowing that He is trustworthy to always do whatever is best for you? Jesus demonstrated unconditional love toward you. He died on the cross, paying the penalty that you should have paid. That's real love…sacrificial love!

You can trust and rely on Jesus to make sense of your life, to teach you truth, and to show you the way. Jesus said,

> *"I am the way and the truth and the life. No*
> *one comes to the Father except through me"*
> (JOHN 14:6).

You can enter into a personal relationship with Christ right now by praying a prayer like this:

God,

I need peace in my life.
I need You in my life.
I admit that I have sinned.
Please forgive me for my sins.

Thank You, Jesus, for dying on the cross
to pay the penalty for my sins.
Please come into my life
to be my Lord and Savior.
I give You control of my life;
make me the person You want me to be.

In Your precious name I pray.
Amen.

Andrea's Epilogue

Once Andrea was placed back on the medication necessary to restore a chemical balance within her brain, she returned to a non-psychotic state. But, she then had to face the horrendous fact that she had taken the lives of her five precious children.

The harsh reality of her actions resulted in overwhelming emotional, psychological, and spiritual pain. How would she process, how would she think through the unthinkable? In a psychotic state of mind, she had done that which was inconceivable in a right state of mind.

The consequences were catastrophic to the children she cherished and devastating to her own mind and heart. Her mind could be restored to rightness, but her children could never be restored to life. She would never be without them in her mind and heart, yet she would never be with them in her lifetime.

Andrea's struggle through the darkness of depression to the life-giving light of redemption was indescribably difficult. Christians who minister to prisoners have reached out to her with the reality of

God's love and forgiveness, and His ability to comfort her and carry her through the all-consuming litany of losses in her life—her five children, her marriage, her entire way of living. Never would she be the same; never would her life be the same.

As Andrea opened her heart to God and to His healing hand, she began to experience a new life—His life. And she began to reach out to other women in the prison who also needed a new life in Christ. Never a day goes by that she doesn't think of and long for her children. But now she misses them without falling back into that deep hole of depression. She lives in the strength of the Lord knowing that one day she will be united with them in heaven. She—and every believer—can cling to the promise that in heaven,

> *"He will wipe every tear from their eyes. There will*
> *be no more death or mourning or crying or pain"*
> (REVELATION 21:4).

IV. STEPS TO SOLUTION

God has a purpose for everything. Even the storm clouds in your life are no accident. Depression can open your eyes to God's unique design for you before, during, and after your bouts with despondency. Remember: Storms replenish dry and parched ground, and they give birth to flowers and new life in the spring.

A. Key Verse to Memorize

If you encounter a violent storm while traveling, you are faced with two choices: keep going, or pull over to a safe spot and wait it out. The storm clouds of depression are no different. You face the choices of seeking help, riding it out alone, seeing God's perspective, or becoming drenched in bitterness. No matter how long the sky has been overcast or your soul has been downcast, you can rest in the words of the psalmist, who said,

> *"I am still confident of this:*
> *I will see the goodness of the LORD*
> *in the land of the living"*
> (PSALM 27:13).

B. Key Passage to Read and Reread

While we can't choose what we inherit genetically, we can choose what we dwell on cognitively. In the medical world, brain scans of those suffering from depression show marked improvement when words of hope, affirmation, and purpose are continually reinforced. In this respect, *life is a series of choices.* You can choose today to put the Word of God into action.[49]

=========== *1 Thessalonians 5:16-24* ===========

—*"Be joyful always."*
   Choose to write down and continually
   focus on the positives in your life . . . . verse 16

—*"Pray continually."*
   Choose to talk to God about everything . . . . . . verse 17

—*"Give thanks in all circumstances."*
   Choose to thank God for what you are
   learning right now . . . . verse 18

—*"Do not put out the Spirit's fire."*
   Choose to change when God's Spirit convicts
   you to make a change . . . . verse 19

—*"Do not treat prophecies with contempt."*
   Choose to take God's Word seriously . . . . verse 20

—*"Test everything."*
   Choose to ask, "Is this right in God's sight?" . . . . verse 21

—*"Hold on to the good."*
   Choose to do right, even when you are
   tempted to do wrong . . . . verse 21

—*"Avoid every kind of evil."*
   Choose to turn immediately from
   temptation . . . . verse 22

—*"May God himself, the God of peace,
   sanctify you through and through."*

Choose to see how God has set you apart (sanctified you)
to be what He intended you to be . . . . verse 23

—*"May your whole spirit, soul and body be kept blameless."*
Choose to commit your whole being to doing
what God created you to do . . . . verse 23

—*"The one who calls you is faithful and he will do it."*
Choose to rely on God's power to do what
you are called to do . . . . verse 24

C. How to Take Off the Mask of Masked Depression

As we endure painful events in our lives, we can sweep them under the rug and ignore them. However, in doing so, we fail to grieve over our hurts and losses. By masking our depression, we try to protect our hearts and hide who we really are and what we don't want to face. But this kind of masquerade blocks our maturity and our ability to have intimacy with God and others.

Don't ever fear admitting your personal disappointments, the painful truths about your life, directly to God. Allow Him to help you see the reality of your pain from His perspective. He will reveal how He will work through your pain to give you wisdom about life and true depths of understanding. As David said to God,

> *"Surely you desire truth in the inner parts; you*
> *teach me wisdom in the inmost place"*
> (PSALM 51:6).

My Time Line

- *Draw* a long time line representing your life.
- *Divide* the time line into three sections: childhood, youth, adult.
- *Denote* the major changes in your life. Draw short horizontal lines extending from the time line and write, on each line, all significant events in your life—both positive and negative—including all major hurts and griefs. For example:

LIFE STAGES	EVENTS
Childhood	Birth of siblings
	Change of school
	Death of a favorite pet
	Abuse (verbal, emotional, physical, sexual)
	Best friend moved away
Youth	Death of a close relative
	Rejection from a romantic relationship
	Relocation, family moves (loss of "roots")
Adulthood	Broken engagement, crisis pregnancy
	Marriage
	Miscarriage
	Childlessness, infertility
	Hurts by loved ones
	Empty nest, children leaving the home
	Marriage of children
	Separation/Divorce
	Job loss/new job
	Illness/injuries
	Financial Difficulties
	Retirement
	Death of spouse

- *Determine* whether there are any sad experiences or significant losses and hurts that you have not faced, such as...

  —failures   —thwarted goals

  —false accusations   —unjust criticism

  —rejection   —unrealized dreams

- *Discover* the source of your masked pain through earnest prayer.

Prayer for Discovery

Heavenly Father,

As Your child, I come to You for help.
Calm my heart.
Enable me to see what I need to see.
Make me aware of my need
for healing and show me Your truth.
Bring to my mind any hidden hurt
in my heart and the exact
circumstances that caused it.

In Your holy name I pray. Amen.

- *Define* the emotional impact each event had on you with specific statements, such as...

    "This made me feel like..."

    "I am grieving over..."

    "I was so embarrassed when..."

    "I felt abandoned by..."

    "I was really hurt when..."

    "I've been determined to never let (_____) happen again."

- *Decide* to allow deep, genuine grieving over your losses.

    "You, O God, do see trouble and grief; you consider it
    to take it in hand. The victim commits himself to you"
    (PSALM 10:14).

- *Defuse* the power that the event has over your emotions by sharing it with someone you trust and with God.

    "There is a time for everything...a time
    to be silent and a time to speak"
    (ECCLESIASTES 3:1,7).

- *Deepen* your dependence on the Lord to set you free emotionally.

*"In my anguish I cried to the LORD, and
he answered by setting me free"*
(PSALM 118:5).

═══════════ *Prayer for Healing* ═══════════

Dear Lord Jesus,

*Help me to allow You to minister
to my wounded heart.
I know that You understand my pain.
And I know You have the power
to make me whole.*

*Thank You for loving me.
Thank You that I can have confidence
that You will set me free.*

In Your holy name I pray. Amen.

*"Heal me, O LORD, and I will be healed; save me
and I will be saved, for you are the one I praise"*
(JEREMIAH 17:14).

D. Depression and the Whole Person[50]

The Three Parts of a Person

As portrayed below, every person is created with a tangible body, an intangible soul, and an intangible spirit, which makes us all *trichotomous* beings. As a tri-part (three-part) person, the following is true:

- *Your body* is your physical makeup (your flesh, bones, and blood)
- *Your soul* is your personality (your mind, will, and emotions)
- *Your spirit* is your innermost part that needs salvation, craves gratification of your deepest needs (for love, significance, and security), and, in the believer, houses the Holy Spirit[51]

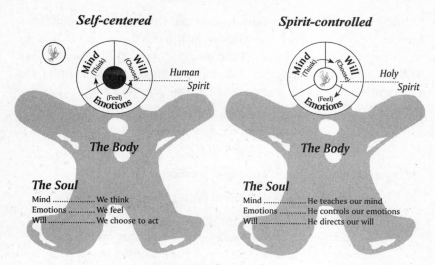

Self-centered

Mind (Think)
Will (Choose)
Emotions (Feel)

Human Spirit

The Body

Spirit-controlled

Mind (Think)
Will (Choose)
Emotions (Feel)

Holy Spirit

The Body

The Soul

Mind .... We think
Emotions .... We feel
Will .... We choose to act

The Soul

Mind .... He teaches our mind
Emotions .... He controls our emotions
Will .... He directs our will

Adam and Eve were privileged to have perfect oneness with God. They had spiritual life because their human spirits were alive to God. Warned by God that eating from the tree of the knowledge of good and evil would bring death, Adam and Eve disobeyed God and indeed something died— they lost spiritual oneness with God.

You and I are born in the likeness of Adam, dead to God's Spirit until we receive His gift of a new life in Christ Jesus.

> *"Count yourselves dead to sin but*
> *alive to God in Christ Jesus"*
> (ROMANS 6:11).

Medical doctors have long stated that how you respond to life's disappointments has a direct impact on your body. Likewise, depression can have a profound effect on both your soul and spirit. God encourages us to seek Him for healing and health in all three areas of life—body, soul, and spirit.

> *"May God himself, the God of peace, sanctify you through*
> *and through. May your whole spirit, soul and body be*
> *kept blameless at the coming of our Lord Jesus Christ"*
> (1 THESSALONIANS 5:23).

1. COMBATING DEPRESSION IN THE BODY
The increase in cases of depression today may be directly related to

unhealthy eating habits. Consider, for example, that Jesus probably ate fresh fish every day because fish was a common and healthy staple eaten in the region where He lived. Jesus fed the multitudes of 5,000 men and then 4,000 as well as the women and children by taking 12 loaves of bread and a few small fish. And He often mentioned fish in his teaching analogies:

> *"Which of you fathers, if your son asks for a*
> *fish, will give him a snake instead?"*
> (LUKE 11:11).

If you are suffering with prolonged depression...

- *Get a thorough medical checkup.* First, tell the doctor you feel unusually depressed. Be specific.

- *Ask your doctor to evaluate all medications* you are taking and eliminate what is unnecessary. Ask your doctor if any of your medications could contribute to depression. If so, could a substitute be prescribed?

- *Develop regular sleep habits.* Sleep is therapeutic. Only during deep sleep does the brain produce serotonin, which alleviates depression. Set a regular time to go to sleep and to rise.

- *Maintain a regular, active schedule.* Be actively involved in outside functions, such as spiritual and social functions, which impact brain function. Accept invitations to be with others, even if you don't feel like it.

- *Eliminate stress.* Avoid being overly fatigued. Set aside regular quiet times of relaxation.

- *Eat nutritious meals.* Researchers have discovered a link between diet and the rise of depression. A key role in normal brain development and function is played by the chemical mechanism called fatty acid metabolism. A.J. Richardson writes, "Omega-6 and Omega-3 fatty acids are crucial for normal brain structure and function, and must be derived from the diet."[52] Lack of Omega-3s is believed to be linked to lower levels of serotonin and norepinephrin in the brain, and these lower levels are known to have a correlation to depression.[53]

  —Avoid caffeine, alcohol, salt, fast food, and junk food

—Especially avoid foods containing trans-fats found in cereals, cookies, chips, and margarine which block the absorption of Omega-3s and other nutrients for several days after consumption

—Stay away from sugar (including sugary sodas) to avoid "the sugar blues"—a condition caused when sugar consumption temporarily boosts sugar levels, which then plummet just as quickly.

—Drink six to eight glasses of water a day

—Include in your diet, on a regular basis, cold-water fish containing Omega-3s—mainly salmon, trout, sardines, mackerel, and tuna—and dark, leafy green vegetables containing Omega-6s

- *Contact an informed nutritionist.* Find out about the therapeutic amounts of fish oil, Vitamin D, zinc, magnesium, and other vitamins and minerals that help combat depression through increased levels of serotonin.

    —Adopt a Vitamin D regimen to increase levels of serotonin

    —Take a good daily multivitamin with zinc and magnesium

    Research trials have indicated that increased consumption of Omega-3 fatty acids can result in a significant reduction of symptoms for bipolar disorder, antisocial and violent behavior, as well as unipolar depression.[54]

- *Exercise regularly.* Walk, jog, or swim at least four days a week. Twenty minutes of brisk walking releases endorphins—a natural mood elevator.

- *Spend time in the sun* enjoying God's beautiful creation. Research reveals that 30 minutes of sunshine can help alleviate depression. Too little sun produces melatonin, which can cause lethargy.

- *Pet a pet.* Giving affection to an animal lowers blood pressure, relieves stress, and allows an increase in good mood chemicals.

- *Laugh out loud!* At least one good belly laugh a day releases a helpful amount of serotonin and norepinephrin. Try reading funny stories or watching a funny movie or comedy on TV for therapy. Proverbs 17:22 says that a "cheerful heart is good medicine."

This prayer from the Bible should encourage each of us to care for and take responsibility for our physical health:

*"I pray that you may enjoy good health and that all may
go well with you, even as your soul is getting along well"*
(3 JOHN 2).

Question: "Recently I moved to a town that has gloomy weather and now I'm feeling gloomy. Everything else in my life is positive. What can I do? It's as if the fog outside my window has invaded my mind and muddled my thinking."[55]

Answer: Seasonal affective disorder, or SAD, is a form of depression associated with deprivation of sunlight. SAD, also called the winter blues, typically begins in the fall when the days become shorter and there is less sunlight. It subsides in the spring as the days get longer. Too little sunlight entering the eye produces in the brain a hormone called *melatonin*, which is released with the onset of darkness. Too much melatonin creates a biochemical imbalance in the hypothalamus region of the brain. In animals, melatonin controls hibernation and causes a decrease in activity. In humans, SAD causes symptoms such as excessive sleep, lethargy, overeating, and depression.

The best treatment for SAD is light—light is therapeutic.

- Avail yourself of any and every opportunity to spend time in natural sunlight (outdoor reading or exercise, morning or afternoon walks).
- You could purchase a specially designed light box that produces artificial light and expose your eyes to that light for 30 minutes to two hours daily.
- Vacation in places where you can enjoy sunshine.

"Light is sweet, and it pleases the eyes to see the sun"
(ECCLESIASTES 11:7).

2. COMBATING DEPRESSION IN THE SOUL

When you have lost a significant relationship, whether by rejection, divorce, or death, it is normal for you to be depressed. However, after a period of time, normal healing should occur. If your heart has not "resumed its natural shape," your heart could be in a state of depression. Because the entire soul (mind, will, and emotions) is affected by depression, recovery involves taking steps to treat depression in all three areas of the soul. Each part touched by depression needs to be reached with healing.

THE MIND

What your mind dwells on can be a key ingredient to overcoming chronic depression. Research verifies that what a person chooses to think about literally changes the chemistry of the brain![56] You need to fill your thinking with God's thinking—fill your mind with God's perspective and promises. Romans 12:2 says that you are "transformed by the renewing of your mind."

- Write several Scriptures on index cards and read them several times a day.
- Make a list—"My Thanksgiving List"—of seven blessed aspects of your life and spend time every day thanking God for those specifically.
- Next week, list seven specifics for which you can thank God.
- Each week thereafter, keep adding to the list.

By looking at God's Word, you can discover God's purpose for allowing the painful losses in your life. God is your Redeemer, and He has a purpose for allowing everything—even the storms in your life.

"He sent forth his word and healed them"
(PSALM 107:20).

═══════ *Bring Light into the Darkness* ═══════

In order to combat depression, first write out your dark thoughts. Then, as your rebuttal, write out what God says. Ask the Lord and a friend for help with the wording. Then whenever dark thoughts come, use cognitive therapy on yourself, which simply means replacing your *dark thoughts of despair* with the *light of truth*.

*"You are my lamp, O LORD; the LORD
turns my darkness into light"*
(2 SAMUEL 22:29).

—**Dark thoughts:** "I cannot escape this darkness."
Light of truth: "The Lord will bring light into my darkness."

"My God turns my darkness into light"
(PSALM 18:28).

—**Dark thoughts:** "I feel like I have no refuge, no safe haven."
Light of truth: "The Lord will be my refuge."

"Keep me safe, O God, for in you I take refuge"
(PSALM 16:1).

—**Dark thoughts:** "I feel like I'm in too much trouble."
Light of truth: "The Lord is my help in trouble."

*"God is our refuge and strength, an
ever-present help in trouble"*
(PSALM 46:1).

—**Dark thoughts:** "I can't help feeling so restless."
Light of truth: "My God gives my soul rest."

*"My soul finds rest in God alone; my
salvation comes from him"*
(PSALM 62:1).

—**Dark thoughts:** "I can't see the path I should take."
Light of truth: "The Lord will direct my path."

*"Trust in the LORD with all your heart and lean not on
your own understanding; in all your ways acknowledge
him, and he will make your paths straight"*
(PROVERBS 3:5-6).

—**Dark thoughts:** "My burden is too heavy to bear."
Light of truth: "The Lord is my Burden-Bearer."

"Praise be to the Lord, to God our Savior,
who daily bears our burdens"
(PSALM 68:19).

—**Dark thoughts:** "I'm afraid to be around people."

Light of truth: "The Lord will give me strength to be around people."

"The LORD is my light and my salvation—
whom shall I fear? The LORD is the stronghold
of my life—of whom shall I be afraid?"
(PSALM 27:1).

—**Dark thoughts:** "My confidence is completely shaken."

Light: "The Lord will keep my life from being shaken."

"I have set the Lord always before me. Because
he is at my right hand, I will not be shaken"
(PSALM 16:8).

THE WILL

People who have prolonged depression often have a paralysis of the will and feel that life has stripped them of their choices. They feel stranded in the middle of the storm with no real options. But that is far from the truth. While it is true that life is sprinkled with unavoidable discouragement, you *can* avoid letting your mind become drenched with discouragement. That is your choice; it's an *act of the will.*

After an initial downpour, you can choose to stay in bed, procrastinate, and *rely on yourself* for relief, or you can choose to get underneath God's umbrella of protection and *rely on Him.* Jesus said, "Do not let your hearts be troubled. Trust in God; trust also in me" (John 14:1). You can choose to trust the Lord with your life; He is worthy of your trust.

Even if you don't feel like it...

- *Listen* to uplifting and inspirational music.
- *Keep* your living environment bright and cheerful.
- *Maintain* a clean, uncluttered environment.

- *Clear* your home of objects associated with activities related to the demonic or the occult.

- *Resist* long periods of time on the telephone, which keep you from accomplishing what is needed.

- *Avoid* spending too much time watching television.

- *Write* thank-you and encouragement notes to others.

- *Set* small, attainable goals every day.

- *Look* for something you can do for someone else each day, and you will experience God's truth that, indeed, "it is more blessed to give than to receive" (Acts 20:35).

> *"Preserve sound judgment and discernment, do*
> *not let them out of your sight; they will be life*
> *for you, an ornament to grace your neck"*
> (PROVERBS 3:21-22).

THE EMOTIONS

Often people who are depressed have difficulty expressing their feelings in a healthy way. A common cause of depression is buried feelings as a result of loss or past hurts. Yet ignored or denied feelings won't go away. They are buried alive, deep inside your soul, where they fester and create an infection that produces poison in your body. That is why it is vital to face your feelings.

Bring your heartache and hurts, your anger and anxieties, your fear and frustrations to Jesus. Pour out your heart to Him and receive His comfort. He alone understands the depth of your pain. The Bible assures us that

> *"we do not have a high priest who is unable to*
> *sympathize with our weaknesses, but we have one who*
> *has been tempted in every way, just as we are—yet*
> *was without sin. Let us then approach the throne of*
> *grace with confidence, so that we may receive mercy*
> *and find grace to help us in our time of need"*
> (HEBREWS 4:15-16).

Question: "What is anniversary depression?"

Answer: Anniversary depression is a yearly, recurring depression related to the anniversary date of a traumatic event. Triggered by painful memories, this involuntary, emotional reaction lasts for only a limited period of time.

Examples:

— Many women dive into a depression each year around the anniversary of the abortion of their child or the anniversary of placing their child into another home for adoption.

— Widowed men and women can have anniversary depression around the date of their mate's death.

The Bible speaks of being mired in the pain from the past, but also offers the key to getting unstuck and restoring our hope. We have to make the choice to change our focus.

> *"I remember my affliction and my wandering, the*
> *bitterness and the gall. I well remember them, and my*
> *soul is downcast within me. Yet this I call to mind and*
> *therefore I have hope: Because of the LORD's great love*
> *we are not consumed, for his compassions never fail.*
> *They are new every morning; great is your faithfulness"*
> (LAMENTATIONS 3:19-23).

Here are some ways to deal with anniversary depression:

— Understand that your depression is rooted in a real loss from your past and that what you are experiencing is not uncommon.

— Acknowledge your emotions. Write out all painful memories and process them with a helpful person you can trust.

— Release your pain to the Lord, and receive His comfort and healing.

Lord,

You know the pain I've felt over
(specifically list each hurt, each failure,
and each person associated with the pain).

I now release all this pain into Your hands.

Set me free in my soul and spirit.
Thank You for wanting to heal me and make me whole.

In Your precious name I pray. Amen.

"The LORD is close to the brokenhearted and
saves those who are crushed in spirit"
(PSALM 34:18).

- Anticipate any upcoming anniversary and plan ahead for ways to counter possible depression. For instance, plan a trip with someone or arrange a social event so you will not be alone and so your mind will be focused on something other than the past event.

- Turn your anniversary date into an occasion that will produce new, positive memories by serving others in a meaningful way.

"It is more blessed to give than to receive"
(ACTS 20:35).

3. THE SPIRIT

The security and strength of every Christian is the day-by-day indwelling presence of the Holy Spirit. Zechariah 4:6 reveals that God plans for you to be an overcomer—"not by might nor by power, but by [His] Spirit." Since He is literally God living within you, you are to live dependently on Him for everything.

Even in the depths of your despair and the darkness of your depression, God is with you, for His Spirit is within you. When you cry in the night, He sees every teardrop and holds your soul as a mother holds her crying infant to her heart. Though you do not see Him with your physical eyes, nor feel Him with your physical touch, you can see Him with your spiritual eyes and you can experience His joy and His "peace...which transcends all understanding" (Philippians 4:7). He promises to give you hope for your heart. To overcome depression, look not to yourself, but to Him who is the God of hope.

"May the God of hope fill you with all joy and
peace as you trust in him, so that you may overflow
with hope by the power of the Holy Spirit"
(ROMANS 15:13).

E. Learn to Conquer Depression

When darkness enters into our lives, we can too easily become consumed with the situation that causes our darkness. At such times, we have difficulty seeing all that God wants for us to see. During those days when we are shrouded in darkness, we must not trust in our own perspective. Instead, we need to see life from God's perspective. And the only way to have that view is to confront our losses, offer our hearts to God, and allow Him to shed His light on our lives.

> *"Let him who walks in the dark, who has no light,*
> *trust in the name of the LORD and rely on his God"*
> (ISAIAH 50:10).

How can you C-O-N-Q-U-E-R depression?

C Confront all the losses in your life.
Allow yourself to grieve and be healed.

> *"[There is] a time to weep and a time to laugh,*
> *a time to mourn and a time to dance"*
> (ECCLESIASTES 3:4).

O Offer your heart to Christ and give Him control.
Confess your sins and He will cleanse you.

> *"If we claim to be without sin, we deceive ourselves*
> *and the truth is not in us. If we confess our sins,*
> *he is faithful and just and will forgive us our*
> *sins and purify us from all unrighteousness"*
> (1 JOHN 1:8-9).

N Nurtur.e the thoughts of God's love for you.
God's love for you will never end.

> *"I have loved you with an everlasting love; I*
> *have drawn you with loving-kindness"*
> (JEREMIAH 31:3).

Q Quit all negative thinking.
Replace all negative self-talk by focusing on the positive.

*"Whatever is true, whatever is noble, whatever
is right, whatever is pure, whatever is lovely,
whatever is admirable—if anything is excellent
or praiseworthy—think about such things"*
(PHILIPPIANS 4:8).

U Understand God's purpose for allowing your personal pain.
God promises to use your heartaches for your ultimate good.

*"We know that in all things God works for
the good of those who love him, who have
been called according to his purpose"*
(ROMANS 8:28).

E Exchange your hurt for thanksgiving.
Choose to give thanks, even when you don't feel thankful.

*"Give thanks in all circumstances, for this
is God's will for you in Christ Jesus"*
(1 THESSALONIANS 5:18).

R Remember God's sovereignty over your life.
He promises hope for your future.

*"For you have been my hope, O Sovereign
LORD, my confidence since my youth"*
(PSALM 71:5).

Question: "Is forgiveness always right? I was severely hurt by someone I completely trusted. Now I find myself staying in a bad mood because of how much he hurt me. I can't just let him off the hook!"

Answer: Because your thinking impacts your feelings, if you are harboring unforgiveness in your heart toward someone, you may be experiencing symptoms of depression as a result of failing to extend forgiveness and not letting go of negative thoughts and feelings. Forgiving someone who has grievously wronged you is not easy, but it is right, and it is possible to do. It is the doorway that God has made through which you must walk in order to gain emotional and spiritual freedom. The Bible says,

> *"Bear with each other and forgive whatever*
> *grievances you may have against one another.*
> *Forgive as the Lord forgave you"*
> (COLOSSIANS 3:13).

- Imagine a meat hook around your neck.
- Imagine a burlap bag hanging from the hook, carrying all the pain you are harboring inside.
- Imagine your offender being attached to that hook as well. Ask yourself, *Do I really want to carry this person and all this pain with me for the rest of my life?*

The Lord wants you to take the offender and all the pain and release them into His hands. He wants you to take them off your emotional hook and place them onto His hook. The Lord knows how to deal with people who wrong you. He says,

> *"It is mine to avenge; I will repay"*
> (ROMANS 12:19).

═══════ *Prayer to Forgive Your Offender* ═══════

Lord Jesus,

Thank You for caring about how much
my heart has been hurt.
You know the pain I have felt
because of (list every offense).
Right now I release all that pain
into Your hands.
Thank You, Lord, for dying on the cross
for me and extending Your forgiveness to me.

As an act of my will, I choose to forgive (offender's name).
Right now, I move (name) off
my emotional hook and onto Your hook.
I refuse all thoughts of revenge.
I trust that in Your time and in Your way,
You will deal with (name) as You see fit.

*And Lord, thank You for giving me
Your power to forgive so that I can be set free.*

In Your precious name I pray. Amen.

F. Discover God's Purpose for Permitting Depression

God has a purpose for everything that touches your life. Even the times of painful pruning are useful in the hands of God. Depression can heighten your awareness of God and increase your dependency on Him. It can open your eyes to His unique design for you before, during, and after your bouts with despondency. Remember, just as storms replenish dry and parched ground and give birth to flowers and new life in the spring, so the storms in your life can revitalize your relationship with God and give birth to greater fruit of the Spirit in your life.

> *"He cuts off every branch in me that bears no fruit, while
> every branch that does bear fruit he prunes so that it will
> be even more fruitful...This is to my Father's glory, that
> you bear much fruit, showing yourselves to be my disciples"*
> (John 15:2,8).

Your depression has been permitted by God to...

- warn you that something is wrong

> *"Before I was afflicted I went astray,
> but now I obey your word"*
> (Psalm 119:67).

- slow you down and cause you to reflect inwardly

> *"We do not lose heart. Though outwardly we are wasting
> away, yet inwardly we are being renewed day by day"*
> (2 Corinthians 4:16).

- reveal your weakness

> *"He [the Lord] said...'My grace is sufficient for
> you, for my power is made perfect in weakness.'*

*Therefore I will boast all the more gladly about my
weaknesses, so that Christ's power may rest on me"*
(2 CORINTHIANS 12:9).

- bring you to Himself

   *"Let us draw near to God with a sincere heart
   in full assurance of faith, having our hearts
   sprinkled to cleanse us from a guilty conscience and
   having our bodies washed with pure water"*
   (HEBREWS 10:22).

- develop your trust in Him

   *"Why are you downcast, O my soul? Why so
   disturbed within me? Put your hope in God, for I
   will yet praise him, my Savior and my God"*
   (PSALM 43:5).

- be a healing process for damaged emotions

   *"Heal me, O LORD, and I will be healed; save me
   and I will be saved, for you are the one I praise"*
   (JEREMIAH 17:14).

- develop your perseverance and maturity

   *"Consider it pure joy…whenever you face trials
   of many kinds, because you know that the testing
   of your faith develops perseverance. Perseverance
   must finish its work so that you may be mature
   and complete, not lacking anything"*
   (JAMES 1:2-4).

- affirm worth and value in your life

   *"Are not five sparrows sold for two pennies? Yet
   not one of them is forgotten by God. Indeed, the
   very hairs of your head are all numbered. Don't be
   afraid; you are worth more than many sparrows"*
   (LUKE 12:6-7).

- cause you to rely on His resources

> *"His divine power has given us everything we need for*
> *life and godliness through our knowledge of him who*
> *called us by his own glory and goodness. Through these he*
> *has given us his very great and precious promises, so that*
> *through them you may participate in the divine nature and*
> *escape the corruption in the world caused by evil desires"*
> (2 PETER 1:3-4).

- increase your compassion and understanding for others

> *"The Father of compassion and the God of all*
> *comfort...comforts us in all our troubles, so that*
> *we can comfort those in any trouble with the*
> *comfort we ourselves have received from God"*
> (2 CORINTHIANS 1:3-4).

A Positive Perspective on Depression

The famous English pastor Charles Haddon Spurgeon (often referred to as the greatest preacher of the nineteenth century) openly reflected on his own bouts with depression, and from him we can gain much insight.

The times most favorable to fits of depression, so far as I have experienced, may be summed up in a brief catalogue. First among them I must mention *the hour of a great success.* When at last a long-cherished desire is fulfilled, when God has been glorified greatly by our means, and a great triumph achieved, then we are apt to faint...

Before any great achievement, some measure of the same depression is very usual. Surveying the difficulties before us, our hearts sink within us...This depression comes over me whenever the Lord is preparing a larger blessing for my ministry...

In the midst of a long stretch of unbroken labor, the same afflic-tion may be looked for. The bow cannot be always bent without fear of breaking. Repose is as needful to the mind as sleep to the body...

This evil will also come upon us, we know not why, and then it is all the more difficult to drive it away. Causeless depression is not to be reasoned with...If those who laugh at such melancholy did but feel the grief of it for one hour, their laughter would be sobered into compassion...

If it be enquired why the Valley of the Shadow of Death must so often be traversed by the servants of King Jesus, the answer is not far to find. All this is promotive of the Lord's mode of working, which is summed up in these words: "Not by might nor by power, but by my Spirit, saith the Lord"...Heaven shall be all the fuller of bliss because we have been filled with anguish here below, and earth shall be better tilled because of our training in the school of adversity."[57]

When your heart is pressed down to the ground and living life makes you feel depressed, allow your depression to press you closer to the Lord. Let Him lead you into the light. The Bible reveals His promise for the times we feel depressed...

> *"We are hard pressed on every side, but not crushed;*
> *perplexed, but not in despair; persecuted, but not*
> *abandoned; struck down, but not destroyed"*
> (2 CORINTHIANS 4:8-9).

G. Do's and Don'ts for Family and Friends

Be aware of the power of your words. If you express kindness in what you say, you can be God's instrument of hope to help change the disposition of one who is depressed.

> *"An anxious heart weighs a man down,*
> *but a kind word cheers him up"*
> (PROVERBS 12:25).

Don't say: "You shouldn't feel that way."

Say: "I care about what you are feeling."

—Ask, "Would you like to share your feelings with me?"

—Say, "If ever you want to talk, I'm here for you."

"The purposes of a man's heart are deep waters,
but a man of understanding draws them out"
(PROVERBS 20:5).

Don't say: "You must eat! Think of all the starving children in Africa."

Say: "Even if we're not hungry, we both need to eat. Just as a car needs gas for energy, we both need food for energy."

—Take nutritious food to the person's home.

—Take him or her out to eat or perhaps on a picnic.

—Encourage healthy eating habits (no junk food, minimize sugar). The Bible says we need to have...

"food for the stomach"
(1 CORINTHIANS 6:13).

Don't say: "You need to quit taking that medicine."

Say: "Not all medicines work the same for everyone. I'll go with you to get a thorough medical evaluation so that the doctor can make sure the medicine is working for you."

—Talk specifically to a competent doctor who specializes in depression.

—Don't be afraid to get a second opinion.

"Plans fail for lack of counsel, but with
many advisers they succeed"
(PROVERBS 15:22).

Don't say: "You just need to pray more."

Say: "I'm praying for you, and I'm going to keep praying."

—Pray *with* the person, and say you are praying for him or her.

—Ask specifically, "How can I pray for you today?"

"Far be it from me that I should sin against
the LORD by failing to pray for you"
(1 SAMUEL 12:23).

Don't say: "You just need to read the Bible more!"

Say: "There are several passages in the Bible that have given me much hope, and I've written them out for you. May I share them with you?"

— Give hope-filled scriptures for the person to read three times a day: upon awakening, midday, and at bedtime (see Psalm 130:5; Jeremiah 29:11).

— Help the person memorize Scripture (see Philippians 4:6-8,13,19).

"They cried to the LORD in their trouble, and he saved them from their distress. He sent forth his word and healed them; he rescued them from the grave"
(PSALM 107:19-20).

Don't say: "You need to get involved in a church."

Say: "I'm involved in a church where I've been learning how meaningful life can be. I would love for you to come with me next Sunday and afterward we can have lunch together."

— Invite the person to come to church with you.

— Involve the person in a small group Bible study.

"Let us not give up meeting together, as some are in the habit of doing, but let us encourage one another"
(HEBREWS 10:25).

Don't say: "Snap out of it! Get over it!"

Say: "I'm going to stick with you, and we'll get through this together."

— Admit, "I don't know everything I wish I knew, but I'm willing to help."

— State, "If you can't hold on to God, hold on to me because I'm holding on to God."

"There is a friend who sticks closer than a brother"
(PROVERBS 18:24).

H. How You Can Help

When you have depressed loved ones in your life, you want to do something that will make a difference. But the question is, *what?*

Most important of all, *do not avoid them*. Find ways to show you care—plan a fun activity together, read together, exercise together (walk, jog, swim). Invite them to outside events or even to run errands with you.

Because their tendency is to withdraw from others, help your depressed loved ones get *involved* in activities, and not just as a spectator. Perhaps you could help them find a hobby. Just realize, you may be their only lifeline of hope for staying connected. Do what you wish someone else would do for you if you were the one struggling with depression.

> *"Do to others as you would have them do to you"*
> (LUKE 6:31).

- Learn all you can about depression—read books, watch videos, attend seminars.

> *"Apply your heart to instruction and*
> *your ears to words of knowledge"*
> (PROVERBS 23:12).

- If suicide is a concern, ask, "Are you thinking about hurting yourself or taking your life?" Your friend may get mad, but it's better to have a *mad* friend than a *dead* friend.

> *"The tongue has the power of life and death"*
> (PROVERBS 18:21).

- Take all threats of suicide seriously—15 percent of those who are depressed ultimately kill themselves.[58]

> *"The words of a man's mouth are deep waters"*
> (PROVERBS 18:4).

- Be an accountability partner—"I'm with you in this and I won't abandon you."

> *"If one falls down, his friend can help him up"*
> (ECCLESIASTES 4:10).

- Initiate dialogue regularly—make frequent phone calls and keep intentional contact.

> *"The wise in heart are called discerning, and*
> *pleasant words promote instruction"*
> (PROVERBS 16:21).

- Listen and hear your friend's pain—listening affirms his or her value.

> *"Everyone should be quick to listen, slow*
> *to speak and slow to become angry"*
> (JAMES 1:19).

- Talk about depression—talking helps remove the stigma of depression.

> *"A word aptly spoken is like apples*
> *of gold in settings of silver"*
> (PROVERBS 25:11).

- Verbally encourage your friend—sincerely and often.

> *"Encourage one another and build each other up"*
> (1 THESSALONIANS 5:11).

- Realize the power of touch—a hand on the shoulder and appropriate hugs and kisses are powerful affirmations that you care.

> *"Greet one another with a kiss of love"*
> (1 PETER 5:14).

- Play inspirational praise music to lift your friend's spirits— music is therapeutic.

> *"Speak to one another with psalms,*
> *hymns and spiritual songs"*
> (EPHESIANS 5:19).

- Bring laughter into your friend's life through fun games, outings, cultural activites, movies, and people.

> *"A cheerful heart is good medicine"*
> (PROVERBS 17:22).

- Recommend nutritional therapy—for example, vitamins B-6 and E, calcium, magnesium, and folic acid are helpful for combating depression. Ask your doctor and a nutritionist for other suggestions.

> *"[God made] leaves for healing"*
> (EZEKIEL 47:12).

- Help your friend set small, daily goals that require minimum effort, and check on his or her progress regularly.

> *"The desires of the diligent are fully satisfied"*
> (PROVERBS 13:4).

- Enlist help from other family members and friends—be specific about your concerns.

> *"Carry each other's burdens, and in this*
> *way you will fulfill the law of Christ"*
> (GALATIANS 6:2).

The Most Miserable Man Living

His was a dominant presence—a somber, statuesque figure—yet clothed from head to toe in sadness and gloom. At the same time, to many thousands, he brought great joy and jubilation. He is believed to be the most beloved politician in American history—heralded as a national hero and credited with uniting a weary, war-torn country.

Through him came freedom from slavery—the hard-fought-for Emancipation Proclamation.

But the sixteenth president of the United States seldom experienced himself the joy that he brought to so many. Instead, Abraham Lincoln's life was marked by melancholy, darkened by depression.

Like other members of his family, Lincoln struggled with chronic depression. But it was after his great personal loss in 1835 that he emotionally collapsed, some people going so far as to call him crazy.

The untimely death of Anna Rutledge, whom he deeply loved, proved too much to bear. She lost her life most likely to typhoid fever. Afterward came his repeated talk of suicide...his rambling through the woods with a deadly gun in hand...his broken heart and dreams.

But what pushed Abe Lincoln over the edge was the weather at Anna's funeral. As the day turned gray, cold, and wet, grief-stricken Lincoln couldn't face the reality of rain falling on her grave. One observer noted, "As to the condition of Lincoln's mind after the death of Miss R, after that event he seemed quite changed."[59]

Lincoln's second emotional breakdown came in the winter of 1840, triggered by a traumatic trio of circumstances. First, he was physically and emotionally exhausted from long periods of intense work. Second, thoughts of his lost love wrenched his soul—he would never be with the one whom he loved. And third, he found himself in a "stretch of bleak weather" that, like the first emotional collapse, was the domino that caused his world to tumble. Back again was the talk of suicide and speaking openly of the hopelessness in his heart.

Imagine—*this* is the same man who—decade after decade—has inspired countless millions. This is the same man who—during that dreary Illinois winter—feared he couldn't recover from the depths of his despair. On January 23, 1841, Lincoln wrote these words in a letter to his law partner, John Stuart: "I am now the most miserable man living...to remain as I am is impossible. I must die or be better."[60]

Unlike Vincent van Gogh, who less and less turned to the Bible for help, Abraham Lincoln more and more opened the Bible for peace. There he not only found solace, but also a sense of purpose. He once wrote about a Bible given to him: "I doubt not that it is really...the best cure for the 'Blues.'"[61]

What kind of gift was the Bible to Lincoln? "But for this Book we could not know right from wrong. I believe the Bible is the best gift God has ever given to man."[62] To endure the pangs of depression, Abe Lincoln needed a sense of purpose.

He needed to know the God of hope would use his pain to make a difference.

"I know the plans I have for you," the Lord says in Jeremiah 29:11, "plans to prosper you and not to harm you, plans to give you hope and a future." Lincoln's life reflects this passage. He acquired a growing understanding of the sovereignty of God, and surrendered to it. His surrender was sweet, because therein he found peace.

His faith refreshed and his hope restored, all was put to the test in the summer of 1863 following the dismal news from the War Department. Things were dark—everywhere.

Elizabeth Keckly, dressmaker for Lincoln's wife, Mary, recalled watching the president "drag himself into the room"[63] where she was fitting the First Lady. "His step was slow and heavy, and his face sad. Like a tired child he threw himself upon a sofa, and shaded his eyes with his hands. He was a complete picture of dejection."[64]

But then Lincoln reached over to a stand near the sofa and pulled out a small Bible. Fifteen minutes passed, and the dressmaker observed a noticeable change in expression. "The dejected look was gone, and the countenance was lighted up with new resolution and hope."[65]

Curious, she peeked over Lincoln's shoulder to see what he was reading—the book of Job, equal to none in reconciling human suffering and the sovereignty of God. Lincoln undoubtedly sensed a kinship with Job, a relationship forged through sharing the fiery trials of life.

In addition to his losses in love and losses in war, Lincoln experienced the painful loss of little Eddie, his three-year-old son, to a lengthy illness in 1850. And more so, his wife, known for her violent temper and mood swings—indicative of manic depression—eventually was committed to an insane asylum.

But the book of Job both comforted Lincoln and strengthened him. One of the many biographies on the life of Lincoln observed, "What distinguished Lincoln was his willingness to cry out to the heavens in pain and despair, and then turn, humbly and determinedly, to the work that lay before him."[66]

As was the case with Vincent van Gogh, Lincoln's life would end from a gunshot wound. But it would not come from his own hand...for unlike the despairing artist, Lincoln's final days were lived with a sense of divine purpose—*and fulfillment.*

It was Good Friday, the morning of April 14, 1865. After putting on his slippers, Lincoln read a few pages of his Bible. His spirit was cheerful. Following a late-morning meeting, Lincoln enjoyed an afternoon carriage ride and then readied himself for a trip to the theater that evening. *His post-dinner plans had been announced in the morning papers...*

Three days earlier, handsome young actor John Wilkes Booth had been present at a Lincoln speech in which the president expressed support of the right of African-Americans to vote. Booth recoiled at the prospect and declared, "Now, by God, I'll put him through. That is the last speech he will ever make."[67]

And it was. Lincoln had to be carried out of the theater that evening after he was shot. But the final days of the great president were not characterized by the darkness and gloom that governed so much of his life. Secretary of the Interior James Harlan described it this way:

> That indescribable sadness which had previously seemed to be an adamantine element of his very being, had been suddenly exchanged for an equally indescribable expression of serene joy as if conscious that the great purpose of his life had been achieved...[68]

Depression—Answers in God's Word

Question: "What should I do when I feel down?"

Answer: "Why are you downcast, O my soul? Why so disturbed within me? Put your hope in God, for I will yet praise him, my Savior and my God" (Psalm 42:11).

Question: "When I am depressed, in what can I put my hope?"

Answer: "I wait for the LORD, my soul waits, and in his word I put my hope" (Psalm 130:5).

Question: "When I am depressed, will it really help to get counsel from others?"

Answer: "Plans fail for lack of counsel, but with many advisers they succeed" (Proverbs 15:22).

Question: "When I am depressed, who sustains me?"

Answer: "Surely God is my help; the Lord is the one who sustains me" (Psalm 54:4).

Question: "What must I remember as I pass through the waters of deep depression?"

Answer: "When you pass through the waters, I will be with you; and when you pass through the rivers, they will not sweep over you. When you walk through the fire, you will not be burned; the flames will not set you ablaze" (Isaiah 43:2).

Question: "When I am depressed, what should I think about and focus on?"

Answer: "Whatever is true, whatever is noble, whatever is right, whatever is pure, whatever is lovely, whatever is admirable—if anything is excellent or praiseworthy—think about such things" (Philippians 4:8).

Question: "When I feel depressed with unrelenting pain, can I find any consolation or joy?"

Answer: "Then I would still have this consolation—my joy in unrelenting pain—that I had not denied the words of the Holy One" (Job 6:10).

Question: "When I am depressed, what will guard my heart and mind?"

Answer: "Do not be anxious about anything, but in everything, by prayer and petition, with thanksgiving, present your requests to God. And the peace of God, which transcends all understanding, will guard your hearts and your minds in Christ Jesus" (Philippians 4:6-7).

Question: "When I've lost all hope for the future, does the Lord still have any plans for me?"

Answer: "'For I know the plans I have for you,'" declares the LORD, "'plans to prosper you and not to harm you, plans to give you hope and a future'" (Jeremiah 29:11).

Question: "When I feel depressed, what will motivate me to persevere under this trial?"

Answer: "Blessed is the man who perseveres under trial, because when he has stood the test, he will receive the crown of life that God has promised to those who love him" (James 1:12).

FEAR

Moving from Panic to Peace

I magine being terrorized—your life continually threatened, your heart gripped with fear. Imagine every day waking to the thought, *This day could be my last day—the last for my family, the last for my friends!* Imagine living in the constant fear of being burglarized and brutalized...vandalized and victimized...mauled and murdered.

Suddenly, someone appears out of the blue instructing you to do the unthinkable—*take action and fight those whom you fear!* But such an idea is impossible—even preposterous—especially for Gideon, who is inclined to *flee* in the face of fear.

Now, imagine trying to thresh wheat in a *winepress* of all places! After the threshing, in order to separate the chaff from the wheat, a gentle outdoor breeze is needed. As both are thrown up into the air, the wind blows away the lightweight chaff and the heavier wheat falls to the ground. But...the center of a winepress is protected from the breeze by its surrounding walls. With little wind, your efforts yield only paultry results.

So here you are in hiding, fearing for your life, fighting an uphill battle, for a few grains of wheat. At this point, the angel of the Lord appears, saying, "The Lord is with you, mighty warrior." He addresses you as...what? *A mighty warrior?*

Who...you?

I. DEFINITIONS OF FEAR

A. What Is Fear?

Imagine being asked to do something you know you can't do. Like

Gideon, rather than attempting to meet the challenge, you find yourself responding, "Thanks, but no thanks. You've got the w-r-o-n-g person."

However, the angel announces that *you* are to lead the battle against your greatest enemy—one vastly outnumbering your army, one greatly feared by your people, and feared for good reason! The mammoth Midianites ravage and ransack your nation at will, leaving death and destruction in their wake: "Whenever the Israelites planted their crops, the Midianites [and other enemies]...ruined the crops all the way to Gaza and did not spare a living thing for Israel, neither sheep nor cattle nor donkeys."[1]

Understandably, you feel terrorized and your heart is filled with fear.

- *Fear* is a strong emotional reaction to a perceived imminent danger characterized by a fight, flight, or freeze response.[2]
- *Fear* can be real or imagined, rational or irrational, normal or abnormal.
- *Fear* acts as a protective reaction, placed in us by our Creator to activate all our physical defense systems when we face real danger. Fear triggers the release of adrenaline in the body, which both prepares and propels us to action, often called "fight or flight."
- *Fear* is a natural emotion designed by God. However, *fearfulness* is not designed by God, for fearfulness means living in a state of fear.
- *Fear,* in Hebrew, is *yare,*[3] which means "to be afraid, stand in awe or fear." The Bible says about Gideon that

"he was afraid"
(Judges 6:27).

B. What Is Anxiety?

After the heavenly messenger delivers his initial instructions, Gideon begins to wonder: *If the Lord is really with us, why has all this evil happened?* And Gideon makes it most clear that if God wants a deliverer, the fragile farmer definitely is not the man for the job! After all, he is the *least* in his family, belonging to the *weakest* clan, in the *small* tribe of Manasseh. Cowering with the angst of anxiety, Gideon exclaims, "How can I save Israel?"

Gideon knows the monstrous Midianites have a new weapon that enables them to make swift, long-range attacks against the Hebrews, rendering them virtually powerless. This terrible weapon is nothing other than *the camel!*

Without food or water and with a heavy load, a camel can travel 300 miles in just three or four days. During Israel's harvest time, the Midianites would ascend from the desert and quickly cover the land "like swarms of locusts." The Midianite troops and their camels, both "impossible to count," would strip Israel bare of everything edible. They would return to the desert with their plunder, and wait until the next harvest season to return.

Existing like this for seven years reduced Gideon and all the people to threshing meager amounts of grain in winepresses. They hid themselves and their food in mountain dens and caves. No wonder Gideon is fearfully anxious and fully persuaded "the LORD has abandoned us and put us into the hand of Midian" (Judges 6:13).

Gideon's fear has a "close cousin" called *anxiety.*

- *Anxiety,* in the psychological/psychiatric world, is the umbrella word used to refer to varying degrees of worry and fear from mild to extreme.

- *Anxiety* is an uneasiness or distress over a real or perceived threat and is characterized by extreme worry or brooding fear.

- *Anxiety* stems from *uncertainty*—hoping something will happen but having no guarantee that it will, or fearing something will happen, but having no control over whether it will or not.

- *Anxiety* can lead to "catastrophic thinking" that overestimates the likelihood of danger or a negative outcome.

- *Anxiety* becomes a disorder when it becomes so intense that it dominates a person's thoughts, feelings, and actions, thus preventing the person from living a normal life.

Anxiety Disorders

phobias	post-traumatic stress disorder
panic disorders	acute stress disorder
obsessive-compulsive disorders	generalized anxiety disorder
anxiety due to a medical condition	substance-induced anxiety

C. What Is a Panic Attack?

When the Lord gives Gideon the directive, "Go in the strength you have and save Israel out of Midian's hand,"[4] He is not giving Gideon a pep talk or a lesson in positive thinking. Rather, He is referring to His own strength operating inside Gideon. This becomes clear with His promise, "I will be with you, and you will strike down all the Midianites together."[5]

Nevertheless, Gideon wants proof that both the message and the messenger are truly from God—and indeed, he receives it.

Gideon presents to God an offering of meat and unleavened bread, and the moment the angel touches the offering with His staff, fire flames from the rock, the offering is incinerated, and the angel disappears—vanishes—without a trace! "When Gideon realized that it was the angel of the LORD, he exclaimed, 'Ah, Sovereign LORD! I have seen the angel of the LORD face to face!'" (Judges 6:22).

Now Gideon realizes his encounter is with *the* angel of the Lord—meaning he saw a manifestation of the Lord God Himself, not merely an angel. Gideon knew this could mean sudden death![6] God had told Moses, "No one may see Me and live" (meaning seeing God in His essential glory).[7]

> *"But the LORD said to [Gideon], 'Peace! Do*
> *not be afraid. You are not going to die'"*
> (JUDGES 6:23).

Fortunately, the Lord's assurance prevents Gideon from experiencing profound panic. Yet there are many things in life that can cause us to feel overwhelmed with fright or filled with terror. And we feel the sense of panic expressed in this scripture:

> *"Fear and trembling have beset me;*
> *horror has overwhelmed me"*
> (PSALM 55:5).

- *Panic attacks* are sudden, brief episodes of intense fear with multiple physical symptoms (such as heart palpitations and dizziness) but without any precipitating external threat.[8]

- *Panic attacks* are typically unexpected, "out of the blue" experiences. The first time they occur, people are usually involved in normal activities such as shopping or walking outdoors.

Suddenly a barrage of frightening sensations strikes them, lasting just a few seconds to a few minutes.[9]

- *Panic attacks* can recur at any time. Sufferers know that just the fear of having another attack can trigger one—and so these episodes take on a life of their own.

- *Panic attacks* can be considered fear out of control.

Question: "Can I do anything to stop a panic attack?"

Answer: Yes. When you first begin to experience shallow, rapid breathing, recognize these symptoms as the onset of *hyperventilation.* This state reduces the insufficient carbon dioxide in your blood, which in turn produces classic symptoms of a panic attack: lightheadedness, dizziness, tingling of the extremities, palpitations of the heart, feelings of faintness, and respiratory distress. You can consider the onset of rapid breathing to be a warning signal, and these symptoms can be stopped by using the following techniques:

- Take slow deep, deep breaths and hold the air in your lungs for a number of seconds. Then slowly release the air.

- Place the open end of a paper bag around your nose and mouth. Breathe normally into the bag, being sure to breathe in the same air being expelled.

- Place a blanket or sheet totally over your head, which will increase the amount of carbon dioxide being taken into your lungs and will ward off the frightening symptoms produced by too little carbon dioxide in your blood.

When experiencing a panic attack, you may feel as though you will die! But that feeling is not based on fact. The truth is, *you will not die.* Whatever your perceived "threat," claim this truth as you go to war against your panic attacks. The Lord says,

> *"Do not be fainthearted or afraid; do not be terrified*
> *or give way to panic before them. For the LORD*
> *your God is the one who goes with you to fight for*
> *you against your enemies to give you victory"*
> (DEUTERONOMY 20:3-4).

D. What Is a Phobia?

Gideon has a very real and legitimate fear that he will die, and his fear doesn't go away entirely despite God's assurances and call on his life. After the spectacular episode involving the offering, God instructs Gideon to tear down his father's altar to Baal and cut down his Asherah pole—items of pagan worship—and build an altar to Him.

Gideon obeys, but only under the cover of night because "he was afraid of his family and the men of the town" (Judges 6:27). Oddly enough, God calls this man to defeat an entire army—of well over 100,000—yet this same man is afraid of his own family.

And while some people, such as Gideon, experience profound fear in response to specific circumstances, others experience paralyzing fear without the slightest provocation. Such unwarranted fear is called a *phobia*.

- *Phobias* are persistent, irrational fears of an object or situation that, in reality, presents no real threat.[10]
- *Phobia*, the English word, comes from the Greek word *phobos,* which means "fear, flight or dread."[11] In the New Testament, the word for fear is usually *phobos,* which, in the Greek language, first had the meaning of "flight," and then later it referred to "that which may cause flight."[12]
- *Phobias* grow out of fear when...[13]

  —the fear is clearly *excessive and irrational* (being out of proportion to the actual degree of threat)

  —the fear is associated with *avoidance behaviors* (deliberately doing things differently to avoid becoming afraid)

  —the fear is associated with *decreased quality of life* (curtailing enjoyment in life)

- *Phobic disorders* consist of persistent, *irrational* fears that impair a person's ability to function normally.[14]

  —If a phobia causes no major disturbance in a person's lifestyle, it is not considered a disorder (such as having an excessive fear of snakes, but rarely ever seeing a snake).

  —However, a phobic disorder occurs when a phobia gains such power in a person's life that it drives that person's thoughts, perceptions, and actions to the point that his or her entire life is affected (such as a fear of darkness or of people).

—Those who suffer from a phobic disorder experience the most extreme form of fear.

—Not only do those with a phobic disorder live in a constant state of hyper-alertness, their fear also continuously controls their activities, limits their lives, and drastically diminishes their quality of life.

The one who suffers in this way could easily say,

> *"Fear and trembling seized me and*
> *made all my bones shake"*
> (Job 4:14).

E. What Are Examples of Phobias? [15]

The type of phobia a person experiences is determined by the focus of that person's fear. There are three primary types of phobias, all of which are painfully fear-producing for the sufferer. Typically, those with phobias avoid any thought or sight of the stimulus that triggers a panic attack.

> *"When I think about this, I am terrified;*
> *trembling seizes my body"*
> (Job 21:6).

Specific Phobias (formerly known as Simple Phobias)

This type of phobia is marked by a persistent fear experienced in the presence of or in the anticipated encountering of the feared object or situation.

Examples of feared objects: elevators, spiders, knives, snakes, cats, fire, insects

—*Zoophobia* is the fear of animals, characterized by a sense of danger in the presence of even nonthreatening animals.

Examples of feared situations: flying, heights, darkness, driving over bridges or through tunnels

—*Acrophobia* is the fear of heights, characterized by feelings of extreme insecurity and of falling even when there is no danger of doing so.

—*Claustrophobia* is the fear of closed spaces, characterized by a sense of being smothered in a confined environment.

Social Phobias (sometimes called Social Anxiety Disorder)

This type of phobia is a fear of public embarrassment and is characterized by a paralyzing fear of appearing stupid or being judged as shameful in a social situation.

Examples: A persistent fear of social situations such as initiating and maintaining a conversation, eating in public, attending a party; also a persistent fear of performance situations such as stage fright and fear of public speaking.

Agoraphobia (literally, "fear of the marketplace")

This phobia is the fear of having a panic attack in a place where escape could be difficult or embarrassing. It comes as a result of experiencing repeated panic attacks and is the fear of having yet another panic attack. Therefore, any situation that could cause a sense of panic is avoided.

Example: Being so afraid of having a panic attack in a public or unfamiliar place that a person becomes homebound or even room bound.

> *"I so feared the crowd and so dreaded the contempt of*
> *the clans that I kept silent and would not go outside"*
> (Job 31:34).

When I first met Patsy Clairmont, I saw her "spiritual sparkle." Then as we talked in in depth, I saw her spiritual heart.

=== *Patsy Clairmont*[16] ===

What qualifies a person to speak fearlessly before audiences of tens of thousands, to author more than 20 books, to offer life-changing hope? How about a résumé that includes high school dropout, teenage runaway, prescription drug addict, and a fear-based female with multiple debilitating phobias? Not exactly what you'd consider a likely candidate! But that's God's specialty—healing everyday folks and helping them move from fear to faith, from panic to peace.

When Patsy ran away from home, it was all about control. She hated being out of control and wanted to be in control of her life. She partied into the night, smoked, and drank. Though just five feet tall, she wanted to go her own way in a big way. Still, she yearned for stability. So she soon became a teenage bride. But instead of being swept away to an impressive castle to live happily ever after, she found herself living in a depressing tenement infested with rats.

After Patsy's husband left for 18 months of military duty, their first child was born. Experiencing a sense of wonder and the value of life, Patsy realized there had to be a God. She began attending church...then gave her life to God.

Although she felt a change, her everyday existence remained the same. Disillusioned, she began to blame God for her circumstances. The control she thought she had relinquished to Him resulted in out-of-control behavior.

Patsy's emotions swung back and forth between anger and fear until one day she grabbed her son's small chair and threw it at her husband. Although he caught it before it could hit him, Patsy was embarrassed and humiliated. She was overcome by fear, and experienced her first full-blown panic attack. She writes, "Oh, how hard that was for me to wake up in the morning already filled with fear, this ominous thing that I could not touch but that seemed to surround me on all sides. I would think, 'I haven't even done anything yet and already it's hard for me to open my eyes and face yet another day.' The dread was consuming my energy, the disorder was obvious in my home, in my mind, and in my emotions..."[17]

At times Patsy's panic attacks were so severe her husband would take her to the hospital. She would need an injection to help calm her. She said, "The panic attacks were so frightening that I began to feel like I was allergic to my anger, so I tried to push down the anger. As I pushed down the unresolved anger and my unrelenting guilt, what came forth from my life was unreasonable fear."[18]

When Patsy realized she was not gaining control of her life, anger seethed inside her from the past. Although she couldn't remember the early years of her childhood, the signs of trauma—of childhood victimization—began to surface.

Patsy tried desperately to escape her reality. To numb her pain and mute overwhelming fears, she became chemically dependent on tranquilizers, smoked two packs of cigarettes a day, and consumed large amounts of caffeine. Patsy depended on other people and addictive behaviors to attain a measure of control in her life.

Patsy's mother and husband tried to care for her, but her destructive tendencies began to choke the life out of them as well. Trying to hold onto them as her life raft, Patsy instead started pulling them under. "I seemed to be spiraling down deeper and deeper into this darkness as I would have one fear and give into that. It would call to its friends—'Over here, you guys!' And there would be more and more and more."[19]

Patsy's fear escalated to the point that she was afraid of heights, storms, riding in cars, hospitals, elevators, crowds of people, and being all alone. Patsy had no knowledge of diagnosable mental conditions, much less any idea of what the term *agoraphobia* meant, but that did not stop this crippling condition from dominating her life. She isolated herself from society, choosing to live in near-solitary confinement in her home while her mother and husband watched and cared for her as best they could.

Patsy's condition worsened. Finally her doctor suggested she attend a self-help program. Out of desperation for help, she went. Patsy learned that though her situation was deeply distressing, it wasn't dangerous. In spite of her fears, she wasn't going to die. She was given a plan, and that plan gave her hope.

As Patsy began to achieve small successes, she discovered that people liked her. And although the swings between her high and low points were great, she began to get a handle on her symptoms.

Then a friend called with an idea and prefaced it by saying that she wanted Patsy *to consider what God wanted her to do.* Suddenly Patsy became responsible *to God* instead of to her friend. Her friend's idea was for Patsy to go to a weekend retreat.

"For someone with agoraphobia, that was a major decision," she admitted, "to leave the safety of home and to make sure I had enough tranquilizers to be in control of the situation, to purposefully put myself in the midst of over three thousand women. Just the thought of hours in a car to reach my destination frightened me because just to go from my home to the grocery store was a major trip and I could only go if my husband drove me."[20]

However, Patsy did find the courage to attend the retreat—courage in the face of her fear. And while she was there, she heard truth that challenged her to be set free: "Do not conform any longer to the pattern of this world, but be transformed by the renewing of your mind. Then you will be able to test and approve what God's will is—his good, pleasing and perfect will" (Romans 12:2).

Patsy knew she needed to be transformed. Romans 12:2 told her she could accomplish that by the renewing of her mind—and that with a renewed mind, she would not live the rest of her life controlled by fear, but be able to experience God's perfect will for her.

Patsy began to apply the truths of the Bible to her everyday living. Her addictive and destructive choices were replaced with Bible study, prayer, and changed patterns of thinking. Her life became transformed as she kicked the smoking habit, overcame her dependency on tranquilizers, and gained control over her panic attacks. With a renewed mind and with renewed hope from Christ, she experienced total transformation.

Patsy was once fearful of leaving her own home. But since her transformation, she has shared her story with over three million people—providing hope for healing, humor for the heart, and *fearlessly* standing tall.

II. Characteristics of Fearfulness

Time and time again, fear arises in Gideon's heart. A vast army of Midianites has gathered again, ready to raid the land of Israel at harvest time. Meanwhile, the Lord has promised Gideon total victory. Yet Gideon *still* asks for divine confirmation concerning his call. "Gideon said to God, 'If you will save Israel by my hand as you have promised—look, I will place a wool fleece on the threshing floor. If there is dew only on the fleece and all the ground is dry, then I will know that you will save Israel by my hand, as you said'" (Judges 6:36-37).

God exercises great patience with Gideon's fragile faith, and the next morning, His reluctant servant finds a damp fleece and a dry floor. *But wait a minute,* Gideon must have pondered, *Might not that have happened naturally? Of course the floor would dry before the fleece.* So Gideon asks God to participate in a second test, and this time to reverse the outcome. He asked for a dry fleece and a damp floor. And

"that night God did so"
(Judges 6:40).

A. What Are Symptoms of *Normal* Versus *Abnormal* Fear?

The fear Gideon feels is completely understandable. His enemy is real, and his life is in real danger. He has "normal" fear. However, God has proven Himself to be both powerful and trustworthy. So why does God seem absent in this situation? It isn't that God doesn't see Gideon's circumstance or denies his dilemma. God knows neither is a problem for Him, and Gideon needs to know that too! No fear—normal or abnormal—is beyond God's ability to resolve.

What are the differences between normal and abnormal fear?

Normal Fear

Why would God give us the emotion of fear if it could be detrimental to us? The answer is found in asking another question: If at this moment you were surprised by an assailant with a knife in his hand, would you not want the "*benefits* of fear?"

Put a check mark (√) next to the symptoms you exhibit when you experience fear. These benefits include...

☐ Apprehension (to proceed with caution)

☐ Increased breathing (to deliver more oxygen to your body)

☐ Increased energy (to provide the fuel to take immediate action)

☐ Increased heart rate (to fuel your muscles with blood)

☐ Hyper-alertness (to increase awareness of danger)

☐ Racing mind (to provide options to consider)

☐ Contracting muscles (to prepare for the "fight or flight" reaction)

☐ Increased perspiration (to cool your body and prevent overheating)

☐ Dilated pupils (to increase vision, especially at night)

☐ Heightened senses (for the purpose of dealing with the feared object)

☐ Lessened sleep (to provide more "awake" time)

☐ Increased talking (to aid in communication about the problem)

Abnormal Fear[21]

With abnormal fear, the level of fear a person feels is way out of proportion to the actual situation—in fact, the fear may be totally unrelated to the situation. Abnormal fear can lead to a panic attack. The person with abnormal fear can identify with this anguished cry:

> *"My heart is in anguish within me; the terrors of*
> *death assail me. Fear and trembling have beset me;*
> *horror has overwhelmed me. I said, 'Oh, that I had*
> *the wings of a dove! I would fly away and be at*
> *rest—I would flee far away and stay in the desert'"*
> (PSALM 55:4-7).

A person experiences a panic attack when four or more of the following symptoms reach a peak within a period of ten minutes or less. (The body cannot sustain the "fight or flight" mode for longer than that amount of time.) Place a check mark (√) next to symptoms you have experienced:

☐ Chest pain or discomfort (feeling like you are having a heart attack)

☐ Chills or hot flashes (feeling like you *must* get to the hospital)

☐ Choking sensation, difficulty swallowing (feeling like your throat is closing)

☐ Cold hands, tingling sensation (feeling like you are going numb)

☐ Detached sensation (feeling like you are losing touch with reality or yourself)

☐ Dizziness, lightheaded (feeling like you are going to faint)

☐ Fear of losing control (feeling like you are going crazy)

☐ Hyperventilating, shortness of breath (feeling like you are being smothered)

☐ Nausea, diarrhea, or abdominal pain and cramping (feeling like you have a life-threatening disease)

☐ Rapid heart rate, pounding heartbeat (feeling like your heart is going to jump out of your chest)

☐ Sweating, excessive perspiration (feeling embarrassed and conspicuous)

☐ Terror of dying (feeling like you are *sure* to die)

☐ Trembling or shaking (feeling like you are unable to control your body)

People with abnormal fear are not as afraid of the *object* of their fear as they are of the *symptoms* of their fear.[22] And indeed, their fear is great. They experience the same feelings that Job did.

> *"Terrors overwhelm me; my dignity is driven away*
> *as by the wind, my safety vanishes like a cloud"*
> (JOB 30:15).

B. What Are the Two Levels of Anxiety?

Gideon will gradually come to realize that *God's call to a person is never dependent on that person's strength or ability.* God's call is always determined by His own plan and power, and we are asked to respond with faith in His strength. The more Gideon comes to believe God will give the Midianites into his hands, the more he is able to go forth in complete faith and follow

God's plan for the future. Though initially afraid, Gideon moves forward in faith!

Fear can paralyze or mobilize. Gideon could have been paralyzed by doubting God, by fearing that the problems would never change, by wallowing in his bottom-of-the-rung status of being the least in his family. Negative doubt-filled messages could have played over and over in his mind. If that had been the case, his response to being addressed as a mighty warrior would have been, "Mighty warrior? Not a chance!"

Like Gideon, we all experience times of anxiety, but not all of us experience it in the same way, for the same reason, or to the same degree. Typically, we want to avoid anxiety like the plague! However, anxiety is not to be feared, but to be understood and to be used as a prompt to trust in the Lord all the more. The Lord Jesus Christ advises,

> *"Do not let your hearts be troubled.*
> *Trust in God; trust also in me"*
> (JOHN 14:1).

Moderate Anxiety

Normal, fearful concern can be healthy and helpful:

—It motivates us and leads to increased efficiency.

—It forces us out of our comfort zone.

—It helps us avoid dangerous situations.

—It can cause us to live more dependently on the Lord.

Notice that the psalmist, who put these words to music, turned his focus to the Lord when he was anxious:

> *"When anxiety was great within me, your*
> *consolation brought joy to my soul"*
> (PSALM 94:19).

Intense Anxiety

Abnormal, fearful obsession is more profound and problematic:

—It makes concentration more difficult.

—It causes us to be forgetful.

—It hinders our performance.

—It blocks our communication with others.

Notice that Solomon—called the wisest man on earth—said,

"Banish anxiety from your heart"
(ECCLESIASTES 11:10).

Question: "I have had a number of panic attacks during which I thought I was going to die. How can I overcome my irrational fear of death?"

Answer: You can experience peace—a lasting peace—when you realize that you have absolutely no control over the moment of your death. Based on the Bible, God has already determined the exact number of your days on earth. Therefore, face the fact of your death head-on.

Say to the Lord:

—"I choose to trust You with Your perfect plan for my life, and my death."

—"I yield my will to Your will."

—"Thank You for giving me Your perfect peace."

"All the days ordained for me were written in
your book before one of them came to be"
(PSALM 139:16).

Question: "How can I overcome my overwhelming fear that my children might die?"

Answer: Unquestionably, your children *will* die. The question that no one can answer with certainty is *when*. That is, no one but God. Realize that God knew and ordained the length of each of your children's lives before they were conceived. Your fear can't change that fact. Instead of having fear, which is not beneficial, you can benefit your children in the following ways:

—Pray that you will be a Christlike example for your children

—Pray that you will draw your children to the Lord by the life you live

—Pray a prayer of trust:

Lord,

Thank You for loving my children.
And thank You that I can trust You
to do what is best for them.
Since the length of their lives
is already in Your sovereign hands,
I choose to be controlled by fear no longer.
I choose instead to trust You
and thank You for every day
they are here on earth.
And I commit myself to helping them
grow in Christlike character.

In Your holy name I pray. Amen.

❧

"Man's days are determined; you have decreed the number
of his months and have set limits he cannot exceed"
(JOB 14:5).

III. CAUSES OF FEAR

What causes Gideon—the man God destines to be one of the greatest leaders in history—to fear the army God promises to defeat? First, Gideon lacks military experience; and second, Gideon has lived under the oppression of the savage Midianites for seven years. These facts alone are enough to cause Gideon to doubt God's promise of victory.

God's next charge, however, would leave anyone completely paralyzed with fear. Gideon is to go against an army "thick as locusts"[23] numbering 135,000.[24] And he is to do this not with a larger army, or even one of the same size. Nor is he to do it with his small army of 32,000—just one-fourth the size of the Midianite army. Rather he is to fight with the help of a drastically reduced and *much* smaller army! Why? So...

> *"Israel may not boast against me that*
> *her own strength has saved her"*
> (Judges 7:2).

God gives Gideon an unimaginable directive: Those who are fearful about fighting the Midianites can return home. Instantly, 22,000 men are eliminated! While these men had enough faith to fight, they did not have enough faith to fight *fearlessly*—something God required of Israel when going into battle. The fundamental principle? *Fear contaminates faith.*[25]

Now only 10,000 men remain in Gideon's ranks. Then God makes a seemingly more absurd statement: "That's still too many men!"

A. What Are the Common Causes of Fear?[26]

Situations that evoke no fear in some people are the same situations that evoke great fear in others. What makes the difference? Perception! A person's perception of a situation and of God determines whether or not fear or faith will rule. Notice that Gideon is *not* one of the fearful men who returns home! His perception of his situation has begun to change.

Likewise, your perception of a situation affects both the degree of your fear (how much fear you will feel), and the way you will *respond* to your fear (what you will do because of the fear).

Fear is a natural human reaction to a perceived threat—either physically or emotionally—in one or more of these three areas: love, significance, and security.

Your Love from Others Feels Threatened

Examples of situations that might threaten your need to feel loved include:

- Primary relationship: "If I lose my marriage partner, I don't know what I will do or how I can go on living."
- Talents and abilities: "If I don't do well enough, I'll lose my friends. Then I'll be all alone."
- Physical attractiveness: "If I start looking older and put on more weight, I will lose the affection I need so badly."
- Position in a relationship: "If you spend time with other people, then you don't really love me."

Solution: Learn that you are loved by the Lord beyond measure.

*"As high as the heavens are above the earth, so
great is his love for those who fear him"*
(PSALM 103:11).

Your Significance Feels Threatened

Examples of situations that might threaten your sense of significance include:

- Identity: "If I lose my position at work, I will lose all that I have worked to achieve. Then what reason will I have to live?"
- Self-esteem: "If I embarrass myself in front of people, I will never be able to face them again. I'll be too ashamed."
- Reputation: "If others find out about my compulsive habit, I'll lose face with them."
- Self-fulfillment: "If I don't achieve my goals, my life will be a failure."

Solution: Learn that you are so significant that the Lord chose to save you and has future plans for you.

*"God is my salvation; I will trust and not be
afraid. The LORD, the LORD, is my strength
and my song; he has become my salvation"*
(ISAIAH 12:2).

Your Security Feels Threatened

Examples of situations that might threaten your sense of security include:

- Financial security: "If I don't do well on this presentation, I might lose my job. Then I won't be able to support myself or my family."
- Physical safety: "If I drive too far from home, I might have an accident and possibly even be killed."
- Physical health: "If I am not careful about what I eat or touch, I may get sick. I could even die!"
- Possessions: "If I lose my home, I will have nowhere to live and I won't be able to survive."

Solution: Learn that your security is in your personal relationship with the Lord.

> *"In God I trust; I will not be afraid.*
> *What can man do to me?"*
> (Psalm 56:11).

B. What Are the Key Contributors to Fear?[27]

Fear does not appear in a vacuum. Just as Gideon's seven years of terror at the hands of the Midianites set him up to be fearful, something set you up to be controlled by fear, and something serves to trigger that fear. The setup occurred in the past, while the trigger occurs in the present. Finding the truth about your past fearful setup will provide wisdom as to why you are being controlled by fear in the present.

> *"Surely you desire truth in the inner parts; you*
> *teach me wisdom in the inmost place"*
> (Psalm 51:6).

Fear-producing Experiences

Traumatic experiences:
—Childhood sexual abuse or rape
—Tragic accident
—Divorce or the death of a loved one or a cherished pet

Scare tactics used on you by others:
—Threats of violence by a parent
—Threats of violence by siblings
—Threats of violence by others

Underdeveloped sense of self-worth:
—Neglect, criticism, or ridicule
—Poor school performance
—Lack of musical, artistic, or athletic abilities

Parents or family members who displayed excessive fear:

—"My aunt had a panic disorder."

—"My father worried constantly."

—"My mother was fearful and overprotective."

Realize the reason for your fear and tell yourself the truth about both the past and the present.

> *"When I was a child, I talked like a child, I*
> *thought like a child, I reasoned like a child. When*
> *I became a man, I put childish ways behind me"*
> (1 CORINTHIANS 13:11).

Emotional Overload

Denial of your feelings:

—"I must suppress my pain."

—"I must deny my disappointments."

—"I must reject my anger."

Excessive need to please people:

—"I must keep everyone from getting angry."

—"I must keep everyone happy."

—"I must be at peace with everyone."

Internalization of stress:

—"I have a lot of hidden anxiety."

—"I fail to admit stressful situations."

—"I have no outlet for venting my emotions."

Strict or perfectionist parents or authorities:

—"I never pleased my parents."

—"I never was good enough."

—"I received harsh punishments."

Realize the reason for your fear, acknowledge it to the Lord, and let Him help heal you from your emotional hurts.

> *"Humble yourselves, therefore, under God's mighty*
> *hand, that he may lift you up in due time. Cast all*
> *your anxiety on him because he cares for you"*
> (1 PETER 5:6-7).

Avoidance of Threatening Situations

Refusing to face your fears:
—"I minimize my fearfulness."
—"I think it will go away in time."
—"I think that I can avoid fearful situations."

Giving no opportunity for change:
—"I don't seek help or talk to anyone."
—"I don't try to figure out why I am fearful."
—"I don't try to learn to confront my fear."

Continuing to reinforce your fears:
—"I accommodate my fears rather than challenge them."
—"Everything I do is contingent on my fearfulness."
—"I don't go anywhere that might raise my anxiety level."

Reinforcing your negative thought patterns:
—"Fear dominates all of my decisions."
—"I evaluate everything through the filter of fear."
—"My thoughts are dominated by fear."

Realize the reason for your fears and let the Lord help you face them.

> *"I am the LORD, your God, who takes hold of your right*
> *hand and says to you, Do not fear; I will help you"*
> (ISAIAH 41:13).

Runaway Imagination

Expecting life to be threatening:
—"I always expect hostility and hatred."

—"I always expect resistance and roadblocks."

—"I always expect danger and disaster."

Assuming the worst will happen:

—"I always assume rejection and ridicule."

—"I always assume hurt and heartache."

—"I always assume frustration and failure."

Believing you can never change:

—"I have given up thinking my life will ever be good."

—"I think I will be controlled by fear forever."

—"I don't believe God can or will help me."

Thinking you have no control over the situation:

—"I am overwhelmed when I experience fear."

—"I am powerless when I experience fear."

—"I can't think clearly when I experience fear."

Realize the reason for your fear and take the lies you are believing and replace them with the truth.

> *"Whatever is true, whatever is noble, whatever*
> *is right, whatever is pure, whatever is lovely,*
> *whatever is admirable—if anything is excellent*
> *or praiseworthy—think about such things"*
> (Philippians 4:8).

C. What Are the Physical Causes of Fear and Anxiety?

So again, Gideon's troops are thinned! This time God is looking for fearless men who are fervently committed to engaging the enemy in battle—men who will keep pursuing the enemy even when hungry, thirsty, and exhausted.

God has Gideon lead the remaining thirsty men to a body of water, where He narrows ther ranks again. This time Gideon is to select only the 300 who scoop water into their hands and lap it while maintaining vigilance. These become God's chosen army to defeat the Midianites:

"The LORD said to Gideon, 'With the three hundred men
that lapped I will save you and give the Midianites into
your hands. Let all the other men go, each to his own place'"
(JUDGES 7:7).

We see no indication here of a physical cause for Gideon's fear—no coronary condition, no blocked arteries, no heart attack. However, God sees something in Gideon's heart that is fatal to faith—a fortress of fear, albeit crumbling, but still standing after living so many years under terror and tyranny. Gideon's fear continues to result from how he views his situation, how he views his insufficiency, and how he views God. He still lacks complete trust in God, whom Gideon sees as having no real commitment in spite of His promises and miraculous assurances.

Some people, however, experience fear and anxiety when no fearful situation exists, and they become further frustrated when they try to talk themselves out of their anxious feelings but to no avail. They have no idea their feelings are simply a reaction to something physical, such as a particular medication or illness.

If you are suffering with a level of anxiety that is interfering with your ability to function normally, consider taking the following steps:

Obtain a Thorough Medical Check-up

—Tell the doctor that you feel unusually anxious. Be specific. While you cannot be *genetically* predisposed to panic attacks, you may be *psychologically* predisposed to having them.

—If you do not get substantial help, get a second opinion from a medical doctor who specializes in anxiety disorders.

"The heart of the discerning acquires knowledge;
the ears of the wise seek it out"
(PROVERBS 18:15).

Consider Your Medical Condition

—Especially to be evaluated are heart, endocrine, respiratory, metabolic, and neurological conditions. Identify any possible deficiency in B-vitamins, niacin, pyridoxine, calcium, or magnesium.

—The medical world has identified a condition called Anxiety Disorder

Due to a General Medical Condition. That such a condition exists clearly indicates that a person's poor physical health can contribute to anxiety or even panic attacks.

Consider Your Exposure to Substances

—There is a form of anxiety that is called Substance-induced Anxiety Disorder.

—Any exposure to toxins, drugs, medications, vitamins, and minerals—legal and illegal, over-the-counter and prescription—should be evaluated, along with food substances (for example, caffeine or sugar).

In the midst of your affliction, know that your heavenly Father loves you, listens to you, and will help you.

> *"He has not despised or disdained the suffering*
> *of the afflicted one; he has not hidden his face*
> *from him but has listened to his cry for help"*
> (PSALM 22:24).

D. What Are the Spiritual Causes of Excessive Fear?

Gideon's greatest weakness eventually becomes his greatest strength. He discovers that when he acknowledges he is weak and inadequate, God's strength and adequacy prevail in him. Imagine God having an encounter with a fear-filled Gideon, revealing truth to him about the fearsome man of God he will become and the plan God has for him—*then* supplying him with only 300 men against an army of 135,000—so the victory would clearly be the Lord's! And though no one man could ever defeat 450 men in his own strength, Gideon wholeheartedly goes!

And the last kernel of fear is removed from Gideon's heart as he creeps among the sleeping Midianites and hears one man give the interpretation of a certain dream to another man:

> *"This can be nothing other than the sword of*
> *Gideon son of Joash, the Israelite. God has given the*
> *Midianites and the whole camp into his hands'"*
> (JUDGES 7:14).

E. What Is the Root Cause of Being Controlled by Fear?

Once Gideon hears words of his upcoming victory from the mouth of a Midianite, he is immediately filled with praises toward God and the courage of God. Quickly, in the dark of night, he summons his men.

"Get up!" commands Gideon. "The LORD has given the Midianite camp into your hands" (Judges 7:15). Obviously, something has changed in Gideon! His words could not be more direct, decisive, and divinely inspired. The stronghold of fear in his heart—that formidable fortress of fear—has finally fallen!

Wrong Belief:

"I have no control over my fear. My only recourse is to avoid all fearful situations."

Right Belief:

"As I face my fear in the strength of the Lord, fear will not control me. Christ lives in me, and as I focus on His perfect love and His perfect truth, I will feel His perfect peace in the midst of every fear-producing situation."

> *"There is no fear in love. But perfect love drives*
> *out fear, because fear has to do with punishment.*
> *The one who fears is not made perfect in love"*
> (1 JOHN 4:18).

======= *How to Have Freedom From Fear...Forever!* =======

Throughout the Bible, God repeats the instruction over and over and over: "Do not fear...do not be afraid...fear not." God tells us not to fear circumstances, people, or things. Rather, we are told, "Fear the LORD your God, serve him only."[28] This fear is not fright in the sense that we would be afraid *of* God. The meaning of this kind of fear is *reverence* and *awe* for God.

How can you know freedom from fear forever? First, acknowledge that God is worthy of your reverence. Second, submit your life and your fears to His authority by receiving His Son, Jesus, as your Savior and Lord. What does that involve?

1. GOD'S PURPOSE FOR YOU...IS *SALVATION*

—What was God's motive in sending Christ to earth? To express His love for you by making salvation available to you!

> *"God so loved the world, that he gave his one and only*
> *Son, that whoever believes in him shall not perish but have*
> *eternal life. For God did not send his Son into the world to*
> *condemn the world, but to save the world through him"*
> (JOHN 3:16-17).

—What was Jesus' purpose in coming to earth? To make everything perfect and to remove all sin? No, to forgive your sins, empower you to have victory over sin, and enable you to live a fulfilled life!

> *"I [Jesus] have come that they may have*
> *life, and have it to the full"*
> (JOHN 10:10).

2. YOUR PROBLEM...IS *SIN*

—What exactly is sin? Sin is living *independently* of God's standard—knowing what is right, but choosing wrong.

> *"Anyone, then, who knows the good he*
> *ought to do and doesn't do it, sins"*
> (JAMES 4:17).

—What is the major consequence of sin? Sin produces death, both physical and spiritual separation from God.

> *"The wages of sin is death, but the gift of God*
> *is eternal life in Christ Jesus our Lord"*
> (ROMANS 6:23).

3. GOD'S PROVISION FOR YOU...IS THE *SAVIOR*

—Can anything remove the penalty for sin? Yes. Jesus died on the cross to personally pay the penalty for your sins.

> *"God demonstrates his own love for us in this:*
> *While we were still sinners, Christ died for us"*
> (ROMANS 5:8).

—What is the solution to being separated from God? Belief in Jesus Christ as the only way to God the Father.

> *"Jesus answered, 'I am the way and the truth and the*
> *life. No one comes to the Father except through me'"*
> (JOHN 14:6).

4. YOUR PART...IS *SURRENDER*

—Place your faith in (rely on) Jesus Christ as your personal Lord and Savior and reject your good works as a means of gaining God's approval.

> *"It is by grace you have been saved, through*
> *faith—and this not from yourselves, it is the gift of*
> *God—not by works, so that no one can boast"*
> (EPHESIANS 2:8-9).

—Give Christ control of your life, entrusting yourself to Him.

> *"Jesus said to his disciples, 'If anyone would come after*
> *me, he must deny himself and take up his cross and follow*
> *me. For whoever wants to save his life will lose it, but*
> *whoever loses his life for me will find it. What good will*
> *it be for a man if he gains the whole world, yet forfeits his*
> *soul? Or what can a man give in exchange for his soul?'"*
> (MATTHEW 16:24-26).

Prayer of Salvation

Father,

I want a real relationship with You.
I admit that many times I've chosen
to go my own way instead of Your way.
Please forgive me for my sins.
Thank You for sending Your Son to die
on the cross to pay the penalty for my sins,
and for His rising from the dead
to provide new life.
Come into my life
to be my Lord and my Savior.

I'm giving control of my life to You
so that I live by faith rather than fear.

In Jesus' name I pray. Amen.

If you have placed your trust in the completed work of Jesus Christ, then the following promise from God applies to you:

"The LORD himself goes before you and will be
with you; he will never leave you nor forsake you.
Do not be afraid; do not be discouraged"
(DEUTERONOMY 31:8).

IV. STEPS TO SOLUTION

Dividing his men into three companies, Gideon gives each of them a trumpet for one hand and an empty jar with a torch inside for the other. Now, in yet another test of faith, God calls Gideon and his men to war—*weaponless!* They will face an army of 135,000 with not a sword, spear, or shield in sight!

God asks us to stand in His strength when we're afraid—and that's exactly what Gideon does.

"Watch me," Gideon further instructs, "Follow my lead"
(JUDGES 7:17).

These are not the words nor the actions of the Gideon first introduced at the winepress. The once-cowering man has now become courageous. Clearly he is operating in the strength of Another, in the power of Almighty God Himself!

The battalion of 300 proceeds to encircle the vast Midianite camp in the dark of night, with all eyes trained on their leader like a hawk.

"When I and all who are with me blow our
trumpets, then from all around the camp blow yours
and shout, 'For the LORD and for Gideon'"
(JUDGES 7:18).

A. Key Verse to Memorize

A bone-chilling blast of trumpets startles the enemy camp, and the terrifying smashing of jars exposes blazing torches that now encircle the Midianites in a ring of fire. Bedlam breaks loose, and absolute chaos consumes the camp.

Of course, the strategic mastermind of this brilliant battle plan was Gideon's commander-in-chief—the Lord Himself!

Whenever you find yourself in a fearful situation, realize, like Gideon, that you are not alone. Rely on the Lord's presence in your life, focus on His strength, and claim and memorize the promise in this verse:

> *"Do not fear, for I am with you; do not be dismayed,*
> *for I am your God. I will strengthen you and help you;*
> *I will uphold you with my righteous right hand"*
>
> (ISAIAH 41:10).

B. Key Passage to Read and Reread

The result is that 120,000 of the mighty enemy lie dead[29] without Gideon ever even raising a shield or losing a single one of his 300 men—*and God gets all the glory!*

All the Israelites, along with all their surrounding enemies, know that only God could achieve such an awesome feat! Surely the God of Israel is the one true God!

In the blackness of night, the Midianites can't see their opponents. Nevertheless, they draw their swords and attack...and attack...and attack...*one another!* Pandemonium runs rampant, and "the LORD caused the men throughout the camp to turn on each other with their swords" (Judges 7:22). Brother fought against brother; friend fought against friend.

As a result, Gideon learned to rely totally on the Lord, his Shepherd, even when he walked through the valley of the shadow of death. Gideon feared no evil because from the beginning, he was told, "The Lord is with you" (Judges 6:12).

When you are stricken with fear, open your Bible to the twenty-third Psalm. This psalm is the most beloved in all the Bible, and for good reason. It is full of truths we need to focus on so we can know comfort, restoration, and peace rather than fear. Every verse in the psalm reminds us of truths that can calm our hearts.

The Psalm 23 Strategy

"The Lord is my shepherd, I shall not be in want.
He makes me lie down in green pastures,
he leads me beside quiet waters, he restores my soul.
He guides me in paths of righteousness for his name's sake.
Even though I walk through the valley of the shadow of death,
I will fear no evil, for you are with me;
your rod and your staff, they comfort me.
You prepare a table before me in the presence of my enemies.
You anoint my head with oil; my cup overflows.
Surely goodness and love will follow me all the days of my life,
and I will dwell in the house of the Lord forever."

Certain situations are more fearful than others. Sometimes it is enough to read the psalm once to settle your fears. At other times you may need to move to a quiet place without distractions so you can exchange panic for peace by thoroughly focusing on the psalm and its promises.

Verse 1: *"The Lord is my shepherd, I shall not be in want."*
Imagine a grassy, pastoral scene and the Lord there with you. Slowly say "The Lord is my Shepherd" five times, each time emphasizing a different word:

THE Lord is my Shepherd.
The LORD is my Shepherd.
The Lord IS my Shepherd.
The Lord is MY Shepherd.
The Lord is my SHEPHERD.

Verse 2: *"He makes me lie down in green pastures, he leads me beside quiet waters."*
Imagine yourself lying down beside a calm pool of water.

Verse 3: *"He restores my soul. He guides me in paths of righteousness for his name's sake."*

Take several deep breaths and say, "My Shepherd restores my soul" five times. Say it slowly, each time emphasizing a different word:

MY Shepherd restores my soul.

My SHEPHERD restores my soul.

My Shepherd RESTORES my soul.

My Shepherd restores MY soul.

My Shepherd restores my SOUL.

Verse 4: *"Even though I walk through the valley of the shadow of death, I will fear no evil, for you are with me; your rod and your staff, they comfort me."*

Realize that you are not trapped. Say, "I will fear no evil; the Lord is with me" five times, repeating it slowly.

Verse 5: *"You prepare a table before me in the presence of my enemies. You anoint my head with oil; my cup overflows."*

Repeat the following statement five times, each time emphasizing a different word:

THE Lord is my Protector.

The LORD is my Protector.

The Lord IS my Protector.

The Lord is MY Protector.

The Lord is my PROTECTOR.

Verse 6: *"Surely goodness and love will follow me all the days of my life, and I will dwell in the house of the LORD forever."*

Thank the Lord for the way He will use each fearful situation for *good* in your life.

> *Dear God,*
>
> *I thank You that You are my Shepherd.*
> *You guide me, You protect me,*
> *and You give me Your peace.*
> *You are the One who restores my soul.*

*You know my weaknesses and
the times I've caved in to fear.*

*Now, in my weakness,
I will choose to rely on Your strength.
You are my Shepherd.
I am choosing to rely on
Your power to move me from fear to faith.*

*As I turn my fear over to You,
use it for good in my life
to remind me of my continual need for You.*

In Your holy name I pray. Amen.

---

*Focus on your fear, and your panic will increase.
Focus on your Shepherd, and your heart will be at peace.*

—June Hunt

C. Why Are You Afraid?

Now there is no knocking of knees, no trembling of hands. Gideon not only leads the charge against the Midianites: In the Lord's strength, he and his 300 men boldly stand up to criticism and relentlessly pursue what remains of the enemy. Along the way, despite physical exhaustion. When Gideon asks the men in the town of Succoth for sustenance so he can continue his quest, they scoff at his potential for success and refuse him.

Sometimes after a great success, we often revert back to an old habit—an attitude filled with fear and doubt—simply because someone treats us as we were treated in the past.

When the men of Succoth scoffed at Gideon, he could have collapsed emotionally—even though he had just experienced a miraculous victory. That is why it's helpful for us to pause and evaluate our situation each time a new situation has the potential to fill our hearts with old fears.

Examining your fear, its origin, its legitimacy, and its pattern can help you understand it and develop a strategy to resolve it. First, go before God, who is the Source of wisdom, and pray this prayer from your heart:

> *"Search me, O God, and know my heart; test me and*
> *know my anxious thoughts. See if there is any offensive*
> *way in me, and lead me in the way everlasting"*
> (PSALM 139:23-24).

Identify Your Specific Fear

Of what are you truly afraid?

Evaluate Your Specific Fear

—Is my fear tied to recent events, or did it originate from some specific situation in the past?

—Is my fear based on a real threat or merely a perceived one?

—Is my fear wrongly associated with an event or object that should not be feared?

—Is my fear coming from certain places, people, or things that remind me of possible fearful consequences?

—Is my fear due to a persistent fear-based mentality even though the circumstance, relationship, or lifestyle in which it was rooted no longer exists?

—Is my fear a result of continuously faking fear over such a long period of time that it has now become real to me? Have I come to believe my own lie?

> *"The wisdom of the prudent is to give thought to*
> *their ways, but the folly of fools is deception"*
> (PROVERBS 14:8).

D. What to Do When You Feel Afraid

Gideon makes the same request for supplies at a second town, Peniel, and once again is refused. Resuming their pursuit, Gideon and his men rout the entire remaining army of 15,000 and capture their cruel kings. Gideon continues living out his personal transformation from fear to faith as he completes the task God has called him to accomplish. And he does it in the face of criticism and opposition not only from his enemies, but from his own countrymen! And he does it because he knows his God is trustworthy.

God desires to fill you with the same assurance as you complete the following steps to overcoming your fears.

Identify Your False Assumptions

Knowing the truth and then acting on it is critical to conquering fear. The source of truth is the One who does not lie—our God who *cannot* lie.

The first step in applying truth is to identify the false assumptions behind the fears you are experiencing and to replace them with the truth.

> *"You will know the truth, and the truth will set you free"*
> (JOHN 8:32).

Ask Yourself These Helpful Questions

IS THAT WHICH I AM AFRAID OF ACTUALLY LIKELY TO HAPPEN?

—Realize that fixating on your fear most often guarantees its repetition.

—Understand that most fears have nothing to do with what's happening now.

IS MY FEAR ROOTED IN THE PAST, OR IS IT CURRENT?

—What past trauma(s) first instilled my fear?

—What past fear am I bringing into the present?

—When did I first experience this fear?

—How old am I emotionally when I am feeling this fear?

—Where am I when I am feeling this fear?

—What is going on when I am feeling this fear?

—How is this fear affecting my life now? What is it costing me?

AM I DETERMINED TO GET OUT OF THE GRIP OF FEAR?

—Do what it takes to control your fear and to change from being fearful. Tell yourself, "I will not let this fear run my life. I will not let past fears control me."

—Decide to live in the here and now and act in a way that is not based on fear. Repeat this phrase over and over: "That was then, and this is now. That was then, and this is now."

—Share with a trustworthy person your fear and your plan for change.

As you choose to face your fear with faith, claim this Scripture as your own:

> *"I sought the LORD, and he answered me;*
> *he delivered me from all my fears"*
> (PSALM 34:4).

E. How to Move from Fear to Faith

Gideon moves from the testing of God to triumph with God, from a fear-based fleece to a faith-based foundation. Previously, Gideon kept asking God for supernatural signs that affirmed God would do what He clearly and repeatedly said He would do.[30] Ultimately, Gideon moves from weakness to strength, from doubt to faith, from vacillating to victorious—and he does so by trusting in the one true God and taking action based on that trust. It is God who gives Gideon victories in defeating both his foes and his fears.

Gideon's successes in saving his people from perishing, conquering enemy kings, and gaining victory over vast armies cause the people of Israel to ask him to rule over them. However, Gideon tells them,

> *"I will not rule over you...The LORD will rule over you"*
> (JUDGES 8:23).

God's call on Gideon's life is clear: He is to go forth in the Lord's strength and "save Israel out of Midian's hand."[31] But that call does not include ruling over Israel. Gideon knows this, and he also knows that God is not to be replaced by the man He made into a mighty warrior and empowered to accomplish His purposes. Gideon is still just a man, and God is still the almighty Ruler of the universe.

As you seek to follow Gideon's example in moving from fear to faith...

Begin with a healthy fear (awe) of God

Believe that God...

—created you because He loves you.

—has a purpose and a plan for your life.

—has the right to have authority over you.

—wants you to entrust your life to Him.

—has the power to change you.

—will keep you safe as you trust in Him.

> *"The fear of the LORD is the beginning of knowledge,*
> *but fools despise wisdom and discipline"*
> (PROVERBS 1:7).

Realize that fear is not God's plan for you

Fear-based thinking…

—reveals you are not trusting God.

—does not appropriate the grace of God.

—keeps you in bondage to fear.

—is physically, emotionally, and spiritually damaging.

> *"In God I trust; I will not be afraid.*
> *What can mortal man do to me?"*
> (PSALM 56:4).

Analyze your fear and discover its source

Are you fearful of experiencing…

—rejection: Do you need to be loved?

—failure: Do you need to feel significant?

—financial loss: Do you need to feel secure?

> *"Fear of man will prove to be a snare, but*
> *whoever trusts in the LORD is kept safe"*
> (PROVERBS 29:25).

Know the extent of God's love for you

God's love provides you with…

—complete acceptance.

—a realization of your true value.

—the power to overcome fear.

—true security.

> *"I have loved you with an everlasting love; I*
> *have drawn you with loving-kindness"*
> (JEREMIAH 31:3).

Develop your faith in the Lord

Ask God to help you be...

—actively involved in a Bible study (2 Timothy 2:15).

—in daily prayer, truly talking with God (Philippians 4:6).

—active in a local church that teaches the Word of God (Hebrews 10:25).

—committed to memorizing and meditating on God's Word (Philippians 4:8).

—obedient to God's promptings in your spirit (Philippians 4:5).

> *"His delight is in the law of the LORD, and*
> *on his law he meditates day and night"*
> (PSALM 1:2).

Be involved with other believers

As you cultivate fellowship, be...

—engaged with fellow Christians (Hebrews 10:25).

—willing to testify to God's faithfulness in your life (Lamentations 3:22-23).

—focused on serving others (Philippians 4:10).

—aware of the twofold responsibility (Christ's and yours) in assisting others in need (Philippians 4:13-14).

—accountable to a small, close group of growing Christians.

> *"As iron sharpens iron, so one man sharpens another"*
> (PROVERBS 27:17).

Use God's Word to rein in your fears

Meditate on these truths:

—"When I am afraid, I will trust in you" (Psalm 56:3).

—"The LORD is my light and my salvation—whom shall I fear? The

Lord is the stronghold of my life—of whom shall I be afraid?" (Psalm 27:1).

—"God is our refuge and strength, an ever-present help in trouble" (Psalm 46:1).

Put your faith in the power of Christ

Ask God for the grace to...

—know that Christ is always ready to respond to your needs.

—acknowledge Christ's presence in your life and call for His help.

—release your fear to Him and receive His powerful love.

—act in love toward others by focusing on their needs and relying on God.

> *"The one who calls you is faithful and he will do it"*
> (1 Thessalonians 5:24).

Become free from fear and strong in faith

As you do, you will also become...

—more trusting.

—more peaceful.

—more thankful.

—more Christlike.

> *"Just as you received Christ Jesus as Lord,*
> *continue to live in him, rooted and built up*
> *in him, strengthened in the faith as you were*
> *taught, and overflowing with thankfulness"*
> (Colossians 2:6-7).

From Fear to Faith

Imagine what it must have been like: the disciples, in a boat, on the lake, in the darkness, before the dawn.

Imagine their wavering emotions, their startled surprise. They saw "something"...something not seen before, something fearful, something terrifying. They saw a ghost!

Is their fear based on fantasy or fact? Myth or truth? Is their perception of the situation true or false? Notice how quickly they move back and forth from fear to faith to fear to faith. It all depended on what they *perceived* to be true.

Fear: "When the disciples saw Jesus walking on the lake, they were terrified. 'It's a ghost,' they said, and cried out in fear. But Jesus immediately said to them: 'Take courage! It is I. Don't be afraid.' 'Lord, if it's you,' Peter replied, 'tell me to come to you on the water.' 'Come,' he said" (Matthew 14:26-29).

Faith: "Then Peter got down out of the boat, walked on the water and came toward Jesus" (verse 29).

Fear: "But when he saw the wind, he was afraid and, beginning to sink, cried out, 'Lord, save me!' Immediately Jesus reached out his hand and caught him. 'You of little faith,' he said, 'why did you doubt?' And when they climbed into the boat, the wind died down" (verses 30-32).

Faith: "Then those who were in the boat worshiped him, saying, 'Truly you are the Son of God'" (verse 33).

What the disciples *perceived* as true controlled their emotions—though at times their perception was false. Of course, when Truth entered the boat, they moved from fear to faith, and His truth set them free.

F. How to Decrease Your Fear through Desensitization[32]

In spite of his enormous initial fear, Gideon eventually accomplishes the supernatural in the power of God because he believes in the promises of God and acts on them in faith. At first he sees himself as a weak thresher, but God sees him as a mighty warrior. Then as Gideon takes God at His word and acts out of faith rather than fear, his faith in God grows, his courage as a warrior grows, and finally he comes to see himself as God sees him. With each progressively more fearful situation, God's reassurance helps Gideon to choose, as an act of his will, to trust God and move forward in victory. With each new step, Gideon's fear becomes weaker and his faith becomes stronger.

Identifying your fear and its "triggers" will help deprive those triggers of their power. Your regular, repeated exposure to a trigger (something that initiates a sense of fear or danger) can help to desensitize you to it. If your fear is situational or if you are under medical care for panic attacks, you can move toward victory as you walk one step at a time through the following process.

After repeating a specific step day after day for a week or two, or until you no longer have a strong emotional reaction, move on to the next step. A slight reaction is expected and permissible before moving to the next step.

Gradually increase your exposure to the fear
Example of a specific phobia: fear of elevators

—Stand near an elevator and watch people get on and off.

—Push the button *as if* getting ready to step inside.

—Step inside when other people are not around. Hold the "Door Open" button, count to five and step out.

—Step inside again (when others are not around). Hold the "Door Open" button, count to ten, then step out.

—Step inside, ride to only one floor, and exit.

—Ride to two floors…three…eventually all the way up and down for ten minutes.

A supportive person can be present for each step, initially also doing the activity—then later not participating, but remaining present to encourage and praise.

Practice facing your fear
Example of a social phobia: fear of initiating conversation

—Initiate by simply saying hello with a smile.

—Practice being genuinely interested in each person you speak with. Ask yourself, *What is truly meaningful to that person?* Then mention it or ask about it.

—Listen carefully to what is said by others.

—Ask follow-up questions.

—Ask simple, open-ended questions of others about themselves—questions that can't be answered with just a yes or no.

—Intentionally use the words *you* and *yours* more in conversations than you use *I* and *my.*

—Make brief comments about yourself.

—Practice by asking a salesperson questions.

—Every day, practice saying general questions you could ask anyone:

"Who has been the most influential person in your life?"

"What was your favorite subject in school?"

"What do you enjoy doing more than anything else?"

"Of all that you have done, what has given you the greatest satisfaction?"

Repeat each step until it evokes little reaction

Example of agoraphobia: *fear of a panic attack (fear in open spaces)*

—Open your front door and leave it open.

—Stand in the open doorway for as long as possible.

—Go out the door and stand on the porch—breathe deeply.

—Walk down the sidewalk to the edge of your property.

—Walk around the outside of your house.

—Sit in the car while it is in the driveway.

—Have someone drive you around the block.

—Drive yourself around the block.

—Go to the mall and sit in your car in the parking lot.

—Go to the mall when it is not too crowded and walk around.

—Go into a store and greet a sales clerk.

—Make a small purchase.

Each step of the way, say,

> *"The LORD is with me; I will not be afraid"*
> (PSALM 118:6).

> *"Be strong and courageous. Do not be afraid or terrified because of them, for the LORD your God goes with you; he will never leave you nor forsake you"*
> (DEUTERONOMY 31:6).

Note: For serious phobic reactions, the process of desensitization is almost always used in combination with medical help.

G. How to Counter Your Fears with Facts

If you had grown up in an environment where fear reigned, as Gideon did, you could have easily developed a fear-based mentality as a child and then grown into an adult who is now controlled by fear. At times, you may feel powerless to confront or match someone strength-for-strength. You will remain, as did Gideon, at the mercy of those around you who are "master manipulators" with their arsenal of fear tactics *unless* you come to recognize the bondage you are in and accept the fact that the Lord came to free the oppressed. Yes, He came to set you free—just as He set Gideon free centuries ago.

> *"The Spirit of the Lord is on me, because he has anointed*
> *me to preach good news to the poor. He has sent me*
> *to proclaim freedom for the prisoners and recovery*
> *of sight for the blind, to release the oppressed"*
> (LUKE 4:18).

—*Fear:* "I can't help this feeling of intense fear!"

   Fact: "This feeling is a bluff to my mind and body. It is not grounded in truth."

> *"Though an army besiege me, my heart*
> *will not fear; though war break out against*
> *me, even then will I be confident"*
> (PSALM 27:3).

—*Fear:* "I have this feeling of doom—a feeling that I am going to die."

   Fact: "The time of my death is in God's hands. I will choose to trust Him."

> *"Man's days are determined; you have decreed the number*
> *of his months and have set limits he cannot exceed"*
> (JOB 14:5).

—*Fear:* "I'm afraid of what others are thinking about me."

   Fact: "My peace comes from pleasing God, not in pleasing others."

> *"We make it our goal to please him"*
> (2 CORINTHIANS 5:9).

—*Fear:* "I am hopeless and can never change."
　Fact: "In Christ, I am a new person. Nothing is hopeless."

> *"If anyone is in Christ, he is a new creation;*
> *the old has gone, the new has come!"*
> (2 Corinthians 5:17).

—*Fear:* "I am so nervous, I can't think clearly."
　Fact: "God will guard my mind and give me peace."

> *"The peace of God, which transcends all understanding,*
> *will guard your hearts and your minds in Christ Jesus"*
> (Philippians 4:7).

—*Fear:* "To be safe, I have to be in control."
　Fact: "God is in control of my life, and He is with me step by step."

> *"The Lord himself goes before you and will be*
> *with you; he will never leave you nor forsake you.*
> *Do not be afraid; do not be discouraged"*
> (Deuteronomy 31:8).

—*Fear:* "I feel trapped with no way of escape."
　Fact: "God always makes a way of escape."

> *"No temptation has seized you except what is*
> *common to man. And God is faithful; he will*
> *not let you be tempted beyond what you can bear.*
> *But when you are tempted, he will also provide*
> *a way out so that you can stand up under it"*
> (1 Corinthians 10:13).

Question: "I want to conquer my fears…what do I need to do first?"

Answer: Certain general things to consider when dealing with fears are often overlooked just because they are so simple and "obvious." It's like looking at the forest but missing the trees. The following suggestions may seem simplistic, but they can be the foundation on which to build an effective plan for overcoming fear and anxiety.

- Get a thorough medical check-up, and ask if any condition could be causing you anxiety.

- Ask your doctor to evaluate all your medications.
- Get adequate sleep.
- Get regular exercise.
- Plan for times of laughter, fun, and recreation.
- Be around encouraging people, and remove yourself from negative ones.
- Adopt a healthy diet. Avoid alcohol and drugs.
- Develop the habit of living one day at a time.
- Listen to inspirational Christian or classical music.
- Ask a trusted friend to help you imagine the worst that could happen to you in a particular situation and consider why it wouldn't be as bad as you feared it would be.

> *"Let us then approach the throne of grace with*
> *confidence, so that we may receive mercy and*
> *find grace to help us in our time of need"*
> (HEBREWS 4:16).

H. Do's and Don'ts for Family and Friends[33]

A key lesson we can learn from Gideon is that he does exactly what God requires. In time, he refuses to focus on his fear and chooses to step forward in faith. He knows he is not a mighty warrior, but he learns that God can be the warrior within him! It's not complicated—Gideon's supernatural victory comes simply because he walks both *fearfully* with God by faith and *fearlessly* with God by faith.

Sometimes God chooses a specific person, such as a friend or family member, to walk with the one who needs more faith. Just as God told Gideon to take Purah with him into the Midianite camp, fearful people need fearless friends to walk alongside to help them find the road to freedom.

Those who are fearful need a friend; those who are timid need a team-mate; those who are worried need someone wise; those who are anxious need an exhorter; those who cower need an encourager. Those who are tormented by fear need inspiration from those who have found freedom from fear.

To support a loved one who is struggling with fear, learn what to do and not to do. You can very well be that person's answer to prayer.

"There is a friend who sticks closer than a brother"
(Proverbs 18:24).

Don't become impatient when you don't understand their fear.
Do understand that what fearful people *feel* is *real.*

"A patient man has great understanding, but
a quick-tempered man displays folly"
(Proverbs 14:29).

Don't think the person is doing this for attention.
Do realize he or she is embarrassed and wants to change.

"I do not understand what I do. For what I want
to do I do not do, but what I hate I do"
(Romans 7:15).

Don't be critical or use demeaning statements.
Do be gentle and supportive, and build up the person's self-confidence.

"Encourage one another and build each
other up, just as in fact you are doing"
(1 Thessalonians 5:11).

Don't assume you know what is best.
Do ask how you can help.

"We urge you, brothers, warn those who are idle, encourage
the timid, help the weak, be patient with everyone"
(1 Thessalonians 5:14).

Don't make the person face a threatening situation without advance planning.

Do give the person instruction in positive self-talk and relaxation exercises.

"Hold on to instruction, do not let it go;
guard it well, for it is your life"
(Proverbs 4:13).

Don't make the person face the situation alone.

Do be available and assure the person of your support.

> *"Two are better than one, because they have a*
> *good return for their work: If one falls down,*
> *his friend can help him up. But pity the man*
> *who falls and has no one to help him up!"*
> (ECCLESIASTES 4:9-10).

Don't begin with difficult situations.

Do help the person to begin facing a particuar fear in small increments.

> *"Consider it pure joy, my brothers, whenever you*
> *face trials of many kinds, because you know that*
> *the testing of your faith develops perseverance"*
> (JAMES 1:2-3).

Don't constantly ask, "How are you feeling?"

Do help the person see the value of having other interests.

> *"Each of you should look not only to your own*
> *interests, but also to the interests of others"*
> (PHILIPPIANS 2:4).

Don't show disappointment and displeasure if the person fails.

Do encourage the person and compliment efforts to conquer fear.

> *"Do not withhold good from those who deserve*
> *it, when it is in your power to act"*
> (PROVERBS 3:27).

Don't say, "Don't be absurd; there's nothing for you to fear!"

Do say, "No matter how you feel, tell yourself the truth and say, 'I will take one step at a time.'"

> *"The wise in heart are called discerning, and*
> *pleasant words promote instruction"*
> (PROVERBS 16:21).

Don't say, "Don't be a coward; you *have* to do this!"

Do say, "I know this is difficult for you, but it's not dangerous. You have the courage to do this."

> *"A wise man's heart guides his mouth,*
> *and his lips promote instruction"*
> (PROVERBS 16:23).

Don't say, "Quit living in the past; this is not that bad."

Do say, "Remember to stay in the present and remind yourself, 'That was then, and this is now.'"

> *"Pleasant words are a honeycomb, sweet to*
> *the soul and healing to the bones"*
> (PROVERBS 16:24).

I. The Result of Moving from Fear to Faith

Among the thousands and thousands of people mentioned in the Bible, Gideon is selected by God to be one of the few in His famous "Hall of Faith" in Hebrews chapter 11. The individuals mentioned here demonstrated in their lives the power of living by faith. Fewer than 20 names are listed on this Honor Roll of Old Testament Saints, with Gideon being one. In fact, we are told specifically that it was "through faith" that Gideon "conquered kingdoms, administered justice, and gained what was promised" (Hebrews 11:32-33).

Gideon's transformation from being fearfully timid to being fearlessly triumphant is evident as he confronts the captive kings of Midian. Asking what kind of men they had killed at Tabor, Gideon's once fearsome enemies reply, "Men like you...each one with the bearing of a prince" (Judges 8:18).

The once-weak man from the small clan of Manasseh now bears a princely posture and has become a powerful warrior—the "mighty warrior" God called him to be.

=========== *Fear—Answers in God's Word* ===========

Question: "Is it possible to be delivered from fears that I've lived with for years?"

Answer: "I sought the LORD, and He answered me; he delivered me from all my fears" (Psalm 34:4).

Question: "What does the Bible tell me to do when I'm overcome with anxiety?"

Answer: "Humble yourselves, therefore, under God's mighty hand, that he may lift you up in due time. Cast all your anxiety on him because he cares for you" (1 Peter 5:6-7).

Question: "Who can I count on when I'm afraid and discouraged?"

Answer: "The LORD himself goes before you and will be with you; he will never leave you nor forsake you. Do not be afraid; do not be discouraged" (Deuteronomy 31:8).

Question: "How can I guard my heart and mind when I have no peace?"

Answer: "And the peace of God, which transcends all understanding, will guard your hearts and your minds in Christ Jesus" (Philippians 4:7).

Question: "Why do I have fear in my relationships, and what can I do about it?"

Answer: "There is no fear in love. But perfect love drives out fear, because fear has to do with punishment. The one who fears is not made perfect in love" (1 John 4:18).

Question: "Can my fear and anxiety be controlled by training my mind?"

Answer: "Set your minds on things above, not on earthly things. For you died, and your life is now hidden with Christ in God" (Colossians 3:2-3).

Question: "How can the Bible say that I have no one to fear and that I should not be afraid?"

Answer: "The LORD is my light and my salvation—whom shall I fear? The Lord is the stronghold of my life—of whom shall I be afraid?" (Psalm 27:1).

Question: "How can I have the strength to face trouble when no one is present to help me?"

Answer: "God is our refuge and strength, an ever-present help in trouble" (Psalm 46:1).

Question: "When I need strength and help, what assurances do I have from God?"

Answer: "So do not fear, for I am with you; do not be dismayed, for I am your God. I will strengthen you and help you; I will uphold you with my righteous right hand" (Isaiah 41:10).

Question: "Is the Lord really with me? Will He lead, guide, and comfort me so that I will not fear anything?"

Answer: "The LORD is my shepherd, I shall not be in want. He makes me lie down in green pastures, he leads me beside quiet waters, he restores my soul. He guides me in paths of righteousness for his name's sake. Even though I walk through the valley of the shadow of death, I will fear no evil, for you are with me; your rod and your staff, they comfort me" (Psalm 23:1-4).

GRIEF RECOVERY
Living at Peace with Loss

Dear friend, I have felt intense grief…a penetrating grief that cannot be escaped or denied. I know what it's like to feel *unexpected grief*—those times when grief catches me off guard, particularly when, out of the blue, a painful memory floods my mind, raining tears upon my soul.

How well I remember traveling to Indiana to speak at a conference that began with a buffet dinner. As I was standing in line, I noticed a younger woman attentively serving the plate of an older woman with a walker. I couldn't help but notice the tender affection between this mother and daughter. Immediately, a wave of grief swept over me. Tears filled my eyes…I quickly left the room…I cried.

Simply put, that mother-daughter scene evoked precious memories of my mother and me. My mother had died just four weeks before. Never again would I have the privilege of serving her, seating her, sitting with her. Never again could I hug her, kiss her, hold her. Oh, how I missed her!

Unexpected grief can occur anytime and anyplace—especially when we see something that reminds us of the one so dear to our hearts, the one no longer in our lives.

Grief visits us at unexpected times. Like the time I walked into a card shop, saw a bird's nest, and suddenly my eyes filled with tears. I had to turn and walk out of the store.

Again, sorrow had flooded my soul. Although over a year had passed since my mother's death, the moment I saw the bird's nest, I grieved for her. She loved what nests represent: security, family, intimacy.

Once for Mother's Day, I designed a bracelet for her that contained the birthstones of my three siblings that I closely nestled together inside a gold nest. Whenever I found a bird's nest (which was rare), I would get it for her, and she would be utterly delighted. That day, in that card shop, I had found another endearing nest...but this time, it was too late. And my heart grieved.

Periodically you, like me, will go through seasons of grief. And after we lose someone or something immensely meaningful to us, we can expect moments of unexpected grief. No matter what the heartache, realize that God is with you in the midst of your grief. And when you allow Jesus Christ to have control of your life, you can truly live at peace with your loss.

Why are people so drawn to Jesus...especially when their hearts have lost all hope? Why do they assume He will sympathize with their sorrows? Why would He grieve over their griefs? The answer is simple: Jesus was no stranger to grief. He was slandered and scourged, belittled and beaten, criticized and crucified. Yet the Bible says, "When they hurled their insults at him, he did not retaliate; when he suffered, he made no threats. Instead, he entrusted himself to him who judges justly" (1 Peter 2:23).

When you see someone being insulted, when you hear someone being slandered, when you watch someone suffering, you know that person not only *understands* grief, but also *feels* grief. When Jesus lived on earth, His onlookers saw the unjust insults hurled at Him, heard the unjust slander spoken of Him, watched the unjust suffering imposed on Him. Therefore, they knew He was one who could both understand their grief and care about it.

Do you feel as if no one cares about your pain? Jesus cares!

Do you think that no one cares about your sorrow? Jesus cares!

Do you believe that no one cares about your grief? Jesus cares!

> *"Casting all your care upon Him, for He cares for you"*
> (1 Peter 5:7 nkjv).

People are drawn to Jesus because He cares. And because He cares for everyone, you too can turn to Him.

> *"We do not have a high priest who is unable to*
> *sympathize with our weaknesses, but we have one who*
> *has been tempted in every way, just as we are—yet*
> *was without sin. Let us then approach the throne of*

> *grace with confidence, so that we may receive mercy*
> *and find grace to help us in our time of need"*
> (HEBREWS 4:15-16).

I. DEFINITIONS OF GRIEF RECOVERY

Who has not questioned the reason for pain and suffering in the world? Certainly some people have become hardened by their losses, while others have become softened. God used their grief to cultivate in them tender, understanding hearts.

Only days before His own death, Jesus traveled to the grave of Lazarus to comfort Lazarus's two sisters in their loss. Jesus was not only deeply moved in His Spirit, but He was also weeping with Mary and Martha. It may seem paradoxical that Jesus—the Son of God, the One who turned water into wine, the One who multiplied the loaves and the fishes, the One who raised Lazarus from the dead—could not avoid grief in His own life. But the prophet Isaiah foretold that Christ, the coming Messiah, would be a man who would understand grief well for, indeed, He was

> *"a Man of sorrows and acquainted with grief"*
> (ISAIAH 53:3 NKJV).

A. What Is Grief?

—*Grief* is the painful *emotion* of sorrow caused by the loss or impending loss of anyone or anything that has deep meaning to you.

> *"Be merciful to me, O LORD, for I am in distress; my eyes*
> *grow weak with sorrow, my soul and my body with grief"*
> (PSALM 31:9).

—*Grief* begins in your heart as a natural response to a significant, unwanted loss.

—*Grief* is a God-given emotion that increases with knowledge about the sorrows of life. The wiser you are about the grief that people experience, the more you yourself will grieve.[1]

> *"With much wisdom comes much sorrow;*
> *the more knowledge, the more grief"*
> (ECCLESIASTES 1:18).

—In the New Testament, the Greek word *lupe* means "pain of body or mind."[2] When Jesus told His disciples that He would soon be betrayed and killed, they were filled with grief.

> *"The disciples were filled with grief"*
> (MATTHEW 17:23).

B. What Is Mourning?

—*Mourning* is the process of working through the pain of sorrow that follows a significant loss.

> *"Joy is gone from our hearts; our dancing*
> *has turned to mourning"*
> (LAMENTATIONS 5:15).

—*Mourning* (also called grieving) is a normal, healthy process that lasts for a period of time. God uses mourning in order to produce ultimate healing from deep distress and sorrow.

> *"You turned my wailing into dancing; you removed*
> *my sackcloth and clothed me with joy"*
> (PSALM 30:11).

—*Mourning* evokes compassion and expressions of comfort from others. When Lazarus died, Jesus and many others came to comfort Mary and Martha.

> *"Many Jews had come to Martha and Mary to*
> *comfort them in the loss of their brother"*
> (JOHN 11:19).

—*Mourning,* in the Old Testament, can be the Hebrew word *abal,* which means "to mourn or lament."[3] Jacob's favorite son was Joseph. When Joseph's brothers told their father, Jacob, that his favored son had been killed by a ferocious animal, Jacob went into deep mourning for days...and ultimately, for years.

> *"Jacob tore his clothes, put on sackcloth and*
> *mourned for his son many days"*
> (GENESIS 37:34).

C. What Is Chronic Grief?

While we are grieving, a prevalent problem may be that we don't want to talk about our grief or let others see our sadness. Not wanting to appear weak, we mask our emotions.

Yet if we delay sharing our sorrow, our healing will also be delayed. If we are going to be "authentically human," we need to be able to share the truth about the heaviness in our hearts. If we develop chronic grief, we can become emotionally stuck, and we need to be set free. Jesus' words about truth are freeing—even when applied to grieving.

> *"You will know the truth, and the truth will set you free"*
> (JOHN 8:32).

—**Chronic grief** is unresolved, emotional sorrow experienced over a long period of time as the result of not accepting a significant loss or not experiencing closure of that loss.[4]

> *"The troubles of my heart have multiplied;*
> *free me from my anguish"*
> (PSALM 25:17).

—**Chronic grief** (or incomplete grief) can also be unresolved, deep sorrow experienced over a long period of time and characterized by *misconceptions* that result in a failure to move through the grief process.

Misconception: "My grief will never end."

Correction: You will mourn for a season; and then your grief will end.

> *"[There is] a time to mourn and a time to dance"*
> (ECCLESIASTES 3:4).

Misconception: "If I cry, I'm not strong."

Correction: Jesus was strong, yet He wept after Lazarus died.

> *"Jesus wept"*
> (JOHN 11:35).

King David was strong, yet he and his men wept after Saul and Jonathan died.

"They mourned and wept and fasted till
evening for Saul and his son Jonathan"
(2 Samuel 1:12).

Misconception: "If I feel deep sorrow, I must not be trusting God."

Correction: Jesus, the Messiah, never failed to trust God, the Father, yet He was called "a man of sorrows."

"He was despised and rejected by men, a man
of sorrows, and familiar with suffering"
(Isaiah 53:3).

D. What Is Repressed Grief?

Have you seen someone smiling, yet within the smile you recognized sadness? Have you heard someone laughing, though you knew that heart was not healed? This is a picture of repressed grief.

"Even in laughter the heart may ache,
and joy may end in grief"
(Proverbs 14:13).

—*Repressed grief* occurs when a person has reason to grieve and needs to grieve, but does not grieve.[5]

The person with repressed grief exhibits negative lifestyle patterns but does not know why. (Examples may include distancing from others, playing the clown, using mood-altering substances such as alcohol or drugs, engaging in mood-altering behaviors such as gambling or compulsive spending.)

Only by facing the truth of our painful losses in life and going through genuine grief will we have emotional healing.

In the Bible, the psalmist prayed this prayer:

"Send forth your light and your truth, let them guide me"
(Psalm 43:3).

—*Repressed grief* can be overcome and grieving can begin when a person takes the Timeline Test.[6]

The Timeline Test

1. *Draw* a long line representing your life (see sample time line on page 205).

2. *Divide* the timeline into three sections—childhood, youth, and adulthood.

3. *Denote* the major changes in your life, using short phrases...

   —birth of siblings
   —change of school
   —death of loved ones/pets
   —lost friendships
   —abuse (verbal, emotional, physical, sexual)
   —broken engagement
   —abortion
   —marriage
   —relocation
   —miscarriage
   —childlessness, infertility
   —separation/divorce
   —job loss/new job
   —empty nest (children leaving the home or marriage of children)
   —illnesses/injuries
   —financial loss
   —retirement

4. *Determine* whether there are any sad experiences or significant losses and hurts over which you have never grieved or have never finished grieving, such as...

   —abandonment
   —divorce of parents
   —failures
   —false accusations
   —rejection
   —thwarted goals
   —unjust criticism
   —unrealized dreams

5. *Discover* the source of your masked pain through earnest prayer.

Prayer for Discovery

Father,

As Your child, I come to You for help.
Calm my heart. Enable me

> *to see what I need to see.*
> *Make me aware of my need*
> *for healing and show me Your truth.*
>
> *Bring to my mind any buried pain.*
> *Surface any hidden hurt and*
> *the exact circumstances that caused it.*
> *I ask You to help my wounded heart to heal.*
> *I know You have the power*
> *to make me whole.*
> *I am willing to face*
> *whatever You want me to face*
> *so that I can be set free.*
>
> *In Your holy name I pray. Amen.*

6. *Define* the painful events over which you need to grieve by using specific statements.

   —"I've never allowed myself to grieve over _____."

   —"I am grieving over _____."

   —"I was embarrassed when _____."

   —"I felt abandoned by _____."

   —"I was really hurt when _____."

   —"I've been determined to never let (name circumstance) happen again."

7. *Decide* now to allow for deep, genuine grieving over your losses.

   > *"Heal me, O LORD, and I will be healed; save me*
   > *and I will be saved, for you are the one I praise"*
   > (JEREMIAH 17:14).

8. *Defuse* the power these events have over your emotions by sharing your feelings with a trusted person and with God.

   > *"There is a time...to speak"*
   > (ECCLESIASTES 3:1,7).

9. *Deepen* your dependence on the Lord to set you emotionally free.

> *"In my anguish I cried to the LORD, and*
> *he answered by setting me free"*
> (PSALM 118:5).

Sample Timeline

LIFE STAGES / AGE	EVENTS
Childhood	Birth
1	Father abandoned family, parents divorced
5	Mother remarried, stepfather abused me
6	Started to school, brother born
8	Moved to new city, new school
10	Moved again, new school but no friends
Youth　13	Started junior high school
15	Moved to new house
17	Graduated from high school
17	Cousin was killed in auto accident
18	Grandmother died (only one I could trust)
18	Started college
Adulthood　19	Married to leave home, daughter born
22	Pregnant, husband left, son born
23	Divorced, ran away, new job, new city
25	Attempted suicide
27	Remarried, father and two uncles died
31	Accepted Christ as Savior
37	Daughter graduated, went to college
42	Daughter returned pregnant but unmarried
43	Became a grandmother
45	Son graduated, daughter married, empty nest
48	New job, new career
52	Husband lost business of 20 years

52	Mother moved in with us
53	Lost our home, more financial problems
55	Mother died (best friend)

E. What Is "Grief Work"?

Do you feel as if your grief will never end—that your loss is a continual source of sorrow? Moving through the grief process takes time and commitment to stay the course until the goal of grief is recovery. Working through your grief is not an easy task; it is difficult and involves determination. Be assured that God has a plan for you during this season of pain, and God will give you the strength to persevere *through* the pain.

> *"You need to persevere so that when you have done the
> will of God, you will receive what he has promised"*
> (HEBREWS 10:36).

Grief work involves a step-by-step process through which a grieving person walks in order to reach a place of emotional healing.[7]

> *"Though I walk in the midst of
> trouble, you preserve my life"*
> (PSALM 138:7).

Healthy *grief work* will culminate in...[8]

—*accepting* that the past will always be in the past

—*accepting* that the present offers stability and significance

—*accepting* that the future holds new and promising hope

In the end you can say, along with the apostle Paul,

> *"We also rejoice in our sufferings, because we know
> that suffering produces perseverance; perseverance,
> character; and character, hope. And hope does not
> disappoint us, because God has poured out his love into
> our hearts by the Holy Spirit, whom he has given us"*
> (ROMANS 5:3-5).

II. CHARACTERISTICS OF GRIEF

"We don't want to hear it! We don't believe it! We won't accept it!" While Jesus' disciples didn't speak those words literally, these sentiments resounded in their hearts—especially Peter's. The shock, confusion, and fear of Christ's impending death was too great to comprehend. In John 16:18 they protested, "We don't understand what he is saying." Despite their grief, Jesus persisted in telling them the truth. He loved His disciples too much to not prepare them for the harsh realities to come.

Grief over the death of a person significant to you doesn't go away in just a few days, weeks, or even months. Healthy grieving can last for one, two, or even five years.[9] This is especially true with the loss of a beloved child, parent, or mate. Everyone grieves differently, but everyone must grieve in order to heal. As you entrust yourself to the Lord, your grieving gradually lessens and He restores joy to your heart. And someday—if not in this life, then in the life to come—you will understand how God can take even the most unspeakable losses and turn them to joy.

"You will grieve, but your grief will turn to joy"
(JOHN 16:20).

A. How Do You Know Whether You Are Grieving?

Initially when we experience a significant loss, we can plunge into depths of grief and have difficulty "coming up for air." Then eventually, after we surface, we are simply treading water, not swimming toward a real destination. The reason is called *grief.* When you feel engulfed with grief, realize that you have a Deliverer who will keep you from drowning in the depths of despair.

"He reached down from on high and took hold
of me; he drew me out of deep waters"
(PSALM 18:16).

Place a check mark (√) next to all that apply to your situation:

☐ Do you feel alone and isolated?

☐ Do you feel that you are mechanically going through the motions of life?

☐ Do you feel resentful toward God for allowing your loss?

☐ Do you ask, *"Why?"* over and over again?

☐ Do you feel overwhelmed, not knowing what to do or where to turn?

☐ Do you feel emotionally distraught because of your loss?

☐ Do you have frequent daydreams about your loss?

☐ Do you feel angry or bitter over your loss?

☐ Do you have difficulty forgiving those who caused your loss?

☐ Do you frequently dream at night about your loss?

☐ Do you see life as an empty struggle without much reward?

☐ Do you feel helpless knowing how much others must also be suffering?

☐ Do you wonder what kind of God would allow your loss?

☐ Do you view God as uninvolved and lacking compassion?

Regardless of your view of God right now, the Bible says,

> *"The LORD is good, a refuge in times of trouble.*
> *He cares for those who trust in him"*
> (NAHUM 1:7).

B. What Are the Characteristics of Chronic Grief?

Allowing yourself to be open and honest about your sorrow takes great courage.[10] For some, the reality of personal pain has been buried so deeply that the ability to experience real grief is blocked. People do many things to camouflage or ignore their grief so that they don't have to acknowledge and work through it. As a result, they have unhealthy, chronic grief, which is a barrier to emotional maturity. This unresolved sorrow blocks the comfort that Christ wants to give us. In the Beatitudes, Jesus said,

> *"Blessed are those who mourn, for they will be comforted"*
> (MATTHEW 5:4).

Here are the characteristics of chronic grief:

- *Inhibited* grief   denial of grief
  "This is not really happening to me."

- *Isolated* grief
  selective remembering
  "I refuse to think about that car accident again."

- *Insulated* grief
  reduced emotional involvement
  "I'm not going to open myself to being hurt this way again."

- *Intellectualized* grief
  rationally explaining events
  "It could have been worse."

- *Inverted* grief
  returning to immature ways of responding
  "I can't believe it! I just had a temper tantrum like one I had when I was five years old."

- *Immortalized* grief
  inability to let go of the loss
  "He will always be a part of everything in my life."

C. What Are the Stages of Healthy Grieving?

Emotional complications occur when we block the natural process of grieving.[11] You may have made these statements to yourself: *I need to get my act together! I've got to snap out of it. I should be handling this better!* These self-deprecating thoughts reveal unrealistic expectations about grieving and a failure to understand the grief process and the slow journey of restoration.

While stages of grief do exist, they are not "stair-step" stages that you walk through in a specific order. In truth, people do not go through the various stages in a predictable fashion. Every person is unique in terms of his or her grieving. Some stages may be experienced with varying degrees of intensity, some may be missed, and some stages may be repeated. Give yourself permission to experience the inconsistent stages of grieving, and trust God to bring new life again.

> *"Though you have made me see troubles, many and bitter, you will restore my life again; from the depths of the earth you will again bring me up"*
> (Psalm 71:20).

Crisis Stage

This stage of grief can last from two days to two weeks. In this stage, you are mechanically going through daily activities. You will experience many of the following symptoms:

- anxiety/fear
- appetite/sleep loss
- confusion
- denial
- disturbing dreams
- exhaustion
- feeling trapped
- limited concentration
- shock/numbness
- uncontrollable crying

"My eyes will flow unceasingly, without relief"
(LAMENTATIONS 3:49).

Crucible Stage

This stage can last up to a year or two or more, perhaps even until death if the grief is not resolved. This time of sorrow is usually accompanied by many of the following characteristics:

- anger/resentment
- anguish
- appetite/sleep loss
- bargaining with God
- depression/sadness
- guilt/false guilt
- helplessness/lethargy
- impaired judgment
- loneliness/isolation
- low self-worth
- self-pity/victim mentality
- intense yearning

"My soul is in anguish. How long, O LORD, how long?"
(PSALM 6:3).

Contentment Stage

This stage accepts the loss, leaving it in the past. This stage not only accepts that the present offers stability, but also accepts that the future offers new and promising hope. As this time approaches, the following characteristics will become more and more apparent:

- greater compassion toward others
- greater acceptance of others
- greater appreciation of others
- greater humility before others
- greater dependence on the Lord

- new ability to leave the loss behind
- new patterns for living
- new purpose in life
- new hope for the future
- new contentment in all circumstances

> *"One thing I do: Forgetting what is behind and*
> *straining toward what is ahead...For I have learned*
> *to be content whatever the circumstances"*
> (PHILIPPIANS 3:13; 4:11).

D. What Are the Side Effects of Severe Grief?

When your heart breaks over a great loss, intense grief will touch every aspect of your life—your body, soul, and spirit. The effects of this intense grief will vary in degree, ranging from mild to severe, depending on where you are in the grieving process.

While you will not experience all the effects, you will experience at least some of them. Realize that these effects are common to everyone who grieves and are temporary...as long as you face the pain of your loss and work through the grief process. In the Psalms, David recounts both the bitterness of his grief and the assurance of God's presence.

> *"When my heart was grieved and my spirit embittered,*
> *I was senseless and ignorant; I was a brute beast*
> *before you. Yet I am always with you; you hold me*
> *by my right hand. You guide me with your counsel,*
> *and afterward you will take me into glory"*
> (PSALM 73:21-24).

Physical Effects

- exhaustion
- headaches
- inability to sleep
- indigestion
- loss of appetite
- stress-induced illnesses

Emotional/Mental Effects

- depression and anxiety
- dreams about the deceased
- forgetfulness and disorganization
- guilt and anger
- loneliness and withdrawal
- threats of self-destruction/suicide

Social Effects

- antisocial behavior
- awkwardness
- escape behaviors (excessive drinking, drugs, travel, gambling, sex)
- excessive busyness
- tensions in existing relationships
- withdrawal

Spiritual Effects

- anger at God
- doubting the love, fairness, and faithfulness of God
- fear of God and dread about the future
- inability to pray or read the Bible
- withdrawal from spiritual activities
- questions about why God allowed the loss

> *"Why is life given to a man whose way is hidden, whom God has hedged in? For sighing comes to me instead of food; my groans pour out like water. What I feared has come upon me; what I dreaded has happened to me. I have no peace, no quietness; I have no rest, but only turmoil"*
> (JOB 3:23-26).

III. CAUSES OF GRIEF

Imagine a widespread killing of newborn babies, infants, and toddlers in your hometown. How would you feel? Imagine that you know many of their parents. Would they not be grief stricken? Would their hearts not be crushed and their dreams shattered? Now, imagine that all this took place right after you were born, and *you* were the baby targeted for destruction—not the others—yet you escaped (see Matthew 2). No wonder Jesus had great compassion for those who grieved! No wonder He could sympathize with their sorrows. He had been the baby targeted for destruction by King Herod!

When King Herod heard the wise men ask, "Where is the one who has been born King of the Jews?" (Matthew 2:2), he reacted in fear that this up-and-coming king would be a threat to his throne. As a result, Herod plotted to kill all the baby boys in and around Bethlehem—and kill them he did! But Herod's plan did not trump God's plan. For indeed, King Herod died, while King Jesus lived. While your loss may not equate to the widespread slaughter of innocent babies, your pain, nonetheless, is just as real, just as penetrating, and perhaps even paralyzing. Mourning and yet moving on with God's perfect plan for your life may seem impossible. But today, in spite of your deepest trials and trouble, if you are a believer in the Lord Jesus Christ, He lives in your heart to help you, to heal you, and give you His peace. Jesus said,

> *"In me you may have peace. In this world you will have*
> *trouble. But take heart! I have overcome the world"*
> (John 16:33).

Mary, Mary, Mary

Grief is an emotion that touches everyone. Even the very names of familiar people in the Bible are associated with sorrow: *Job* means "he who weeps or cries." *Jabez* means "pain." *Myra* means "pour out, weep," and *Mary*—a derivative of *Mara* or *Marah*, means "trouble, sorrow, bitter." Three of the Marys mentioned in the Bible each encounter and experience grief in profound ways, and we'll read more about their experiences in the pages to come.

First, let's consider the Virgin Mary. She was highly favored and chosen by God from among, all women to be the mother of the Messiah. What an incredible opportunity to serve the Lord…but at what cost? Pregnant by the Holy Spirit, she is awed and astonished that the incarnation is occurring within her womb—God the Son is taking on flesh—but she feels grieved over what is happening around her. Murmuring, whispering, and condemnation are coursing through this close-knit community as word gets out that Joseph's fiancée is pregnant.

Those who have watched the seemingly moral Mary grow up have no idea that from her womb the Savior would be delivered—One who would save them from their sins. Even Joseph considers ending his relationship with Mary until an angel assures him, in a dream, that she has not been unfaithful.

As Mary's belly swells over the nine-month period of pregnancy, so does her "mother's heart," and one must wonder if she grieved over the circumstances surrounding the birth of her son. If only Jesus could have been birthed at home, or at the home of a friend—someplace warm, someplace welcoming and fitting for such an important arrival. Instead, "she wrapped him in cloths and placed him in a manger, because there was no room for them in the inn" (Luke 2:7). On the night of His birth, the Son of God was set down in a feeding trough for animals.

But there would be far greater grief in the future. When the eight-day-old Messiah is presented by his parents at the temple, Simeon speaks the following prophecy directly to Mary:

> *"This child is destined to cause the falling and rising of many...so that the thoughts of many hearts will be revealed. And a sword will pierce your own soul too"*
> (Luke 2:34-35).

And indeed Mary's soul is pierced on the day she watches her son's hands and feet being nailed to a cross and his side being pierced by a sword. This was the very reason He had come into this world. But three days later, Mary's soul overflows with joy upon hearing that Jesus, the Son of God, has risen from the dead!

A. Why Do Losses Generate Such Grief?

Everyone has been created with three God-given inner needs: love, significance, and security.[12] When one or more of these needs is no longer being met, we naturally feel a sense of loss, which, in turn, causes grief.

Unmet need → Sense of loss → Feeling of grief

Throughout our lives we will incur numerous losses. Although we need to feel the pain of our losses, we do not need to be controlled by them. Instead, we must rely on God's promise that He will meet our deepest inner needs. The Bible says,

> *"My God will meet all your needs according*
> *to his glorious riches in Christ Jesus"*
> (PHILIPPIANS 4:19).

Loss of Love

- loss of significant family member (spouse, parent, unborn baby, child)
- loss of a loved pet
- loss of a romantic relationship
- loss of ability to have children (childlessness, infertility)
- loss of a close friend
- loss of an admired mentor or role model

Great Trial: "I'm still in agony over the death of my husband, and I feel like I'm only half a person."

God's Truth: Take comfort in this: Although your loss is severe and even though you have no earthly husband, the Lord says He will be your husband—He will be your Provider and Protector.

> *"Your Maker is your husband—the*
> LORD *Almighty is his name"*
> (ISAIAH 54:5).

Loss of Significance

- loss of employment
- loss of hopes and dreams
- loss of freedom
- loss of achievement
- loss of respect/reputation
- loss of purpose

Great Trial: "Everything that gives my life purpose is gone, and I feel such a sense of loss."

God's Truth: Take comfort in this: As long as you are alive, your life has purpose.

"The LORD will fulfill his purpose for me;
your love, O LORD, endures forever"
(PSALM 138:8).

Loss of Security

- loss of companionship
- loss of health (physical abilities)
- loss of finances
- loss of home
- loss of justice
- loss of family environment

Great Trial: "I've just experienced the greatest rejection of my life, and I feel overwhelmed with grief."

God's Truth: Take comfort in this. While people reject people, the Lord will not reject you. He says,

"I have chosen you and have not rejected you. So do
not fear, for I am with you; do not be dismayed, for
I am your God. I will strengthen you and help you;
I will uphold you with my righteous right hand"
(ISAIAH 41:9-10).

B. What Are Causes of Chronic Grief?

Like feet in hardened cement, our hearts and spirits can get stuck in sadness. Rather than surfacing and facing our pain, we bury it, and thus emotional healing and restored joy are delayed. Don't neglect dealing with your pain, and don't neglect turning to the One who longs to help you work through it. The Lord can help you step out of sadness and on to new purpose and joy.

"Show me your ways, O LORD, teach me your paths;
guide me in your truth and teach me, for you are God
my Savior, and my hope is in you all day long"
(PSALM 25:4-5).

Mary, Mary, Mary

Mary Magdalene waits engulfed in grief as her Lord is publicly humiliated and hung on a cross. A cruel, perplexing end to the story, she thinks...a fatal final chapter, because she has experienced—and witnessed—so much of Jesus' love and power. His death seems all the more painful.

Jesus delivered Mary Magdalene from demon possession, commanding seven evil spirits to leave her. Eventually she would leave her home to travel with Jesus and support His ministry. She had witnessed miracle after miracle, one act of love after another, so to now watch Jesus as He is condemned to a criminal's death sends Mary spiraling downward into grief and despair. And yet by His side she faithfully remains, even after He is buried in the tomb (Matthew 27:61).

At dawn on the first day of the week, she and Mary, the mother of James, go to the tomb to anoint Jesus' body with spices. Upon arrival, they find the tomb empty. A wave of grief sweeps over Mary Magdalene as she describes what she encountered to the disciples: "They have taken the Lord out of the tomb, and we don't know where they have put him!" (John 20:2).

Peter and John then run to the tomb to confirm Mary Magdalene's story. Afterward they "went back to their homes"—everyone except Mary Magdalene, who "stood outside the tomb crying" (John 20:11).

A man then startles her by asking, "Woman…why are you crying? Who is it you are looking for?" (John 20:15). Mary Magdalene doesn't recognize the man until He utters her name—"Mary."

And as with Mary, the mother of Jesus, the indescribable light of joy pervades the darkness of grief as Mary Magdalene exclaims to the disciples, "I have seen the Lord!" (John 20:18).

Common Misconceptions about Mourning[13]

Fallacy: "Mourners need to become busy and laugh a lot in order to keep from thinking about their loss."

Fact: While it is helpful for those who are grieving to be productive in mental and physical activities and to laugh when it is natural to do so, ignoring their loss is counterproductive. They need both to face and to feel their grief. The Bible illustrates this point graphically.

> *"Like one who takes away a garment on a*
> *cold day, or like vinegar poured on soda, is*
> *one who sings songs to a heavy heart"*
> (PROVERBS 25:20).

Fallacy: "Mourners need to move to a new home as soon as possible and focus on finding pleasure."

Fact: Following the death of a loved one who lived at home, consider this as a general rule: Make no major changes for one to two years. Moving to a different home may be appropriate, but only for the right reason at the right time. Before making a major decision such as moving, ask the Lord for wisdom. He will provide.

> *"If any of you lacks wisdom, he should ask*
> *God, who gives generously to all without*
> *finding fault, and it will be given to him"*
> (JAMES 1:5).

Fallacy: "Mourners should keep their grief to themselves."

Fact: Keeping your grief away from others is like keeping the sick away from medical aid. Those who grieve should go to those who can give comfort, help, and healing. The Bible says we are to

> *"mourn with those who mourn"*
> (ROMANS 12:15).

Fallacy: "Mourning is primarily relegated to women, not to men."

Fact: While all cultures have male and female stereotypes, grief is not related to gender, but rather to people. Grief impacts men and women alike, although they may express their grief in different ways. Certainly men grieve too. For example, when Stephen, the first Christian martyr, was stoned to death, the Bible says,

> *"Godly men buried Stephen and mourned deeply for him"*
> (ACTS 8:2).

Fallacy: "If you love someone, you should grieve forever."

Fact: You can love forever, but you don't have to grieve forever. How honorably you live, not how long you grieve, gives the greatest tribute to your loved one. Grieving has a definite beginning, and through God, it can have a definite ending. In a poetic way, David described how his grieving came to an end:

> *"You, O LORD, have delivered my soul from death,*
> *my eyes from tears, my feet from stumbling"*
> (PSALM 116:8).

Fallacy: "Mourners need a major change in their lifestyles."

Fact: Self-imposed, radical changes will only add to present stress and cause greater insecurity. In time, the desire for certain changes will come, and beneficial change will take place...when the time is right.

> *"There is a proper time and procedure for every matter,*
> *though a man's misery weighs heavily upon him"*
> (ECCLESIASTES 8:6).

Mary, Mary, Mary

Mary, the sister of Martha and Lazarus, is well acquainted with the grief that accompanies death even before the crucifixion of Christ occurs.

Lazarus was among Jesus' closest friends. When he fell deathly ill, Mary and Martha knew precisely to whom they needed to send word: "Lord, the one you love is sick" (John 11:3). They assumed that Jesus would immediately head for the small village of Bethany and heal Lazarus on the spot. But He delays his visit by two days and responds, "This sickness will not end in death. No, it is for God's glory so that God's Son may be glorified through it" (John 11:4).

Yet, Lazarus does die.

When Jesus finally arrives in Bethany, Lazarus has been buried for four days. Martha eagerly greets her Lord and Savior as He approaches, "but Mary stayed at home" (John 11:20).

Martha proceeds to make great declarations of faith, telling Jesus that she knows even now He can restore her brother: "I believe that you are the Christ, the Son of God, who was to come into the world" (John 11:27).

Mary, on the other hand, finally goes to Jesus and collapses at His feet, unable to bear the weight of her grief. "Lord, if you had been here, my brother would not have died" (John 11:32). When Jesus sees Mary's tears and those of others all around Him, He is "deeply moved in spirit and troubled." He then asks, "Where have you laid him?" (John 11:33-34).

Jesus instructs that the stone at the entrance to the tomb be removed, then looks up and prays, "Father, I thank you that you have heard me. I knew that you always hear me, but I said this for the benefit of the people standing here, that they may believe that you sent me." Jesus then directs his attention to the tomb and, in a loud voice—one that rings with supreme authority—commands, "Lazarus, come out!" (John 11:41-43).

Wrapped in strips of linen grave clothes, Lazarus emerges from the tomb...and Mary's great grief is suddenly transformed into immense gratitude and joy as her Friend and Savior demonstrates His power and affirms His faithfulness even when all hope seemed gone.

C. How Does God Use Grief and Suffering?

When it comes to grief and suffering, there is always purpose in pain.

> *"See now that I myself am He! There is no god besides*
> *me. I put to death and I bring to life, I have wounded*
> *and I will heal, and no one can deliver out of my hand"*
> (Deuteronomy 32:39).

In His sovereignty, God allows evil, grief, and suffering through...

—The free will of every human being (to make choices that, in turn, can cause suffering)

> *"Do not be deceived: God cannot be mocked. A man reaps*

what he sows. The one who sows to please his sinful nature, from that nature will reap destruction; the one who sows to please the Spirit, from the Spirit will reap eternal life"
(GALATIANS 6:7-8).

—Acts of nature (earthquakes and other natural disasters)

"Then a great and powerful wind tore the mountains apart and shattered the rocks before the LORD, but the LORD was not in the wind. After the wind there was an earthquake, but the LORD was not in the earthquake"
(1 KINGS 19:11).

In His sovereignty, God can use grief and suffering to...[14]

—Produce perseverance, character, and hope in you

"We also rejoice in our sufferings, because we know that suffering produces perseverance; perseverance, character; and character, hope. And hope does not disappoint us, because God has poured out his love into our hearts by the Holy Spirit, whom he has given us"
(ROMANS 5:3-5).

—Save lives

"You intended to harm me, but God intended it for good to accomplish what is now being done, the saving of many lives"
(GENESIS 50:20).

—Develop dependence on Him

"The widow who is really in need and left all alone puts her hope in God and continues night and day to pray and to ask God for help"
(1 TIMOTHY 5:5).

—Encourage you to cry out to Him

"I cry aloud to the LORD; I lift my voice to the LORD for mercy, I pour out my complaint before him;

before him I tell my trouble. When my spirit grows
faint within me, it is you who know my way"
(PSALM 142:1-3).

—Humble your heart

> *"Remember how the LORD your God led you all the*
> *way in the desert these forty years, to humble you and*
> *to test you in order to know what was in your heart,*
> *whether or not you would keep his commands"*
> (DEUTERONOMY 8:2).

—Further your faith

> *"These have come so that your faith—of greater worth*
> *than gold, which perishes even though refined by*
> *fire—may be proved genuine and may result in praise,*
> *glory and honor when Jesus Christ is revealed"*
> (1 PETER 1:7).

—Show His strength in your weaknesses

> *"I [Paul] delight in weaknesses, in insults, in*
> *hardships, in persecutions, in difficulties. For*
> *when I am weak, then I am strong"*
> (2 CORINTHIANS 12:10).

—Cause you to share in Christ's sufferings

> *"Dear friends, do not be surprised at the painful*
> *trial you are suffering, as though something strange*
> *were happening to you. But rejoice that you*
> *participate in the sufferings of Christ, so that you*
> *may be overjoyed when his glory is revealed"*
> (1 PETER 4:12-13).

—Reveal His heart

> *"Those who suffer he delivers in their suffering;*
> *he speaks to them in their affliction"*
> (JOB 36:15).

—Teach and train

"No discipline seems pleasant at the time, but painful.
Later on, however, it produces a harvest of righteousness
and peace for those who have been trained by it"
(HEBREWS 12:11).

—Conform you to Christlikeness

"It is commendable if a man bears up under the pain
of unjust suffering because he is conscious of God. But
how is it to your credit if you receive a beating for doing
wrong and endure it? But if you suffer for doing good and
you endure it, this is commendable before God. To this
you were called, because Christ suffered for you, leaving
you an example, that you should follow in his steps"
(1 PETER 2:19-21).

—Extend Christ's comfort

"[He] comforts us in all our troubles, so that we
can comfort those in any trouble with the comfort
we ourselves have received from God"
(2 CORINTHIANS 1:4).

D. How Does Guilt Produce Grief?

Frequently, grief and guilt walk hand in hand. When we are in the throes of guilt, it is not uncommon for us to lament, "If only I had…" "I should have…" "Why didn't I…!" The problem is that sometimes we can't distinguish whether we are grappling with false guilt or true guilt. We need to be able to discern the difference.

False Guilt

The following question is the kind that's asked when a grieving person unknowingly feels false guilt: "My sister died unexpectedly of a heart attack. How can I ever forgive myself for not being there for her in her time of need?"

When these types of questions arise, it is helpful to point out that obviously, you would have done everything in your power to save your sister's life. But saving her life was not in your power, which means you are struggling with false guilt.

—False guilt arises when you blame yourself, even though you have committed no wrong, or when you continue to blame yourself after you have confessed and turned from your sin.

—False guilt is resolved by recognizing the lie you have believed and by refusing to accept it. Then acknowledge the truth and accept it instead.

In His sovereignty, God has numbered each of our days, and you were not granted power to alter His plan. Clearly, you have a God-ordained season of grieving ahead of you, but don't grieve because of the pain of false guilt. Rather, grieve because of the loss of your beloved sister.

> *"Man's days are determined; you have decreed the number*
> *of his months and have set limits he cannot exceed"*
> (Job 14:5).

True Guilt

The following question is the kind that's asked when a grieving person feels true guilt: "I'm truly grieving. Through a series of bad choices, I made money a higher priority than my wife. Now she has left me. What can I do?"

To the one who is struggling with true guilt, it is helpful to point out that when you know you've been in the habit of majoring on the minors, you have choices. Typically, we learn painful lessons well! Because you have brought this grief on yourself, plan now to change your priorities. Replace your bad decisions with these good decisions:

—Evaluate what you did wrong

—Genuinely repent

—Admit to your wife that you were wrong and ask for her forgiveness

—Then live your life "majoring on the majors"…in line with God's priorities.

Do not pressure your wife. She will see for herself whether you have really changed from focusing on money to focusing on others, particularly her.

> *"The love of money is a root of all kinds of evil. Some*
> *people, eager for money, have wandered from the*
> *faith and pierced themselves with many griefs"*
> (1 Timothy 6:10).

Another question indicating false guilt is this: "I have been told that my young daughter died from cancer because I lacked sufficient faith. Could this be true?"

A helpful response would be no. Consider this: Did Jesus died because He lacked faith? Did Job become ill because he lacked faith? Our faith is to be placed in Jesus, not in *our faith!* We are told to pray that God's will, not ours, be done.

—Before Jesus went to the cross, He prayed to His heavenly Father, "May this cup be taken from me. Yet not as I will, but as you will" (Matthew 26:39).

—Paul prayed three times that his "thorn in [the] flesh" would be removed, yet God did not remove it—not because Paul was lacking faith, but because it was not God's will for healing to happen (2 Corinthians 12:7).

We are to *serve* God, not dictate to Him what He should do. A loved one's death is not caused by your lack of faith.

E. How Do You Resolve the Grief Caused by True Guilt?

The Source of True Guilt

We've all been wrong. We've all been guilty. We've all violated the will of God, going against what His Word tells us.

God created us with an innate need to have a loving relationship with Him. But when we go against His will, a wall is erected between us and God—a spiritual barricade. This wall is called *sin*. Sin is choosing to go our own way instead of God's way and, therefore, sin results in true guilt.

> *"Here we are before you in our guilt, though because*
> *of it not one of us can stand in your presence"*
> (Ezra 9:15).

═══ *Finding God's Forgiveness and Living Guilt Free* ═══

You can understand God's solution for you by reading His Word. His plan can be spelled out in four simple points:

1. GOD'S PURPOSE FOR YOU...IS *SALVATION*

—What was God's motive in sending Christ to earth? To express His love for you by making salvation available to you!

"God so loved the world that he gave his one and only Son,
that whoever believes in him shall not perish but have
eternal life. For God did not send his Son into the world to
condemn the world, but to save the world through him"
(JOHN 3:16-17).

—What was Jesus' purpose in coming to earth? To make everything perfect and to remove all sin, guilt, and grief? No, He came to forgive your sins, empower you to have victory over sin, and enable you to live a fulfilled life without the grief of guilt!

"I [Jesus] have come that they may have
life, and have it to the full"
(JOHN 10:10).

2. YOUR PROBLEM...IS *SIN*

—What exactly is sin? Sin is living *independently* of God's standard—knowing what is right, but choosing wrong.

"Anyone, then, who knows the good he
ought to do and doesn't do it, sins"
(JAMES 4:17).

—What is the major consequence of sin? Spiritual death, which is spiritual separation from God.

"The wages of sin is death, but the gift of God
is eternal life in Christ Jesus our Lord"
(ROMANS 6:23).

3. GOD'S PROVISION FOR YOU...IS THE *SAVIOR*

—Can anything remove the penalty for sin? Yes. Jesus died on the cross to personally pay the penalty for your sins.

"God demonstrates his own love for us in this:
While we were still sinners, Christ died for us"
(ROMANS 5:8).

—What is the solution to being separated from God? Acknowledging and believing in Jesus Christ as the only way to God the Father.

> *"Jesus answered, 'I am the way and the truth and the life. No one comes to the Father except through me'"*
> (JOHN 14:6).

4. YOUR PART...IS *SURRENDER*

—Place your faith in (rely on) Jesus Christ as your personal Lord and Savior and reject your good works as a means of gaining God's approval.

> *"It is by grace you have been saved, through faith—and this not from yourselves, it is the gift of God—not by works, so that no one can boast"*
> (EPHESIANS 2:8-9).

—Give Christ control of your life, entrusting yourself to Him.

> *"Jesus said to his disciples, 'If anyone would come after me, he must deny himself and take up his cross and follow me. For whoever wants to save his life will lose it, but whoever loses his life for me will find it. What good will it be for a man if he gains the whole world, yet forfeits his soul?'"*
> (MATTHEW 16:24-26).

If you choose to believe in Christ and place your faith in Him, He will enable you to live the full, guilt-free life God desires for you. If you want to be fully forgiven by God—if you want to experience His mercy and grace by accepting Him as your personal Lord and Savior—you can tell this to Him in a simple, heartfelt prayer like this:

Prayer of Salvation

God,

I want a real relationship with You.
I admit that many times I've chosen
to go my own way instead of Your way.

*I am genuinely grieved over my sins,
and I deeply regret them.*

*Jesus, thank You for dying on the cross
to pay the penalty for my sins.
Come into my life to be my Lord and Savior.
Make me the person You created me to be.*

In Your holy name I pray. Amen.

If you sincerely prayed the prayer of salvation, then the following truth applies to you! Listen to what God says!

*"Since we have been justified [declared
righteous] through faith, we have peace with
God through our Lord Jesus Christ"*
(ROMANS 5:1).

Having "peace with God" means that you have been brought into a life-changing relationship with Him. You no longer need to grieve over your guilt...because you are now forgiven!

F. Root Cause of Failure to Process Grief

Wrong Beliefs

REPRESSED GRIEF
"I should be able to handle the losses in my life without having to experience and work through deep pain and grief."

CHRONIC GRIEF
"My grief is more than I can bear. If I give in to it, I'm afraid it will consume me."

Right Belief
"Grief is a normal process that I must experience in order to grow emotionally and spiritually and to resolve my losses in life. My hope is in God, my Savior, who provides the strength for me to grieve deeply and honestly."

> *"My flesh and my heart may fail, but*
> *God is the strength of my heart"*
> (Psalm 73:26).

IV. Steps to Solution

Everyone has experienced the grief caused by betrayal. Nothing wounds the heart more deeply than the betrayal of a trusted friend. Jesus understood the grief of betrayal not by just one of his closest friends, but by two: Judas and Peter. These two disciples provide a vivid contrast between *godly sorrow* and *worldly sorrow*.

Both Judas and Peter grieved over the sickening reality of having betrayed Jesus. But Judas's betrayal resulted in further wrong choices. Overwhelmed with grief, Judas rushed headlong into worldly sorrow and ultimately committed suicide.

On the other hand, Peter's betrayal resulted in a godly sorrow. Rather than hardening his heart, Peter's sorrow led him to sincere repentance. This God-honoring repentance, in turn, led to Peter's complete reconciliation with Christ and to a humble yet powerful life that would forever impact the world.

Judas and Peter each had a choice. One chose death, the other chose life. As you face your season of grief, what will your choice be?

> *"Godly sorrow brings repentance that leads to salvation*
> *and leaves no regret, but worldly sorrow brings death"*
> (2 Corinthians 7:10).

A. Key Verse to Memorize

> *"Have mercy on me, O God, have mercy on me, for*
> *in you my soul takes refuge. I will take refuge in the*
> *shadow of your wings until the disaster has passed"*
> (Psalm 57:1).

B. Key Passage to Read and Reread

Jeremiah, known as the weeping prophet, authored the book of Lamentations, in which he lamented (cried aloud) over the enemy's destruction of Jerusalem and the temple. Jeremiah's lament, however, is followed by his hope, which can be your hope when you feel like you are drowning in a sea of grief.

═══════════════ *When Drowning in Grief* ═══════════════
Lamentations 3:19-26

—God lifts me out of the sea of my downcast soul . . . . . verses 19-21

—God's great love and compassion never fail . . . . verse 22

—God's faithfulness comforts me daily . . . . verse 23

—God is all I need...I will wait for Him . . . . verse 24

—God wants all my hope to be placed only in Him . . . . verse 25

—God's goodness is evident to me when I seek Him . . . . verse 25

—God brings healing as I wait for His deliverance . . . . . . verse 26

C. Acceptance—A Place of Healing and Hope

Working through your grief will involve both your mind and your emotions.[15] Even though intellectually you know that a loss has occurred, it's still possible for you to emotionally refuse to accept how your life will be different because of that loss. The work of *accepting the reality* of your unwanted loss may consume all of your energy, but your efforts will succeed when you have the right focus. Rather than trying to feel what others want you to feel, focus on the Lord God. Pray, "Whatever You want me to feel and whatever You want me to do is my desire. My commitment is to be the person You want me to be through this season of sorrow."

> *"Whatever you do, work at it with all your*
> *heart, as working for the Lord, not for men"*
> (COLOSSIANS 3:23).

Accept Your Past

Accept that the past will always be in the past.

—*Pray* for God's help in embracing your grief.

> *"The righteous cry out, and the LORD hears*
> *them; he delivers them from all their troubles.*

The LORD is close to the brokenhearted and
saves those who are crushed in spirit"
(PSALM 34:17-18).

—*Recall* your loss, then write and finish these sentences:

1. "I remember these significant events and memories (list both good and bad)."
2. "I look at these photographs and recall (list memories, good and bad)."
3. "I am grieving over (list all)."

"Surely you desire truth in the inner parts; you
teach me wisdom in the inmost place"
(PSALM 51:6).

—*Allow* yourself to shed tears.

"Weeping may remain for a night, but
rejoicing comes in the morning"
(PSALM 30:5).

—*Complete* the process by reviewing each event on your list and writing the word *past* next to it. This confirms you will be content to leave the past in the past.

"Godliness with contentment is great gain"
(1 TIMOTHY 6:6).

—*Memorize* these verses:

"My soul is weary with sorrow; strengthen
me according to your word"
(PSALM 119:28).

"My comfort in my suffering is this:
Your promise preserves my life"
(PSALM 119:50).

"I have suffered much; preserve my life,
O LORD, according to your word"
(PSALM 119:107).

"Your compassion is great, O Lord; preserve
my life according to your laws"
(PSALM 119:156).

—*Give thanks* for all that God has taught you from the past and how
He will use your past—and your time of grieving—in the future.

"Give thanks in all circumstances, for this
is God's will for you in Christ Jesus"
(1 THESSALONIANS 5:18).

Accept Your Present
The present offers stability and significance.

—*Choose* to live one day at a time.

"Do not worry about tomorrow, for tomorrow will worry
about itself. Each day has enough trouble of its own"
(MATTHEW 6:34).

—*Put* the Lord at the center of your life.

"If anyone would come after me, he must deny
himself and take up his cross and follow me"
(MATTHEW 16:24).

—*Go* to God with your specific questions and concerns (make a list).

"If any of you lacks wisdom, he should ask
God, who gives generously to all without
finding fault, and it will be given to him"
(JAMES 1:5).

—*Thank* God for providing everything you need for life.

"His divine power has given us everything we need
for life and godliness through our knowledge of him
who called us by his own glory and goodness"
(2 PETER 1:3).

—*Praise* God that no matter how your situation changes, He will never
leave you.

"God has said, 'Never will I leave
you; never will I forsake you'"
(HEBREWS 13:5).

—*Focus* on the joy and satisfaction of helping others (make a list).

"Carry each other's burdens, and in this
way you will fulfill the law of Christ"
(GALATIANS 6:2).

Accept Your Future

The future affords new opportunities.

—*Hope* in the plans that God has for your future.

"'I know the plans I have for you,' declares the
LORD, 'plans to prosper you and not to harm
you, plans to give you hope and a future'"
(JEREMIAH 29:11).

—*Know* that your sorrow and grief will not be wasted.

"It was good for me to be afflicted so
that I might learn your decrees"
(PSALM 119:71).

—*Put* all of your hope in God.

"Find rest, O my soul, in God alone;
my hope comes from him"
(PSALM 62:5).

—*Have* faith in God, though you cannot see Him.

"We fix our eyes not on what is seen, but on
what is unseen. For what is seen is temporary,
but what is unseen is eternal"
(2 CORINTHIANS 4:18).

—*Know* that God will fill the void in your life.

"Forget the former things; do not dwell on the
past. See, I am doing a new thing! Now it springs

> *up; do you not perceive it? I am making a way*
> *in the desert and streams in the wasteland"*
> (ISAIAH 43:18-19).

D. Guidelines for Healthy Grieving

Because grieving impacts us emotionally, physically, and spiritually, all three of these areas of our lives need to be considered when we go through the grieving process. If the following guidelines are taken to heart, the potentially harmful effects of grieving can be minimized and the benefits can be maximized.

> *"The prudent see danger and take refuge, but*
> *the simple keep going and suffer for it"*
> (PROVERBS 27:12).

Emotional Guidelines[16]

CULTIVATE A STRONG, SENSITIVE SUPPORT SYSTEM

Having people around you who genuinely care about you is essential—people who accept you wherever you are in the grieving process and who encourage you to share your feelings with them.

> *"As iron sharpens iron, so one man sharpens another"*
> (PROVERBS 27:17).

CULTIVATE THE FREEDOM TO CRY

Expressing emotions honestly, openly, and as frequently as needed is vital in order to walk through grief in a healthy, productive way.

> *"Those who sow in tears will reap with songs of joy"*
> (PSALM 126:5).

CULTIVATE A PLAN FOR SOCIALIZING REGULARLY

One of the helpful factors to feeling good about life, even while mourning, is attending social activities and interacting with others regularly.

> *"Let us not give up meeting together...but*
> *let us encourage one another"*
> (HEBREWS 10:25).

CULTIVATE A TRUSTWORTHY, HONEST CONFIDANTE

Being able to be yourself with someone and share your struggles, your troubled thoughts, and swinging emotions—and then still to be accepted and affirmed—is healing to the soul.

> *"Two are better than one, because they have a*
> *good return for their work: If one falls down,*
> *his friend can help him up. But pity the man*
> *who falls and has no one to help him up!"*
> (ECCLESIASTES 4:9-10).

CULTIVATE THE RELEASE OF RESENTMENT

If you have unresolved issues, anger, or hostile feelings regarding your loss, take the time to list your resentments along with their causes. Journaling can bring to the surface buried emotions. Then release into the hands of God each offender and the pain of each offense:

"Lord, You know the pain I have felt over (situations). I release all that pain into Your hands and, as an act of my will, I choose to forgive and release (person's name). Thank You, Lord Jesus, for setting me *free*."

> *"Be kind and compassionate to one another, forgiving*
> *each other, just as in Christ God forgave you"*
> (EPHESIANS 4:32).

Physical Guidelines[17]

Imagine a very real death threat on your life! Jezebel's edict had Elijah fleeing for his life; he ran until he eventually collapsed beneath a tree. With intense grief over the possible loss of his own life, this godly prophet prayed that he would die. But God sent an angel with food and water. After Elijah ate and drank, he lay down again and rested. Later, the angel awakened him with more food and drink. With increased strength, Elijah was once again able to go on his way (see 1 Kings 19:3-8).

From this account we learn these principles:

GET A SUFFICIENT AMOUNT OF REST

Because grieving often disturbs regular sleep patterns and disrupts prolonged periods of sleep, getting sufficient rest during the grieving process is often a challenge. But doing so is critically important to the body.

GET A GENEROUS INTAKE OF FLUID

Though the sense of thirst frequently goes unnoticed during the grieving process, drinking nonalcoholic and caffeine-free fluids is particularly important. Those help eliminate your body's toxic waste and maintain appropriate electrolyte balance.

GET A BALANCED, NUTRITIONAL DIET

Eat daily portions of food from each of the four basic food groups and avoid skipping meals. Don't become dependent on eating junk foods, smoking, or drinking alcohol.

GET INTO A DAILY EXERCISE ROUTINE

Regular exercise is a natural deterrent to feeling depressed and a natural stimulant to produce a sense of well-being. Exercise carries oxygen to the blood and promotes overall good health.

GET BIG DOSES OF SUNSHINE

Taking a walk in the sunshine is another natural way to fight grief. Light entering through the eyes stimulates the brain to send a message to the body to release antidepressant endorphins.

> *"Light is sweet, and it pleases the eyes to see the sun"*
> (ECCLESIASTES 11:7).

Spiritual Guidelines

DEVELOP A PURPOSEFUL PRAYER LIFE

The grieving process provides a strong impetus for "getting down to business" with God. Have candid conversations with Him about your thoughts and feelings. Listen to Him and lean on Him for comfort and reassurance.

> *"I recounted my ways and you answered*
> *me; teach me your decrees"*
> (PSALM 119:26).

DEVELOP A YEARNING FOR ETERNITY

One of the most hopeful and healing truths is to realize that this present life is being lived in a temporal body, but a permanent body is waiting for you. In that body you will live throughout all eternity, never to grieve again. Grasp God's promise of living eternally!

> *"We fix our eyes not on what is seen, but on*
> *what is unseen. For what is seen is temporary,*
> *but what is unseen is eternal"*
> (2 CORINTHIANS 4:18).

DEVELOP A POSITIVE, PRACTICAL PERSPECTIVE

Maintaining a positive mental attitude based on the practical application of spiritual truths during the grieving process will carry you through the darkest valley and the deepest loss.

> *"Whatever is true, whatever is noble, whatever*
> *is right, whatever is pure, whatever is lovely,*
> *whatever is admirable—if anything is excellent*
> *or praiseworthy—think about such things"*
> (PHILIPPIANS 4:8).

DEVELOP A SENSE OF PEACE ABOUT THE PAST

To resolve any unfinished business from your past, ask God's forgiveness for any failures on your part, and extend forgiveness for any failures on the part of others. Then let go of the past and embrace the present and the future God has planned for you.

> *"If we confess our sins, he is faithful and just and will*
> *forgive us our sins and purify us from all unrighteousness"*
> (1 JOHN 1:9).

DEVELOP A METHOD OF MEMORIZING SCRIPTURE

God spoke the world into existence, and His written Word, the Bible, is powerful enough to create new life in you and to restore joy to your heart, peace to your mind, and hope for your future.

> *"All Scripture is God-breathed and is useful for*
> *teaching, rebuking, correcting and training in*
> *righteousness, so that the man of God may be*
> *thoroughly equipped for every good work"*
> (2 TIMOTHY 3:16-17).

E. Letting Go and Saying Goodbye[18]

The prophet Samuel apparently had difficulty letting go of his sorrow over his beloved King Saul after Saul had violated God's directives and was rejected as king.

> *"Until the day Samuel died, he did not go to see Saul*
> *again, though Samuel mourned for him...The LORD said*
> *to Samuel, 'How long will you mourn for Saul...'"*
> (1 SAMUEL 15:35; 16:1).

Many who grieve never get over the final hurdle of letting go of the pain and saying goodbye. One method of accomplishing this task is to place an empty chair in front of you and imagine that the chair holds whatever or whoever was lost to you, ready to hear and accept whatever you need to say.

For the woman grieving over childhood sexual abuse in her past, this may mean imagining her abuser across from her and then verbalizing her feelings about it. This may allow her to resolve her feelings, forgive the offender, release her pain to God, and move her focus from the past to the present. A woman who was sexually abused as a child often finds she needs the help of a trained professional to walk with her through this process.

For the man who has lost his wife, this may mean verbalizing to her any unresolved feelings about her life or her death. By expressing his feelings as well as his need to move on with his life, he then says a final farewell to her and to their marriage. This act may need to be repeated until there is true relief through letting go, saying goodbye, and embracing the future as a whole person again.

> *"He heals the brokenhearted and binds up their wounds"*
> (PSALM 147:3).

Letting Go

—*Look back* and verbally reflect on the history you have shared with what is now lost. Acknowledge that history as a permanent part of your past but no longer a part of your present.

—*Express* any unfinished business regarding the past and resolve any remaining issues or feelings (such as regrets or resentments), bringing them to closure.

—*Choose* to forgive whatever grievances you may still be harboring and let go of any thoughts of revenge.

—*Release* the past to the past and stop making it a part of your present and future. Put it behind you and leave it there. Allow these words from the book of Job to reflect the disposition of your heart:

> *"You will surely forget your trouble,*
> *recalling it only as waters gone by"*
> (JOB 11:16).

Saying Goodbye

—*Look back* and reflect on the significance of the memories you shared with the one who is no longer in your life—exploring and expressing the depth and breadth of your feelings (such as love, appreciation, anger, and guilt).

—*Acknowledge* the impact this history has had on you as a person. Accept the fact that it will always be a part of who you are. But affirm also that it is time for you to move on with your life and become the person God is making of you *now*.

—*State* that you cannot live in the past and that you have present needs that God plans to meet in new ways. Acknowledge that you need to embrace all that God has for you.

—*Say goodbye* to the past, to the pain, and to all that has been lost. Express your final sentiments that need to be said and say, "Goodbye." Then turn your focus to the present and to the future that God has already planned for you, embracing your life now and your life in the future. Realize that you are ever in process and, therefore, ever changing. Say hello to whatever Jesus has for your life now.

> *"Peace I leave with you; my peace I give you. I*
> *do not give to you as the world gives. Do not let*
> *your hearts be troubled and do not be afraid"*
> (JOHN 14:27).

F. Questions and Answers Regarding Grief

Grieving over the Loss of a Godly Parent

Question: "Ever since the death of my godly dad, I've been angry with God and have turned away from the church. How can I get over my grief and face the future without my father?"

Answer: The loss of a godly parent can be severely painful. Instead of focusing solely on how much you miss him...

—Focus on what would bring honor to his memory.

—Ask yourself, *If my dad were still alive, what would give him the greatest joy?*

Based on the Bible, your dad's greatest joy would be for you to follow in his footsteps, to live a Christlike life, and to grow in the truths of God.

> *"I have no greater joy than to hear that my*
> *children are walking in the truth"*
> (3 John 4).

Grieving over Unforgiveness

Question: "Someone close to me died, and now it is too late for me to ask forgiveness for what I did wrong. What can I do about my heavy guilt?"

Answer: You do not have to live with guilt even though you can no longer speak to the person you wronged. Realize that God is available to you.

—Write down every wrong attitude and action. Then confess your sins to God.

—Ask God's forgiveness, realizing that all sins (even against others) are sins against God because He has told us how we are to treat one another.

—Write a letter to the one you wronged, read it aloud, and ask God to forgive you on behalf of the other person.

God knows your heart, and He can forgive your sins and restore to you a clear conscience.

> *"Create in me a pure heart, O God, and renew a steadfast*

> *spirit within me…The sacrifices of God are a broken spirit;*
> *a broken and contrite heart, O God, you will not despise"*
> (PSALM 51:10,17).

Grieving over Life Not Going Back to Normal

Question: "I have experienced a devastating death in my family, and nothing feels the same. When will life return to normal?"

Answer: When death takes someone dear to your heart, your life will not "return to normal." However, you need to establish a "new normal." When your life is changed by a significant loss, your "old normal" vanishes forever. Yet as you settle into a new routine with a new mind-set, you will develop a new normal—and over time, your comfort level will increase. During this process, remember that…

—God made you to be resilient by equipping you to adapt mentally, emotionally, and spiritually to new situations.

—Life itself consists of never-ending change from the moment of conception to the moment of death.

—Perpetual change brings with it the opportunity to grow in maturity.

Trust the Lord, who created you, and lean on Him as you find your new normal.

> *"Trust in the LORD with all your heart and lean not on*
> *your own understanding; in all your ways acknowledge*
> *him, and he will make your paths straight"*
> (PROVERBS 3:5-6).

Dealing with Anger Toward God

Question: "I have immense anger toward God for taking my child from me when she was the joy and the delight of my life. Why did God take her?"

Answer: Any significant loss results in grief. However, one of the most severe losses is the loss of a child. In the natural order in life, one assumes that children will outlive their parents, not the reverse. Certainly God understands your anguish, and He can shoulder your anger. In order to overcome your anger at God…

—Honestly share your feelings with Him.

—Ask Him to give you insight into His love for you and His plan now for your life.

—Realize the heavenly Father is also a parent and that He has the heart of a parent toward you.

—Trust that God is perfect in His love for you and for your cherished daughter.

—Thank God for every moment He allowed you to spend with your daughter.

—Realize that your daughter has not been lost to you forever—she will spend eternity with you after God's time for you here on earth is complete.

—Focus on what will honor your daughter's memory as you live your life.

—Recognize children actually belong to God, not their parents. He has ultimate authority over their lives.

This grief in your life has not come from a heart of stone, but from a heart of love and compassion. While you may not see it now, God does not find pleasure in bringing grief to His beloved children. But He does what He does from His position as the all-sovereign, all-knowing, all-loving God of the universe.

> *"Though he brings grief, he will show compassion, so*
> *great is his unfailing love. For he does not willingly*
> *bring affliction or grief to the children of men"*
> (LAMENTATIONS 3:32-33).

Dealing with Anniversary Depression

Question: "Every year for the past several years I have become depressed at the anniversary of my spouse's death. Why is it happening, and what can I do to stop it?"

Answer: You are experiencing what is commonly referred to as anniversary depression, a yearly recurring reaction to a past loss or trauma. This involuntary depression correlates to the anniversary date of your loss and lasts for a limited period of time. Because you know when your depression may recur, you might plan ahead. Establish a time to process some of your grief with a wise, caring friend or counselor. And because the depression can be triggered by conscious or unconscious memories, you can choose to create new memories around that date.

—Plan a trip with someone special around the time of the anniversary.

—Go to a Christian seminar or workshop to help keep your focus on the Lord and on His healing Word.

—Attend a social event so that you will not be alone, or invite loved ones for dinner at your home.

—Give loved ones a special remembrance in your spouse's honor (a poem, a picture, or a possession that belonged to him or her).

—Initiate a project in honor of his or her life.

"The memory of the righteous will be a blessing"
(PROVERBS 10:7).

Feeling Guilty Because of Tears

Question: "I have had a major loss in my life, but I should be over it by now. Why can't I stop crying? Why do I cry for no apparent reason at times? I feel guilty about my tears."

Answer: There is no timetable for when you should be "over" grieving a significant loss. Losses are not to be "gotten over." Our losses should be accepted, and our lives should be adjusted to accommodate our losses in such a way that the quality of our lives is not lessened, but is instead enriched. This can be a reality for you because God promises to use all things for good in the lives of those who love Him (Romans 8:28). As you go through the grief process, remember...

—Tears may come sporadically for years after your loss whenever something consciously or unconsciously triggers a memory, a scent, a place, a song, a person.

—Rather than trying to stifle your sorrowful emotions, let them flow freely. Experiencing them will help diminish them.

—Tears are for a reason and for a season. They are the body's way of releasing deep emotional, physical, mental, and spiritual pain. When the pain is released, the tears will subside.

Those who love deeply cry freely at the loss of the object of their love. That you loved deeply is a good thing! You are like God in that way, for He loves deeply, too.

> *"I have loved you with an everlasting love; I
> have drawn you with loving-kindness"*
> (JEREMIAH 31:3).

Dealing with a Most Difficult Time

Question: "It has been almost six months since my loved one died, and instead of getting better, I seem to be getting worse. What is wrong with me?"

Answer: Your grieving process is right on schedule. The sixth month after the loss of a loved one is generally the most difficult time in the grieving process. You will feel as though an unexpected second tidal wave has struck you and sent you reeling just when you thought you might be getting a handle on your grief. As you deal with this second wave of grief, realize...

—What happens at six months is that reality sets in on a much deeper level and opens up more of your soul to acknowledge and accept the significance of your loss.

—God does much of His work in us over a period of time rather than instantaneously.

When your life stays yielded to the Lord, the sorrow you are feeling will complete its work in you, and you will find that it has carved out within you a deep well that God, in His time, will fill with joy and peace and contentment.

> *"May the God of hope fill you with all joy and
> peace as you trust in him, so that you may overflow
> with hope by the power of the Holy Spirit"*
> (ROMANS 15:13).

Dealing with Decisions

Question: "I recently lost my spouse, and I feel like I am in a dense, heavy fog and cannot see my way out of it. I need to make some major decisions about what to do with the house and whether I should stay in it or sell it and move elsewhere. What should I do?"

Answer: Your feelings are completely normal and totally understandable given your situation. The death of a spouse is highly distressing and can leave the mate in a state of shock for weeks and disoriented for months. Therefore, the most commonly given advice to recent widows and widowers is that no major decisions or changes be made for at least a year. Why?

—The task of going through the grief process is a big enough job during that first year and maybe even longer.

—Unless you are some under time constraints, delay making any major decisions and any significant life changes for a year or so. Wait until you are more emotionally replenished and better able to think clearly about the pros and cons of any major decisions.

—Right now you don't know where you will want to live in a year or two or what you will want to pursue.

—The likelihood of regretful decisions are lessened.

The bottom line is that the best thing to do is to wait before you make a major decision. Do not let anyone rush you. A rushed decision can be a deeply regretted decision.

> *"I will instruct you and teach you in the way you*
> *should go; I will counsel you and watch over you"*
> (PSALM 32:8).

Reaching Out to Others

Question: "People keep asking me to socialize with them, but I don't want to be around anyone—I don't want to try to have fun or make conversation. Why can't people understand that in my grief, I just want to be left alone?"

Answer: People do understand your desire for isolation, and that is precisely why they are concerned about your being alone too much. Becoming self-absorbed, losing interest in socializing, and desiring to isolate yourself from others are common when you are in the grieving process. However, there is also the danger you might become reclusive to the point that you become stuck in your grief and fail to reach out to others to stay connected to life. One of the most effective ways to help your own healing is to reach out to others who are grieving.

—Identify with the grief of others.

- Be available as someone who can understand how a grieving person feels.
- Send a card, prepare a meal, bring a flower, run an errand.
- Make periodic phone calls to say, "I care."

—Remember that isolating yourself from others only curtails your own healing. Reaching out will help bring healing to others and, in turn, to yourself.

> *"A generous man will prosper; he who refreshes*
> *others will himself be refreshed"*
> (PROVERBS 11:25).

Grieving the Holy Spirit

Question: "I feel horrible guilt and huge grief. Although I'm a Christian, I've gone against God, and now the damage has been done. Can I ever have peace again with God?"

Answer: When you have unresolved sin, you *should* feel unresolved grief. Why? Because you have actually grieved the Holy Spirit! Realize that because you are an authentic Christian, the Spirit of God resides within you. Therefore...

—When you are in the will of God, you have peace with God (one of the "fruit of the Spirit").

—When you are not in the will of God, you will not have peace with God. The Holy Spirit has removed His peace from you to convict you of sin so that you will correct your course. Do what pleases God, and you will have the peace of God.

> *"Do not grieve the Holy Spirit of God"*
> (EPHESIANS 4:30).

G. Building Up the Bereaved[19]

What You Can Do

When someone experiences a devastating loss, God most often uses the comfort and encouragement of others to bring healing. As you reach out to others with the compassion of Christ, consider the following helpful hints for building others up when they are in the midst of grief:

- Acknowledge their loss immediately.
- Accept all emotional or verbal responses without judging them.
- Hug with tender affection.
- Expect tears and emotional extremes.
- Find helpful things to do without being asked.
- Give the one grieving many opportunities to talk about the loss.

> *"Encourage one another and build each other up"*
> (1 THESSALONIANS 5:11).

What You Can Say

DEATH OF A CHILD

Don't say, "You can always have another child."

> *Do say,* "I appreciate your special qualities as a parent to your child."

DEATH OF A SPOUSE

Don't say, "A lot of people remarry at your age."

> *Do say,* "I valued his/her (character trait or ability)."

DEATH AFTER A LONG ILLNESS

Don't say, "She's much better off now."

> *Do say,* "I admire the way you encouraged and helped her."

DIVORCE OR SEPARATION

Don't say, "He was never good enough for you."

> *Do say,* "The Lord is here for you, and I will also be here for you."

DISABLED CHILD

Don't say, "Was there something you did to cause the handicap?"

Do say, "I noticed your child's (sweet disposition, nice smile)."

LOSS OF A JOB

Don't say, "You'll find a better job within a week."

Do say, "I feel for you and will pray with you during this time."

LOSS OF A LIMB

Don't say, "Be thankful—you could have died."

Do say, "The adjustment will be difficult, but you can do it. Count on me to be of help."

LOSS OF A HOUSE

Don't say, "At least you're still alive."

Do say, "I know you have many memories of your home. I remember..."

LOSS OF A PET

Don't say, "You can always get another pet."

Do say, "You were so good to your dog."

LOSS OF A FRIEND

Don't say, "You'll make other good friends."

Do say, "A friend is a treasure. I know you will miss him/her."

LOSS AS A RESULT OF ANY TRAGEDY

Don't say, "All things work together for good!" (even though that is ultimately true).

Do say, "Although I don't know why this happened to you, I do know the Lord will stay close to you. One particular Scripture that helped me is Psalm 34:18: 'The LORD is close to the brokenhearted and saves those who are crushed in spirit.'"

> *"A word aptly spoken is like apples*
> *of gold in settings of silver"*
> (PROVERBS 25:11).

H. Finding Comfort

How true the saying, "All sunshine makes a desert." God knows that if you never experience the storms of life—if the rain clouds never release their water—you will never see flower gardens grow. You need to blossom in the areas of sympathy, empathy, compassion, understanding, perspective, and wisdom. Our God is the God of second chances. Whatever is in the past can be used for God's glory. The storms of sorrow should never be wasted. By God's design, grief will ultimately better your heart and life.... Grief will make you grow.

> *"Sorrow is better than laughter, because*
> *a sad face is good for the heart"*
> (ECCLESIASTES 7:3).

When you are in need of C-O-M-F-O-R-T

C Come to the God of all comfort.

> *"Praise be to the God and Father of our Lord Jesus Christ,*
> *the Father of compassion and the God of all comfort"*
> (2 CORINTHIANS 1:3).

O Open your heart to the reality of pain.

> *"In our hearts we felt the sentence of death.*
> *But this happened that we might not rely on*
> *ourselves but on God, who raises the dead"*
> (2 CORINTHIANS 1:9).

M Maintain a clear conscience by confessing past sins and offenses.

> *"He who conceals his sins does not prosper, but*
> *whoever confesses and renounces them finds mercy"*
> (PROVERBS 28:13).

F Find the positive in your grief process.

> *"See what this godly sorrow has produced in you: what*
> *earnestness, what eagerness to clear yourselves, what*
> *indignation, what alarm, what longing, what concern,*
> *what readiness to see justice done. At every point you*
> *have proved yourselves to be innocent in this matter"*
> (2 CORINTHIANS 7:11).

O Obtain comfort from those whom God will send to you.

> *"God, who comforts the downcast,*
> *comforted us by the coming of Titus"*
> (2 CORINTHIANS 7:6).

R Reinforce your faith by giving comfort to others.

> *"[God] comforts us in all our troubles, so that*
> *we can comfort those in any trouble with the*
> *comfort we ourselves have received from God"*
> (2 CORINTHIANS 1:4).

T Trust in the strength of Christ in you for the power to rebuild your life.

> *"I can do everything through him who gives me strength"*
> (PHILIPPIANS 4:13).

> *Just as the farther you are from a flower,*
> *the smaller it seems to your eyes,*
> *so the further your distance from grief,*
> *the smaller your sadness in sorrow. Time indeed is a healer…*
> *a gift of comfort from the God of all comfort.*

—JUNE HUNT

Grief—Answers in God's Word

Question: "Who can I call for help?"

Answer: "O LORD my God, I called to you for help and you healed me" (Psalm 30:2).

Question: "Does anyone see my trouble and grief?"

Answer: "You, O God, do see trouble and grief; you consider it to take it in hand. The victim commits himself to you" (Psalm 10:14).

Question: "How long will my weeping remain?"

Answer: "Weeping may remain for a night, but rejoicing comes in the morning" (Psalm 30:5).

Question: "How can I find rest for my soul?"

Answer: "Find rest, O my soul, in God alone; my hope comes from him" (Psalm 62:5).

Question: "Can I have any consolation in my unrelenting pain?"

Answer: "I would still have this consolation—my joy in unrelenting pain—that I had not denied the words of the Holy One" (Job 6:10).

Question: "Can my broken heart ever heal?"

Answer: "He heals the brokenhearted and binds up their wounds" (Psalm 147:3).

Question: "How can I stop feeling so downcast and disturbed within my soul?"

Answer: "Why are you downcast, O my soul? Why so disturbed within me? Put your hope in God, for I will yet praise him, my Savior and my God" (Psalm 42:11).

Question: "How can I not dwell on the past?"

Answer: "Forget the former things; do not dwell on the past. See, I am doing a new thing! Now it springs up; do you not perceive it? I am making a way in the desert and streams in the wasteland" (Isaiah 43:18-19).

Question: "Will my grief ever turn to joy?"

Answer: "You will weep and mourn while the world rejoices. You will grieve, but your grief will turn to joy" (John 16:20).

Question: "How can I find comfort and compassion?"

Answer: "The Father of compassion and the God of all comfort…comforts us in all our troubles, so that we can comfort those in any trouble with the comfort we ourselves have received from God" (2 Corinthians 1:3-4).

REJECTION
Healing a Wounded Heart 249

REJECTION
Healing a Wounded Heart

Nothing ravages your heart like rejection. The most painful wound you can experience is rejection by a loved one. Even death itself does not pierce as deeply as knowing you have been abandoned, forsaken, rejected.

Rejection chips away at your self-image, chisels your confidence, challenges your hope. Meanwhile, the memory of your loved one lingers on and on in the recesses of your mind, repeating—through whispers and shouts—those haunting messages: "You are not wanted. You are not welcome. You are not worthy."

During those times when your heart is broken and your spirit crushed, nothing is more healing than to know, deep in your soul, the Lord loves you unconditionally...and accepts you eternally.

> *"The LORD is close to the brokenhearted and*
> *saves those who are crushed in spirit"*
> (PSALM 34:18).

Favoritism can be extremely painful. One common example of favoritism is that shown by parents to a specific child. Children catch on quickly when there is a "favorite" in the family.

The favored child often comes late in life—as in the case of young Joseph in the Bible. Jacob favored Joseph over his ten older brothers...and flaunted his favoritism by giving Joseph the infamous coat of many colors—a robe Jacob made himself!

The elder brothers seethed with anger at the sight of the ornate robe, which became a symbol of their father's preferential treatment. Little did

Jacob know that his favoritism had become a breeding ground for jealousy. He had provided the spark that would create a climate of hurt, hostility, and burning hatred. Genesis 37:3-4 describes the scene:

> *"Now Israel [Jacob] loved Joseph more than any of*
> *his other sons, because he had been born to him in*
> *his old age; and he made a richly ornamented robe*
> *for him. When his brothers saw that their father*
> *loved him more than any of them, they hated him*
> *and could not speak a kind word to him."*

I. DEFINITIONS OF REJECTION

A. What Is Rejection?

The first instance of rejection is recorded for us in the first book of the Bible, after God gives Adam and Eve everything they will ever need. With God's provision came a warning: "Don't eat from that one tree." And what did Adam and Eve do? They ate from that one tree! Their direct defiance was a rejection not only of God's words, but of God Himself (Genesis 2:15-17; 3:6).

To be rejected is to be cast aside, cast off, cast away—to be thrown away as having no value.[1]

—When you are rejected, you can feel useless, abandoned, worthless.

—In the Bible, the Greek verb *atheteo* means "to do away with, to set aside, to cast or throw away as useless or unsatisfactory."[2]

—Jesus challenged the Pharisees and teachers of the law because they were rejecting the laws of God:

> *"You have a fine way of setting aside the commands*
> *of God in order to observe your own traditions!"*
> (MARK 7:9).

Rejection is a refusal to accept a person, consider an idea, or approve of something.[3]

—When you experience rejection, you feel unloved, unwanted, or unacceptable.

—The Greek verb *apodokimazo* means "to reject as the result of examination and disapproval"[4] (*apo* = "away from," *dokimazo* = "to approve").

—Jesus felt the pain of rejection. The Bible refers to Christ as the cornerstone—the most essential stone of a major structure—yet He was the cornerstone (or capstone) the builders rejected.

> *"The stone the builders rejected has become the capstone"*
> (Matthew 21:42).

To reject someone means to refuse, shun, despise, or turn away from.[5]

—When you reject others, your judgmental condemning attitude and actions reveal the calloused condition of your heart.

—In the Bible, the Hebrew word *maas* means "to reject, refuse, despise."[6]

—Because God has given each of us free will, we may choose to reject the Word of God and even God Himself.

> *"The wise will be put to shame; they will be dismayed*
> *and trapped. Since they have rejected the word of*
> *the LORD, what kind of wisdom do they have?"*
> (Jeremiah 8:9).

Question: "My father always showed partiality toward my brother, and treated the females in the family—my mother, my sister, and me—like second-class citizens, despite our many accomplishments. How can I stop being so controlled by my anger toward him?"

Answer: Anger has four sources: *hurt, fear, frustration,* and *injustice.* The anger you describe comes from at least three of the four:

- Being rejected by your own father *hurts* deeply.
- Being disfavored simply because you are female is *unjust.*
- Failing to receive well-earned recognition is extremely *frustrating.*

Realize your father's neglect of you has nothing to do with you, but everything to do with him. Something has been severely "broken" in your father, keeping him from being a reflection of the heavenly Father to you. Therefore turn loose of your expectations regarding him. Just as you would not expect a broken watch to keep time correctly, likewise don't expect your "broken" father to treat you correctly. Choose to forgive him so that your anger won't build bitterness in your heart.

> *"See to it that no one misses the grace of God and that no bitter root grows up to cause trouble and defile many"*
> (HEBREWS 12:15).

B. What Is Acceptance?

Clearly, Joseph understands rejection. The fact that he is his father's favorite results in him being betrayed by his jealous brothers and sold to strangers, to foreigners. Imagine Joseph, as a teenager, being sold by his own brothers as a common slave and carted off to a foreign land. His grief over losing his loving father and all that was familiar to him must have been overwhelming. He must have been terrified.

Still, Joseph accepts the will of God in his life...he accepts the sovereignty of God over what happens. Despite one betrayal after another, Joseph refuses to become bitter. Instead, he accepts his circumstances and humbly entrusts himself to God.

Years later, Joseph rises to a position of power in Egypt and becomes the prime minister, second only to Pharaoh. When his brothers journey to Egypt in search of grain, they end up at the mercy of Joseph. He immediately knows who *they* are, but they don't know who *he* is!

So what will Joseph do? Will he take revenge and refuse to give them grain? Will he send them off with grain, but not acknowledge them as his brothers? Will he extend his hand of help, but insist they bow before him?

No, Joseph refuses retaliation and instead accepts his brothers, in spite of their past betrayal. His acceptance isn't conditional, but unconditional— possible only because of the condition of his heart. The forgiveness in his heart allows him to focus on the future, which, in turn, allows him to *let the past stay in the past* (Genesis 37:12-29; 41–45).

To accept someone means to think of that person favorably or to receive that person willingly. It can also mean to give approval to another person.[7] We should accept others and value them purely because of their God-given worth.

—Your acceptance of others is based on the disposition of your heart, and expressed through your attitude and actions.

—In the Bible, the Greek word *proslambano* means "to accept, receive, welcome."[8]

—Jesus Christ provides the supreme example of acceptance, as seen in Romans 15:7:

> *"Accept one another, then, just as Christ accepted*
> *you, in order to bring praise to God."*

C. The Three Levels of Acceptance[9]

When we reject someone, if we look closely, we may find that we are doling out the same rejection we ourselves have received. The same is true of those who have learned to be accepting of others. Typically, we give or pass on to others what has been given to us. However, your past rejection by others need not determine your future. You can grow in your ability to become more and more accepting of others even when you yourself have been rejected. The Bible says,

> *"Forget the former things; do not dwell on the past"*
> (ISAIAH 43:18).

1. *Zero Acceptance*—If you habitually receive zero acceptance, you may come to believe that no matter what you do, you will never be accepted.

The person who totally rejects you harbors deep bitterness and extends no grace and mercy. But the Bible says,

> *"Get rid of all bitterness, rage and anger, brawling*
> *and slander, along with every form of malice. Be*
> *kind and compassionate to one another, forgiving*
> *each other, just as in Christ God forgave you"*
> (EPHESIANS 4:31-32).

2. *Performance-based Acceptance*—If you habitually receive performance-based acceptance, you may come to think, "I am accepted only when I perform perfectly."

The person who only accepts you based on how you act demands, "You must meet my requirements," and rarely offers grace and mercy. But the Bible says,

> *"Judgment without mercy will be shown to anyone who*
> *has not been merciful. Mercy triumphs over judgment!"*
> (JAMES 2:13).

3. *Unconditional Acceptance*—If you habitually receive unconditional acceptance, you clearly know that no matter what you do—even when you fail—you will always be accepted.

The person who accepts you—especially when you fail—lives with a heart of grace and mercy, and reflects the heart of God. The Bible says,

> *"Show mercy and compassion to one another"*
> (ZECHARIAH 7:9).

Question: "Can an authentic Christian be rejected by God?"

Answer: No. Based on numerous verses in the Bible, those who have entrusted their lives to Christ, though they may still sin, will never be rejected by God. Romans 8:1 says, "There is no condemnation for those who are in Christ Jesus." Therefore, if you find yourself fearful of being forsaken by God, claim the following truth from God's unchanging Word:

> *"The LORD will not reject his people; he*
> *will never forsake his inheritance"*
> (PSALM 94:14).

II. CHARACTERISTICS OF THOSE WHO FEEL REJECTED[10]

The teenage years can be marked by some of life's most painful rejections. Because of severe insecurity, young people crave acceptance from others, and often overreact to any rejection.

By age 17, Joseph feels the sting of rejection from his older brothers. In truth, Joseph plays a big part in feeding his brothers' jealousy. One day Joseph has a dream that he unwisely discloses to his older brothers. He implies that one day his brothers will bow down to him!

> *"Joseph had a dream, and when he told it to his brothers,*
> *they hated him all the more. He said to them, 'Listen to this*
> *dream I had: We were binding sheaves of grain out in the*
> *field when suddenly my sheaf rose and stood upright, while*
> *your sheaves gathered around mine and bowed down to it'"*
> (GENESIS 37:5-7).

How insulting! How impertinent! How arrogant! Resenting the implication that Joseph will one day "lord" himself over them, his brothers continue to be filled with animosity toward him.

These brothers, who have already felt intense rejection from their father, decide to take revenge and make sure that Joseph will pay dearly. But the brothers don't realize this important fact: Although some say, "Revenge is sweet," it leaves a bitter aftertaste! That is why the Bible says,

> *"See to it that no one misses the grace of God and that no*
> *bitter root grows up to cause trouble and defile many"*
> (HEBREWS 12:15).

A. Are You Controlled by the Fear of Rejection?

If your sense of self-worth is based on the approval of others, you are on a runaway roller coaster with no ability to control when you are up or down. Your feeling of value is at the mercy of what others think about you. Your sense of identity is determined by how others respond to you.

To get off this jerky roller coaster and conquer your fear of rejection, you need to allow the Lord to control your life. He created you and established your worth when He made you in His image. As you put your trust in Him, He will turn your fear into faith because...

> *"Fear of man will prove to be a snare, but*
> *whoever trusts in the LORD is kept safe"*
> (PROVERBS 29:25).

=========== *The Dialogue of the Approval Addict* ===========

If you think you may be living for the approval of others, honestly evaluate the following statements to see if they reflect your self-talk.

"I'm not good enough."	"I'm not acceptable in the eyes of others."
"I have to try to earn love."	"I have to try harder to not be rejected."
"I can never please anyone."	"I have to be perfect to be accepted."
"I'm always the one at fault."	"I always feel stupid."

"I know that what I think isn't as important."	"I know there is nothing likeable about me."
"I don't deserve to be loved."	"I don't feel anyone could really love me."
"I don't feel that God could ever love me."	"I'll do whatever is necessary to be accepted."

Even though you may think such thoughts, they don't reflect God's truth about you. The Bible says,

> *"This is love: not that we loved God, but that **he loved us** and sent his Son as an atoning sacrifice for our sins"*
> (1 John 4:10).

The Fear of Rejection Test[11]

If we are controlled by the fear of rejection, then our focus will be on pleasing people. However, we need to say what the apostle Paul said,

> *"We are not trying to please men but God"*
> (1 Thessalonians 2:4).

If you are uncertain about whether you are living for the approval of others, answer the following questions. They will reveal whether you live with the fear of rejection.

- Do you avoid certain people out of fear they will reject you?
- Do you become anxious when you think someone might not accept you?
- Do you feel awkward around others who are different from you?
- Do you feel disturbed when someone is not friendly toward you?
- Do you work hard at trying to determine what people think of you?
- Do you become depressed when others are critical of you?

- Do you consider yourself basically shy and unsociable around others?
- Do you try to see the negative in others?
- Do you find yourself trying to impress others?
- Do you repeat negative messages about yourself to yourself?
- Do you look for clues as to how others are responding to you in order to avoid the pain of rejection?
- Do you say yes when you should say no to others?
- Do you expect others to respond to situations and conversations in the same way you do?
- Do people close to you say you are a codependent person?
- Are you hypersensitive to the opinions of others but insensitive to your own emotions?
- Do you often feel overly controlled by others?
- Do you struggle with anger and resentment toward others?
- Do you seem to be easily manipulated by others?

If you conclude that you have been controlled by the fear of rejection and you have lived for the approval of others, take this verse to heart:

> *"Am I now trying to win the approval of men, or of*
> *God? Or am I trying to please men? If I were still trying*
> *to please men, I would not be a servant of Christ"*
> (GALATIANS 1:10).

B. What Are Inner Signs of Rejection?[12]

What are the ramifications of rejection? Perhaps you've been unaware of its subtle impact on your soul (your mind, will, and emotions). One way rejection affects you is by altering your self-perception and leaving you feeling insecure.

Rejection can sear the deepest part of your soul and, at the same time, mess with your mind, taint your thoughts, and make you question your ability to function normally. But God, who knows every rejection you will ever encounter, never planned for you to be emotionally or spiritually disabled. Although you will be rejected, the Bible says,

> *"God is able to make all grace abound to you, so that in all things at all times, having all that you need, you will abound in every good work"*
> (2 Corinthians 9:8).

Below are many of the classic symptoms of past rejection and the fear of future rejection...

Ambivalence	"I have difficulty making decisions—if I make the wrong decision, I could be rejected."
Anxiety	"I have real apprehension when someone says, 'Trust me.'"
Bitterness	"I harbor bitterness toward those who reject me, and toward God for allowing it to happen."
Depression	"My heart feels so heavy; the pain has pushed me down."
Distrust	"I can't trust others not to desert me."
Escapism	"Life hurts. I just need to numb the pain."
Fear	"I live in fear of being rejected again."
Flat emotions	"My heart is so deeply hurt that I can't seem to feel excited about anything."
Guilt/false guilt	"I feel so bad about myself—no wonder I was rejected."
Inability to accept love	"Even though others say they love me, I know it's not true."
Inferiority	"I know I'll never measure up!"
Insensitivity	"I can't feel for others who are in pain."
Introspection	"I've got to keep analyzing what's wrong with me."
Low self-worth	"I know I'm not worthy of being accepted."

Resignation	"Whatever will be, will be...so why try?"
Self-condemnation	"I feel terrible. I know I'm to blame whenever I'm rejected."
Self-pity	"I'm always ignored. No one reaches out to me."
Self-rejection	"I wish I'd never been born!"
Withdrawal	"I'm not willing to be vulnerable again."
Worry	"I'm afraid I'll be scarred for life."

C. What Are Outer Signs of Rejection?[13]

While the unseen pain of rejection can sabotage your soul and shatter your spirit, the outer symptoms of rejection can easily be seen—and even felt—by others. For example, when someone special walks out of your life, the joy of living is snuffed out. The darkness of desertion can discolor your perception of others and do untold damage to your relationships. The saddest part of it all is that rejection breeds rejection! In truth, no one can avoid being rejected or treated unjustly at times. However, when you remember that your identity is in the Lord because of your relationship with Him—and not in you having been rejected by others—you will experience the truth that you, like Paul, can be

> *"hard pressed on every side, but not crushed;*
> *perplexed, but not in despair; persecuted, but not*
> *abandoned; struck down, but not destroyed"*
> (2 CORINTHIANS 4:8-9).

Among the outer symptoms of rejection are...

Abuse	mistreating others and even yourself
Addiction	seeking solace in addictive behavior in an effort to numb your pain
Anger	feeling bitterness toward others and even toward God
Apathy	giving up on life, not caring about anything
Arrogance	acting superior to others
Competitiveness	assuming you have to be the best

Critical spirit	being condescending toward others
Defensiveness	arguing with others to protect yourself
Dominance	excessively controlling others and situations excessively
Exaggeration	bragging to impress others
Hatred	loathing (primarily directed toward yourself)
Isolation	becoming a loner as a means of self-protection
Jealousy	resenting suggestions and successes of others
Legalism	complying with rigid rules based on black-and-white thinking
People pleasing	trying too hard to please others
Perfectionism	feeling like a failure unless you do everything perfectly
Performance-based acceptance	believing your acceptance is based only on how well you perform
Rebellion	resisting the authority of others
Subservience	cowering in the presence of others
Undisciplined	lacking self-control and boundaries around others
Vengeful	getting even with others

D. What Are Spiritual Signs of Rejection?

Those who experience childhood rejection often have immense difficulty trusting God because of "projection"—they project onto God the negative characteristics of their childhood authority figures. If their earthly fathers rejected them, they perceive the heavenly Father to be rejecting them as well. If they had an untrustworthy mother, then God must also be untrustworthy.

These wrong perceptions of God make learning His true character essential, yet very often difficult. Nevertheless the Bible says,

> *"The LORD is a refuge for the oppressed, a stronghold in*
> *times of trouble. Those who know your name will trust in*
> *you, for you, LORD, have never forsaken those who seek you"*
> (PSALM 9:9-10).

Periodically, those who have been rejected…

—resent God for allowing the rejection

—regard God as a tyrannical judge and jury

—reflect the negative attributes of childhood authority figures onto God

—rely on self-protection and deny the protection of God

—refuse to accept the authority of God

—rebel against the Word of God

—reject statements about the love of God

—resist the thought of trusting God

—recoil from true fellowship with God

—react to their fear of condemnation from God instead of embracing the love of God

Regardless of the rejection you have experienced from past authority figures, the Bible gives this powerful promise:

> *"Be strong and courageous. Do not be afraid or*
> *terrified because of them, for the LORD your God goes*
> *with you; he will never leave you nor forsake you"*
> (DEUTERONOMY 31:6).

III. CAUSES OF REJECTION

A. What Are the Sources of Rejection?

People reject other people for different reasons. We can be rejected at times because of what *we have done* and at other times because of what *someone else* has done. Then again, we can be rejected merely for who we are—because of something or someone we represent. In Joseph's case, he experienced the rejection of his brothers for all three reasons.

1. *What He Did*

Joseph's brothers knew that Joseph had reported something bad about them to their father—he tattled on them! Being a snitch didn't win Joseph any favors. Then Joseph added fuel to the fire when he told his brothers about his two dreams that foretold how he would one day be in a position of authority over them (Genesis 37:2-9).

2. *What His Father Did*

The brothers envied Joseph because of the "richly ornamented robe" that his father made for him, and not for them (Genesis 37:3).

3. *Who He Was*

Joseph's brothers resented Joseph because of who he was. He was the child of Rachel, their father's beloved and favored wife, born to her after years of barrenness and in Jacob's later years. Thus, Joseph was his father's favorite child.

In reality, Joseph was more of a prophet than a politician or he wouldn't have revealed the content of his dreams to his brothers—they already despised him! And although Jacob rebuked Joseph for what he spoke, he also kept Joseph's dream in mind.

> *"When he told his father as well as his brothers, his father*
> *rebuked him and said, 'What is this dream you had? Will*
> *your mother and I and your brothers actually come and*
> *bow down to the ground before you?' His brothers were*
> *jealous of him, but his father kept the matter in mind"*
> (GENESIS 37:10-11).

B. What Are Overt Causes of Feeling Rejected?[14]

Some reasons people feel rejected are obvious—both to them and to any observant bystander. Think about a difficult time when you felt devalued, dejected, and deserted. Was the reason for your pain obvious? Often the loneliest times of your life can be readily understood because you were *overtly* rejected. But the wonderful Word of God tells us that while others may "cast us away," we are to cast ourselves upon the Lord.

> *"From birth I was cast upon you; from my*
> *mother's womb you have been my God"*
> (PSALM 22:10).

Common causes of feeling rejected are:

Abandonment

Feeling forsaken because someone special is no longer there for you:

"How can I survive without you? You must hate me to leave me helpless and all alone!"

Adoption

Feeling unloved because your focus is on having been given away (instead of on feeling loved because you were placed in a loving home): "I must be a terrible person for my own parents to not want me."

Cast away

Feeling worthless because you were "in the way" and therefore you have been thrown out of the home or sent away (to camp, to boarding school, to other relatives): "I am obviously useless and a burden to everyone."

Childhood sexual abuse

Feeling shamed because your sexual boundaries were violated by abusers inside or outside your family: "My feelings are unimportant and I have no right to be respected or protected."

Disapproval

Feeling flawed because you can't measure up to what is expected of you by others: "I can't do anything good enough to be accepted."

Divorce

Feeling deserted because your parents split up or because you and your spouse divorced (some parents feel deserted by their own children): "I am all alone and those I love the most do not want me anymore."

Domestic violence

Feeling degraded because of physical attacks from one of your family members: "I am no more than a slave and a doormat to my own family."

Excessive punishment

Feeling devalued because your parents were excessively harsh on you: "What's wrong with me that causes my parents to mistreat me?"

Favoritism

Feeling disregarded because someone else is preferred over you: "I don't deserve to be anyone's favorite. I'll never measure up."

Greed

Feeling discredited because someone takes credit for your ideas or work or because someone steals your money or possessions: "I must not deserve recognition no matter how much I achieve."

Hostility

Feeling alienated because of constant fighting and name-calling: "I must bring out the worst in everyone."

Humiliation

Feeling ridiculed because your opinions, actions, choices or values are being attacked: "I must be really stupid to think I could be right about anything."

Indifference

Feeling discounted because your existence is not acknowledged: "I should never have been born."

Infidelity

Feeling betrayed because your bond of trust has been breeched: "I won't ever confide in anyone again."

Jilted

Feeling spurned because of rejection in courtship, friendship, or marriage: "I guess I don't have anything to offer in a relationship."

Prejudice

Feeling ostracized because of merely being different: "I'd be better off as a hermit or not existing at all."

Rape

Feeling violated because of date rape, mate rape, or stranger rape: "I am and always will be damaged goods."

Verbal Abuse

Feeling condemned because you don't deserve such unjust treatment: "What about me is so bad that I can't do enough good to earn a kind word?"

C. What Are Covert Causes of Feeling Rejected?[15]

Just as there are obvious *overt* reasons for people to feel rejected, there are also not-so-obvious *covert* reasons. These covert causes are not easily identifiable because sometimes they are shrouded in secrecy. At other times they are sins of *omission* rather than *commission*.

Whatever the reason, covert rejection cuts just as deeply as overt, if not deeper. Because covert rejection can go undetected, and therefore unchallenged, victims can be left even more devastated. However, God sees everything. Nothing escapes His eye—especially those things concerning each of us whom He carefully crafted and constantly considers.

> *"From heaven the* LORD *looks down and sees all*
> *mankind; from his dwelling place he watches*
> *all who live on earth—he who forms the hearts*
> *of all, who considers everything they do"*
> (PSALM 33:13-15)

Here are some covert causes of feeling rejected:

Absence of nurturing

Feeling *neglected* because of a lack of attention or affection: "There's a hole in my heart because I don't feel loved."

Addictions

Feeling *ignored* because of an addiction (examples: alcohol/drugs, compulsive spending, inappropriate sexual behavior, gambling). The addiction is prioritized above the relationship: "Despite what you say, I know that (the addiction) is more important to you than I am."

Broken promises

Feeling *unimportant* because of a continual lack of commitment: "I'm not worth anything to you. You keep your word to others but not to me."

Comparison

Feeling *inadequate* because of always being measured against others: "I have no intrinsic value."

Cliques

Feeling *unworthy* because of being excluded from a group: "I am not good enough to be accepted."

Critical spirit

Feeling *emotionally* battered because of the relentless judgmental attitudes of others: "I can never measure up to the standards of other people."

Death/critical illness

Feeling *forgotten* because of being left alone (especially in the case of suicide): "Why did you leave me?"

Discounted emotions

Feeling *pushed aside* because what comes from your heart is dismissed: "What I feel isn't important to anyone."

Gender discrimination

Feeling *inferior* because of a bias against your gender: "Nothing I think, say, or do has any validity because I am the wrong sex."

Handicaps

Feeling *inadequate* because of your limitations: "I am defective and not equal to others because I cannot do all that they can do."

Lack of support

Feeling *rebuffed* because of not being believed or helped: "I got no support when I desperately needed it."

Loss of a pet

Feeling *abandoned* because your pet was the only one who accepted you unconditionally: "I just lost my best friend."

Overcontrolling

Feeling *powerless* because your individuality is denied: "I am not allowed to be myself."

Overindulgence

Feeling *helpless* because everything is done for you as though you cannot do anything for yourself: "I feel as though I'm being treated like a child."

Performance-based acceptance

Feeling *unacceptable* because you are valued only for what you do: "I'm accepted only if I perform to the expectations of others."

Sarcasm

Feeling *cut down* because of caustic humor at your expense: "Sharp words, though masked with humor, feel like a sword piercing my heart."

Silent treatment

Feeling *shunned* because a loved one has intentionally stopped communicating with you: "I am treated as if I don't exist."

Question: "My mother doesn't care about me or my problems. She shows no love or affection. Why does she continue to reject me?"

Answer: Sadly, many parents do not know how to nurture their children. Your mother's lack of love reveals that she is not emotionally whole. Her rejection sheds a spotlight on the hole in her heart.

- Ask the Lord to help you stop taking your mother's behavior personally. Her lack of love has nothing to do with you.
- Realize that the void within your mother's heart restricts her from reaching out to your heart.
- Fully receive and focus on God's unconditional love for you. Although you have no power to make your mother express love, God will give you all the love and acceptance you need, empowering you to overcome the pain of rejection.

The Bible gives you this tender assurance:

> *"Though my father and mother forsake*
> *me, the LORD will receive me"*
> (PSALM 27:10).

Question: "How can I overcome my extreme fear of rejection? I'm now isolating myself from people."

Answer: God does not want you to be controlled by fear, but instead to be controlled by Christ, who will enable you to overcome your fear. Therefore, the first step in gaining victory over your fear of rejection is to commit to processing all of the past rejection and giving no more power to that pain. Rely on God's strength within you to face rejection in your life. As you look back at your past...

- Write down every remembrance of rejection from the first instance until the present.
- Take time to feel the pain of each experience and then put into writing how you feel.

- Slowly read back through your list, and with each situation, say, "That was then and this is now. I will not let the pain of my past control my present or my future."

- Release each painful rejection to the Lord, saying, "Lord Jesus, I release this pain and my fear of future pain into your hands. Thank You that You will never reject me."

- Begin talking with a wise, compassionate person whom you think you can trust. (Tell this person what you are trying to overcome and ask if he or she would be willing to help you.)

- Do not focus on what you think others are thinking about you. Instead, trust in God's unconditional acceptance of you.

> *"Fear of man will prove to be a snare, but*
> *whoever trusts in the LORD is kept safe"*
> (PROVERBS 29:25).

D. What Causes Painful Vows Following Rejection?[16]

When you have experienced the pain of past rejection, do you mentally rehearse negative thoughts, feelings, and perhaps even "vows"? Unfortunately, these repetitious thoughts ("I'm not accepted") and emotions ("I feel unwanted") lead to an illogical conclusion ("I vow that no one will hurt me again!").

How we live our lives is based on what we *believe.* Therefore, if we believe we are rejected, we will live a life of rejection in our minds, our hearts, and our emotions, even when we are not outwardly rejected by others.

Repeated Thoughts:	Repeated Feelings:	Repeated Vows:
• "No one loves me." • "No one cares about me."	• "I feel empty inside." • "I feel all alone."	• "I'm not going to get close to anyone again."
• "I don't really matter." • "I'm not good enough."	• "I feel insignificant." • "I feel like I'm not worth anything."	• "I'm not going to let anyone be important to me again."

• "I don't fit in." • "I'm not accepted."	• "I feel unwanted." • "I feel excluded."	• "I'm not going to allow anyone to ever hurt me again."

The progressions depicted above demonstrate the importance of taking your thoughts captive, training your mind, and telling yourself the truth. You are accepted by God; therefore, allow Him to heal your heart from the pain of the past. If you will cancel the vows that are contrary to God's Word, you will lay the foundation needed to experience perfect peace in your life.

> *"We demolish arguments and every pretension that sets*
> *itself up against the knowledge of God, and we take*
> *captive every thought to make it obedient to Christ"*
> (2 CORINTHIANS 10:5).

E. What Is the Root Cause of Rejection?

All of us are created with three God-given inner needs—the needs for love, significance, and security.[17] We experience rejection from our earliest years when we are deprived of having someone who loves us unconditionally, someone who regards us as highly significant, or someone who welcomes us as part of the family (parents divorce, feeling snubbed, deserted by loved one).

Because people fail people, it is essential not to let other people define who you are. Realize that rejection can quickly skew your view of yourself! Even though you may not see the path you should take, the Lord promises to guide all your steps and to meet all your needs.

> *"The LORD will guide you always; he will satisfy your*
> *needs in a sun-scorched land and will strengthen*
> *your frame. You will be like a well-watered*
> *garden, like a spring whose waters never fail"*
> (ISAIAH 58:11).

Wrong Belief:

"Because of being rejected, I feel so unloved, so insignificant, so unwanted. My life isn't worth anything!"

Right Belief:

"I do not like being rejected, but I know my worth isn't based on whether or not others reject me but on the fact that the Lord accepts me. Jesus not only loved me enough to die for my sins, but He also lives inside me and will never leave me nor forsake me."

> *"I trust in your unfailing love; my heart*
> *rejoices in your salvation"*
> (PSALM 13:5).

Question: "Even though I am a Christian, I feel like God rejects me. Others have also rejected me. What can I do about the self-condemnation I feel and the bitterness that is eating me up inside?"

Answer: Bitterness is the result of unresolved, prolonged anger. Self-condemnation is anger turned inward. This means that before you can deal with bitterness or self-condemnation, you need to…

- look into your past and uncover the root cause of your feelings
- determine the cause of your anger: hurt, injustice, fear, or frustration
- examine whether something in your past led you to feel one of these painful emotions
- realize that feelings always follow thinking, so once you have discovered the source of your anger, examine the truthfulness of your thinking, for only the truth can set you free
- once you've established the truth, renew your mind by repeating that truth
- above all, repeat Romans 8:1 and pray, "Thank You, God, that because of Christ you will never condemn or reject me"

> *"There is now no condemnation for*
> *those who are in Christ Jesus"*
> (ROMANS 8:1)

IV. STEPS TO SOLUTION

The strongest lesson to glean from Joseph's life is evident in his response to repeated rejection (see Genesis chapters 37–50). His father, Jacob, sent

Joseph to the fields to find his brothers. When the brothers see him, they first conspire to kill him. But then they decide to sell him to merchants, who cart Joseph off to Egypt, where he is sold as a slave to prominent Potiphar.

In spite of this severe rejection, Joseph never becomes bitter or blames God. He faithfully performs whatever work is given to him, with excellence and integrity.

A day comes when the wife of Potiphar tries to seduce Joseph. Although he resists, Joseph is falsely accused and imprisoned. At any time during Joseph's suffering due to unfair treatment, he could have allowed hatred to fill his heart...but he didn't.

Twenty-two years later, famine spreads to Joseph's homeland, and his family becomes desperate for food. So Jacob sends his sons to Egypt to buy grain. Little do they know that the brother whom they had rejected is now the prime minister of Egypt!

What an opportunity for Joseph to exact revenge! What an opportunity for him to banish his brothers from the land! But rather than returning rejection for rejection, Joseph weeps and reveals his identity. Rather than taking revenge, he accepts his brothers and extends his heart of forgiveness and his hand of help.

Joseph literally saves his family and all Israelites by providing not just food during the famine, but also their new home for the next 400 years. Through what Joseph says to his brothers, it is clear that he is willing to view his years of rejection through the eyes of God. That his heart is filled with mercy is evident in his humble words to his brothers:

> *"You intended to harm me, but God intended*
> *it for good to accomplish what is now being*
> *done, the saving of many lives"*
> (GENESIS 50:20).

A. Key Verse to Memorize

Though banished to a foreign land, falsely accused and forsaken, Joseph never accused God of forsaking him. At the end of his tumultuous ordeal, Joseph acknowledged the hand of the Lord at work in his life even though no "hand" could be seen. During the times you are reeling from rejection, realize the Lord has not rejected you:

> *"The LORD himself goes before you and will be*

with you; he will never leave you nor forsake you.
Do not be afraid; do not be discouraged"
(DEUTERONOMY 31:8).

B. Key Passage to Read and Reread

We who are Christians will be rejected by the world because Jesus was rejected by the world. Sometimes "the world" is within our own families, just as it was within His own family. This means we may be rejected by our own, just as Jesus was rejected by His own. Decide now not to be dismayed or destroyed by rejection, but rather expect it and be strengthened by it. Remember, the heavier the burden, the stronger God's strength to help you bear it.

"Praise be to the Lord, to God our Savior,
who daily bears our burdens"
(PSALM 68:19).

=== *God's Promises in Romans 8:28-39* ===

In spite of the rejection I have faced...

—God will work everything together for my good . . . . verse 28

—God has called me to live according to His purpose . . . . . verse 28

—God has predetermined to conform
   me to Christ's character . . . . verse 29

—God called me, justified me, and will glorify me . . . . verse 30

—God is for me; no one can prevail against me . . . . verse 31

—God did not spare His own Son,
   but gave Him up for me . . . . verse 32

—God will, out of His grace, give me everything I need . . . . verse 32

—God chose me; therefore, no one can condemn me . . . . . . verse 33

—God Himself has vindicated me . . . . verse 33

—God raised Christ from death to life; therefore,
   no one can condemn me . . . . verse 34

—God placed Christ at His right hand
   to intercede for me. . . . . verse 34

—God's plan is that nothing can separate
   me from Christ's love. . . . . verse 35

—God's love compels me to face death willingly. . . . . verse 36

—God has made me more than a conqueror
   through Christ, who loves me. . . . . verse 37

—God's love has convinced me that nothing
   in life or death, ... verse 38

   neither angels nor demons,

   neither the present nor the future,

   nor any powers or principalities,

   neither height nor depth,

   nor anything else in all creation

   can separate me from the love of God . . . . verses 38-39

> *"I am convinced that neither death nor life, neither*
> *angels nor demons, neither the present nor the future,*
> *nor any powers, neither height nor depth, nor anything*
> *else in all creation, will be able to separate us from*
> *the love of God that is in Christ Jesus our Lord"*
> (ROMANS 8:38-39).

C. Do You Feel Rejected by God?

Did you grow up in a home where you never measured up, where you were mistreated, where you were maligned, and as a result, you're convinced God could never approve of you? Have you committed some hidden sin or harbored hatred in your heart such that you now feel beyond the reach of God's forgiveness? Have you ever been told, "You should *never* have been born...you were *never* wanted...you will *never* amount to anything"?

If you are thoroughly persuaded that God has rejected you, then you don't know the God of the Bible and His special plan for you. The Lord says,

> *"For I know the plans I have for you...plans to prosper you*
> *and not to harm you, plans to give you hope and a future"*
> (JEREMIAH 29:11).

What Do You Need to Know About God?

KNOW GOD'S CHARACTER

—God is love.

> *"God is love"*
> (1 JOHN 4:8).

—God loves you.

> *"I have loved you with an everlasting love; I
> have drawn you with loving-kindness"*
> (JEREMIAH 31:3).

KNOW GOD'S HEART

—God wants to adopt you into His family.

> *"How great is the love the Father has lavished on
> us, that we should be called children of God!"*
> (1 JOHN 3:1).

—God wants to be your guide through life.

> *"Trust in the LORD with all your heart and lean not on
> your own understanding; in all your ways acknowledge
> him, and he will make your paths straight"*
> (PROVERBS 3:5-6).

KNOW GOD'S PLAN

—God offers salvation to all.

> *"God did not send his Son into the world to condemn
> the world, but to save the world through him"*
> (JOHN 3:17).

—God wants everyone to be saved, including you.

> *"He is patient with you, not wanting anyone to
> perish, but everyone to come to repentance"*
> (2 PETER 3:9).

KNOW GOD'S PURPOSES

—God uses your suffering to hone your character and increase your
hope.

> *"We also rejoice in our sufferings, because we know that*
> *suffering produces perseverance; perseverance, character;*
> *and character, hope. And hope does not disappoint us"*
> (Romans 5:3-5).

—God gives you compassion and comfort, which, in turn, you can give to others.

> *"The Father of compassion and the God of all comfort…*
> *comforts us in all our troubles, so that we can comfort those*
> *in any trouble with the comfort we ourselves have received*
> *from God. For just as the sufferings of Christ flow over into*
> *our lives, so also through Christ our comfort overflows"*
> (2 Corinthians 1:3-5).

What Is the Key to God's Acceptance?

Have you ever tried to open a door with a key…but the wrong key? It won't work! Unless you use the right key, you cannot get inside. God has already shared the "key" to entering into an everlasting relationship with Him, the key to never being rejected.

Here are four points you need to know about you and God:

1. You have entered through the wrong door. *You, like everyone else, have chosen to sin.*

   You cannot find your way to acceptance with God if you have entered through the wrong door. The Bible says that we all have sinned—not one of us is perfect. Each time we willfully choose to go our own way, and not God's way, we sin.

   > *"All have sinned and fall short of the glory of God"*
   > (Romans 3:23).

2. You have lost the key to God's acceptance. *Your sin separates you from God.*

   You cannot open a locked door without the right key. Your own sin has locked the right door, the door to God, and you have no key to open that door. Because God's character is morally perfect (He is without sin), our sin results in a penalty or consequence. The Bible says that the consequence of our sin is separation from God. Because of your sin, you are separated from God.

> *"Your iniquities [sins] have separated you from your God"*
> (ISAIAH 59:2).

3. You have been given a new key to God's door of acceptance. *God provided the way for you to be forgiven.*

   The heavenly Father sent His own Son, Jesus, to die on the cross to pay the penalty for your sins. You deserved to die, but instead, Christ died for you. God offers to you the only key—the Lord Jesus Christ—that will open the door to God's eternal acceptance.

   > *"God demonstrates his own love for us in this:*
   > *While we were still sinners, Christ died for us"*
   > (ROMANS 5:8)

4. You can open the door of acceptance. *You can receive God's forgiveness and peace by trusting in Jesus Christ now.*

   While you may hold the key to the door, you still have to unlock the door. You need to acknowledge that Jesus Christ died as your substitute, rely on what He did for you, and ask Him to come into your life to take control of your life. If you allow Him to be your Lord and Savior, He forgives you of your sins. And when you are forgiven, not only are you saved from separation from God, but you also are given the peace of God. He is standing at the door of your heart right now.

   > *"Here I am! I stand at the door and knock. If*
   > *anyone hears my voice and opens the door, I will*
   > *come in and eat with him, and he with me"*
   > (REVELATION 3:20).

If you desire to be fully forgiven by God and to receive the peace of God, you can ask Jesus Christ to come into your life right now and give you His peace.

=== *Prayer of Salvation* ===

God,

I want a secure relationship with You.
I admit that many times
I've rejected Your way and gone my way.
Please forgive me for my sins.
Jesus, thank You for dying
on the cross for my sins.
Come into my life to be
my Lord and my Savior.

Thank You for wanting me.
Thank You for accepting me.
Thank You for adopting me.
Thank You that You
will never leave me nor forsake me.

In Your holy name I pray. Amen.

If you sincerely prayed this prayer, this is God's promise to you:

"The LORD himself goes before you and will be
with you; he will never leave you nor forsake you.
Do not be afraid; do not be discouraged"
(DEUTERONOMY 31:8).

Those who will not walk through the door of salvation to God's acceptance may sense God's rejection. In reality, by choosing to reject God they have also chosen to be rejected by God. This fact is illustrated by King Saul's choice to reject God's Word. The godly prophet Samuel told Saul that, as a result, "I will not go back with you. You have rejected the word of the Lord, and the Lord has rejected you as king over Israel!" (1 Samuel 15:26).

D. Replace the Negative Progression with the New

Our core beliefs control every area of our lives. Even when we don't consciously recognize their influence, they are still at work, silently penetrating our thoughts, feelings, and, inevitably, our actions. Identifying and changing our negative core beliefs will help us replace unhealthy, destructive actions with new behaviors that honor God and others. The Bible says,

"Whatever you do, do it all for the glory of God"
(1 CORINTHIANS 10:31).

Progression of Rejection[18]

Negative Core Belief	▶	Negative Thoughts	▶	Negative Feeling	▶	Negative Actions
"I have to have the approval of others."		• "I'm not loved." • "I am not significant." • "I'm not accepted."		*I feel rejected!*		• Rejecting others • Bitterness toward others • Judging others • Withdrawing from others

"Let us stop passing judgment on one another"
(ROMANS 14:13).

Replace the Old Progression with the New[19]

New Core Belief	▶	New Thoughts	▶	New Feeling	▶	New Actions
"I won't always have the approval of everyone, but I have the approval of God."		• "I'm unconditionally loved by God." • "I am significant to God." • "I am unconditionally accepted by God."		*I feel accepted!*		• Accepting others • Forgiving others • Seeing good in others • Reaching out to others

*"Let us consider how we may spur one another
on toward love and good deeds"*
(HEBREWS 10:24).

E. How Does Rejection Breed Rejection?[20]

When you are rejected, a chain reaction can occur that can lead to more rejection. Through a series of conscious choices, a cycle can become a pattern that eventually becomes a way of life. When you are rejected, unless the truth of God's Word is embraced, the cycle broken, and the pattern replaced, the by-product of rejection will always be rejection.

The Rejection Cycle

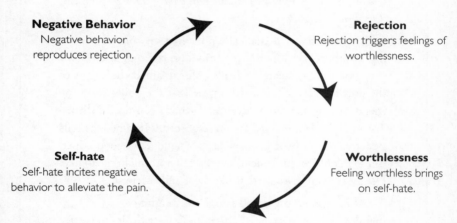

Negative Behavior
Negative behavior reproduces rejection.

Rejection
Rejection triggers feelings of worthlessness.

Self-hate
Self-hate incites negative behavior to alleviate the pain.

Worthlessness
Feeling worthless brings on self-hate.

=== *Rejection Breeds Rejection* ===

Nothing rips the heart apart like rejection—especially rejection from someone near and dear to us. To be rejected by someone we love is a loss like no other.

Many years ago, a friend whom I loved—a friend who helped me immensely—cut off all contact with me, and there never has been a restoration of the friendship. In total candor, I clearly admit I did a number of things wrong in this friendship—I do not question that I was at fault. And with that loss, I felt gut-wrenching pain.

Six months later, I was reading through the Sunday newspaper and came upon the High Profile section, which included a feature spotlighting a notable person. This profiled person was asked many questions, such as, "What is your favorite book? Who would you invite for your last meal? What is the best advice you ever received?"

One open-ended statement caught my attention: "My friends like me because..." Upon reading those words, I tried to give an answer from my own life. However, after a time of serious searching, my heart began to sink. I thought, *My friends really don't like me. There isn't anything in me to like.* I was dead serious. *The only thing they could like is what I could do for them. They really don't like* me.

The next day, I periodically pondered my somber reasoning. I couldn't get it out of my mind. So late that afternoon I called one of my dearest friends and explained the events of the previous day. "It dawned on me that the only reason my friends might like me is because of what I can do for them." Then I expanded, "After all, I am resourceful. If someone needs a doctor, I can help. If someone needs a hand, I'm a good helper. But I've come to this conclusion: There's nothing in me to like. I just want you to know that I know it and accept it."

At that point, my friend said, "June, I am not _____" (naming the other person). "This is me," she said. "It's me you're talking with, not _____. And June, what you're saying is simply not true."

Truthfully, I was surprised at her rebuttal. But then I knew I had to rebut her rebuttal!

"Well, of course you are going to say that," I responded. "You have to say that. I know you're just trying to be nice to me." Ultimately, no matter what she said, I would not believe her attempts to reassure me.

Then she asked, "Can I come over right now?"

"No," I answered...not that I didn't want to see her. "I've got to keep preparing for the Bible study I'm leading in just an hour." (What a dichotomy! Here I am, teaching others about the unconditional love and acceptance of God and how every person is created with God-given worth, but I couldn't just believe it for myself!)

"Well, what about after the Bible study?" she pressed.

"I've got to pack my bags because I'm leaving for California early the next morning," I explained. "I sincerely appreciate what you're trying to do...but it's really not necessary. I'm all right."

After we said our good-byes, I knew I needed to call one other very close friend. Again I recounted the events from the day before: the High Profile section, the "My friends like me because _____" statement, and the fact that there is nothing in me to like, except that I'm resourceful. I assured her, "I really understand it and accept it."

"Why are you saying this?" she asked. "It's just not true... you're believing a lie!"

Again, I knew she was just being "nice." And again, no matter what she said, I wouldn't believe it.

For a period of time, I emotionally retreated away from those who were reaching out to me. Soon I saw that I had fallen into the "rejection breeds rejection" cycle. Because I had been rejected by one significant person, I assumed others would reject me...and I emotionally and unconsciously began to reject their sincere words.

However, the Lord had put sensitive, caring people in my life to be an extension of His love—people who would not let me completely retreat into my "cave." They called...they invited...they affirmed...they included...and they lifted me up when it would have been emotionally easier for me to stay down. What the Bible says is true: "Two are better than one...If one falls down, his friend can help him up" (Ecclesiastes 4:9-10).

How I needed to be reminded that in life, we will all be rejected—but just because *one* person rejects us doesn't mean *everyone* rejects us!

> And when others feel rejected and their hearts are deeply hurt, that is an opportunity for us to reach out to them with the love of Christ, to be the comforter, to be the encourager, to be "the friend who sticks closer than a brother" (Proverbs 18:24).

F. How to Break the Rejection Cycle

Meditate on these statements, and memorize these scriptures.

Rejection

—"Just because someone rejects me doesn't mean everyone rejects me. Jesus loves me and accepts me, no matter how others choose to treat me."

> *"As the Father has loved me, so have I loved you"*
> (JOHN 15:9)

—"Just because someone withholds love from me doesn't mean everyone will withhold love from me. God will always listen to me and will never withhold His love from me. He will always make sure my love needs are met."

> *"Praise be to God, who has not rejected my*
> *prayer or withheld his love from me!"*
> (PSALM 66:20).

Worthless Feelings

—"Just because someone thinks I am worthless doesn't mean everyone thinks I'm worthless. God has already established my worth, and because of Him I will always have worth."

> *"Are not five sparrows sold for two pennies? Yet not*
> *one of them is forgotten by God...Don't be afraid;*
> *you are worth more than many sparrows"*
> (LUKE 12:6-7).

—"Just because someone doesn't value me doesn't mean everyone doesn't value me. God values me enough to send Jesus to die for me so that I can spend eternity with Him."

*"For God so loved the world that he gave his
one and only Son, that whoever believes in
him shall not perish but have eternal life"*
(JOHN 3:16).

Self-hate

—"Just because someone hates me doesn't mean I should hate myself.
God has always loved me, and I can rely on His love—forever!"

"We know and rely on the love God has for us. God is love"
(1 JOHN 4:16).

—"Just because someone condemns me doesn't mean I should condemn myself. God will never condemn me, because I am in Christ's family."

*"There is now no condemnation for
those who are in Christ Jesus"*
(ROMANS 8:1).

Negative Behavior

—"Just because someone has rejected me doesn't mean I should do what
sets me up for more rejection. Because I will pay for my bad choices,
I am going to make good choices."

*"Do not be deceived: God cannot be mocked. A man reaps
what he sows. The one who sows to please his sinful nature,
from that nature will reap destruction; the one who sows
to please the Spirit, from the Spirit will reap eternal life"*
(GALATIANS 6:7-8).

—"Just because others wrongly reject me doesn't give me license to
wrongly reject them. Because God has given me the power to do
what is right, I will master the sinful desires in my life."

*"If you do what is right, will you not be accepted? But
if you do not do what is right, sin is crouching at your
door; it desires to have you, but you must master it"*
(GENESIS 4:7).

Question: "Ever since my closest friend rejected me, I expect other friends to do the same. How can I keep from feeling like a reject?"

Answer: When someone close to you rejects you, be aware of a tendency to overgeneralize and assume that others will reject you, too. Fearing the worst, you might inadvertently begin pushing your remaining friends away in order to prevent further hurt. When they respond negatively, you may interpret their reactions as confirmation of your deepest fears. This vicious cycle can lead to a self-fulfilling prophecy and helps explain the saying, "Rejection breeds rejection."

To stop feeling like a reject…

- Don't assume that one person's opinion reflects everyone's opinion.
- Don't let one person's negative attitude toward you define you.
- Realize that because Jesus calls you friend, you can trust that His love will be with you always.
- Nurture multiple friendships and focus on God's description of how true friends treat one another. A true friend will never reject you.

"A friend loves at all times"
(PROVERBS 17:17).

G. You Are Accepted…Even When Rejected[21]

How can you have faith that you are accepted when, at times, you *feel* rejected?

Basing faith on feelings is disastrous for us all. *Feelings change, but God never changes!* When we exercise faith not in how we feel but in what God has said—based on our faithful God and His faithful Word—our minds and hearts are renewed. Begin telling yourself the truth about your complete acceptance in Christ. During those times when you feel rejected by someone significant in your life, know that the Lord has promised to walk with you in the darkness of your painful journey and shed light on your path. Despite the pain of past rejection, He promises…

"I will turn the darkness into light before them

and make the rough places smooth. These are the
things I will do; I will not forsake them"
(ISAIAH 42:16).

Focus on Facts, Not Feelings

The fact you must remember is that you are A-C-C-E-P-T-E-D.

A Admit the rejection of the past and acknowledge its pain.

—Ask God to bring to mind every rejection from your childhood to the present, and then consider the circumstances of each situation.

—Acknowledge the gamut of feelings you experienced with each past event. Release the pain to God.

—Ask God to heal the physical, emotional, and spiritual damage of each of these painful experiences of rejection.

"I remember my affliction and my wandering, the
bitterness and the gall. I well remember them, and my
soul is downcast within me. Yet this I call to mind and
therefore I have hope: Because of the LORD's great love
we are not consumed, for his compassions never fail.
They are new every morning; great is your faithfulness"
(LAMENTATIONS 3:19-23).

C Claim God's acceptance and unconditional love.

—Confess God's love for you and the various ways He has shown you His love (for example, Christ's death for you).

—Cite Psalm 139:1-18 and praise God for orchestrating your conception, forming you in your mother's womb, and planning each day of your life.

—Convey your appreciation to God for His love of you by loving Him with all your heart, soul, mind, and strength. And love others as He loves you.

"'Though the mountains be shaken and the hills
be removed, yet my unfailing love for you will not

> *be shaken nor my covenant of peace be removed,'*
> *says the LORD, who has compassion on you"*
> (ISAIAH 54:10).

C Choose to forgive those who rejected you.

—Consider all the hurt and anger you feel over your painful rejection.

—Count the cost of withholding forgiveness: a bitter spirit building up inside you, which will cause trouble and spread to those around you.

—Commit to forgiving those who rejected you just as Christ forgave those (including you) who rejected Him. Write down their names, their offenses, and the pain these individuals caused you. Then forgive every one of these people by releasing them to God.

> *"Bear with each other and forgive whatever*
> *grievances you may have against one another.*
> *Forgive as the Lord forgave you"*
> (COLOSSIANS 3:13).

E Expect future rejection as part of living in a fallen world.

—Empty yourself of the pride that drives your desire to be accepted by everyone. Realize that it is impossible for you to gain everyone's approval and, at the same time, commit to pleasing God.

—Empathize with others who feel rejected by friends, family, employers, business associates, or anyone else important to them.

—Embrace the truth that, according to the Bible, sharing in the sufferings of Christ is a privilege. As a believer, you *will* experience rejection just as Jesus did. You are not exempt from being rejected. Even today Jesus continues to be rejected daily by those who refuse to turn to Him for salvation.

> *"Dear friends, do not be surprised at the painful trial*
> *you are suffering, as though something strange were*
> *happening to you. But rejoice that you participate in*

> *the sufferings of Christ, so that you may be overjoyed*
> *when his glory is revealed. If you are insulted*
> *because of the name of Christ, you are blessed, for*
> *the Spirit of glory and of God rests on you"*
> (1 PETER 4:12-14).

P Plant Scripture in your mind to produce new thought patterns.

—Purpose to renew your mind by selecting meaningful scriptures to read, meditate on, and commit to memory. These will help you deal with any past, present, or possible future rejection.

—Plan a specific time each day to read God's Word and to pray.

—Partner with someone who will hold you accountable for applying God's truth to your heart.

> *"Do not conform any longer to the pattern of this*
> *world, but be transformed by the renewing of your*
> *mind. Then you will be able to test and approve what*
> *God's will is—his good, pleasing and perfect will"*
> (ROMANS 12:2).

T Thank God for what you've learned through the rejection.

—"Thank You, Lord, for using my pain to make me more dependent on You and on Your Word."

—"Thank You, Lord, for using my pain to make me less dependent on people."

—"Thank You, Lord, for using my pain to make me more like Christ."

> *"It was good for me to be afflicted so*
> *that I might learn your decrees"*
> (PSALM 119:71).

E Encourage others as an expression of Christ's love.

—Extend compassion to those who are hurting as someone who has also been hurt.

—Embrace those in pain and encourage them to talk.

—Enfold them in prayer, faithfully praying for them and with them.

"Encourage one another daily"
(HEBREWS 3:13).

D Draw on the power of Christ's life within you.

—"I will see Christ as my security whenever I feel insecure."

—"I know that I have all I need, for Jesus will meet all my needs."

—"I will daily set aside my selfish desires in favor of God's desires, saying, 'Not my will, but Yours, Lord.'"

"I can do everything through him who gives me strength"
(PHILIPPIANS 4:13).

Question: "Because of past rejection, I often cling to others too much. Is there anything I can do to help refocus my mind when feelings of rejection begin to rule my heart?"

Answer: You *can* overcome the pain of any and all rejection. The key to being an overcomer is to refocus—to move your attention from the rejection to the fact that the Lord loves you, accepts you, and has a plan for you. The way to change your focus is to repeat these truths over and over again. Be at peace because the Lord not only knows your pain, but He also has plans for you on the other side of your pain.

*"I will be glad and rejoice in your love, for you saw
my affliction and knew the anguish of my soul"*
(PSALM 31:7).

When you are tempted to feel defeated, say to the Lord...

• "Thank You, Lord, that You love me."

*"This is how we know what love is: Jesus
Christ laid down his life for us"*
(1 JOHN 3:16).

• "Thank You, Lord, that You are with me."

"The LORD your God is with you, he is mighty to save.

*He will take great delight in you, he will quiet you
with his love, he will rejoice over you with singing"*
(ZEPHANIAH 3:17).

- "Thank You, Lord, that You forgive me."

    *"I acknowledged my sin to you and did not cover up
    my iniquity. I said, 'I will confess my transgressions to
    the LORD'—and you forgave the guilt of my sin"*
    (PSALM 32:5).

- "Thank You, Lord, that You adopted me."

    *"To all who received him, to those who believed in his
    name, he gave the right to become children of God"*
    (JOHN 1:12).

- "Thank You, Lord, that You will complete me."

    *"He who began a good work in you will carry it
    on to completion until the day of Christ Jesus"*
    (PHILIPPIANS 1:6).

- "Thank You, Lord, that You never leave me."

    *"God has said, 'Never will I leave you; never will I
    forsake you.' So we say with confidence, 'The Lord is my
    helper; I will not be afraid. What can man do to me?'"*
    (HEBREWS 13:5-6).

- "Thank You, Lord, that You care for me."

    "Cast all your anxiety on him because he cares for you"
    (1 PETER 5:7).

H. Replace Rejection with Reaching Out

We have all been rejected, and we all long to be accepted. But rather than focusing inwardly on account of our fear of rejection, we need to focus on reaching out to others, regardless of our differences.

Think about it: We respond positively when we find that others are interested in us. When someone genuinely wants to know more about you, doesn't that warm your heart? When others sincerely reach out to us and nurture us, they are gifts from God to help us grow to our full potential.

If you want to reach out to others but don't know where to start, begin with ordinary questions. Your heartfelt interest will build a bridge to further communication. Gradually ease into the questions.

If you want to talk with someone whom you don't know well, you could start by asking simple questions, such as, "Where did you grow up? What was it like living there? What was the most character-building experience of your childhood?" The Bible poetically affirms the value of well-spoken words:

> *"A word aptly spoken is like apples*
> *of gold in settings of silver"*
> (PROVERBS 25:11).

The following questions can help you initiate conversations with others.

Questions about early family life

—Where were you born and raised? How did you feel about where you lived?

—What kind of work did your mom and dad do?

—What kind of relationship did you have with your father? Your mother?

—Did you have brothers and sisters? Were you emotionally close to them? Where are they now? What do they do? Are you involved in each other's lives?

—Was there an activity your family enjoyed together while you were growing up?

—If you could change anything about your childhood, what would it be?

Questions about school

—What about school did you enjoy most?

—What do you remember most about school?

—Did you have a favorite teacher? What made that teacher special?

—What was your favorite subject in school? Least favorite?

—What extracurricular activities did you enjoy?

—What was your most memorable or embarrassing moment in school?

Questions about growing up

—Who was your childhood hero? Why?

—What did you dream of doing when you grew up?

—Did you have a best friend? What sparked your friendship?

—Who in your childhood encouraged you the most?

—What was the most significant event in your childhood?

—What was the most fearful time in your childhood?

—What was your first job?

Questions about life today

—If you could have any job in the world, what would it be?

—What do you enjoy doing most during your free time?

—What would be your ideal vacation?

—What skill or talent do you wish you had?

—What do you like most about your life today?

—If you could change anything about yourself, what would it be?

Questions about spiritual life

—Do you think God has a purpose for your life?

—How would you describe God?

—Did you attend a church growing up? What was it like?

—Did anything significant occur in your spiritual life when you were young?

—What is the most meaningful experience you've had in your spiritual life?

—If you could come into a true relationship with Jesus Christ, would you want to?

—What do you think God would want you to do that you haven't done yet?

As you talk with others, pray that you will be able to ask the right questions at the right time. As you reach out in positive ways, you'll see positive results in your relationships with others.

> *"The purposes of a man's heart are deep waters,*
> *but a man of understanding draws them out"*
> (PROVERBS 20:5).

I. Knowing When to Reach Out

When Wrong Behavior Is Involved

Should I reject someone who is involved in a behavior contrary to God's Word? The Bible distinguishes between believers and nonbelievers and gives instructions as to how Christians should interact with both groups of people.

—Believers are not to engage in the worldly behavior of unbelievers—behavior that runs counter to God's Word—but are to "come out from them and be separate" (2 Corinthians 6:17).

—Believers are not to isolate themselves from nonbelievers, but are to reach out to them just as Jesus reached out to those in sin when He lived on the earth. In fact, He was ridiculed and rebuked by the religious leaders of His day for associating with sinners and tax collectors (Matthew 9:10-12).

—Believers, however, are instructed to temporarily withhold fellowship from other believers who are living flagrantly sinful lifestyles and to pray that this disciplinary act will bring them to repentance (1 Corinthians 5:9-13).

> *"But now I am writing you that you must not associate*
> *with anyone who calls himself a brother but is sexually*
> *immoral or greedy, an idolater or a slanderer, a drunkard*
> *or a swindler. With such a man do not even eat"*
> (1 CORINTHIANS 5:11).

A major reason for using caution when it comes to people involved in wrong behavior is found in 1 Corinthians 15:33:

> *"Do not be misled: 'Bad company corrupts good character.'"*

When Repentance Is Involved

All Christians will sin from time to time, and repent afterward. To reject those who show remorse and demonstrate true repentance is unbiblical, unproductive, and unkind. Instead, we need to seek to build up a struggling believer with *compassion, truth,* and *encouragement.*

COMPASSION

—Reach out with compassion, recognizing that everyone (including you) has sinned in various ways.

—Pray for God to give you a gentle, nonjudgmental heart as you try to restore those who have gone wayward.

> *"If someone is caught in a sin, you who are*
> *spiritual should restore him gently"*
> (GALATIANS 6:1).

TRUTH

—Help bring to surface the lies the repentant person has believed and exchange each lie with the truth.

—Suggest a positive plan with practical action steps that will help the person to break free of the habit.

> *"You will know the truth, and the truth will set you free"*
> (JOHN 8:32).

ENCOURAGEMENT

—Affirm the person's God-given worth as he or she chooses to live in the strength of Christ.

—Praise the person when he or she makes small steps toward Christ-like behavior.

> *"Encourage one another and build each*
> *other up, just as in fact you are doing"*
> (1 THESSALONIANS 5:11).

J. What if I Deserve to Be Rejected?

If we engage in behavior or activities that grieve the heart of God, someone could rightly reject us. If a relationship is forbidden by God (such as adultery), ending that relationship is *the right thing to do*. Any attempt to continue an unbiblical relationship needs to be rejected.

If you are experiencing rejection because you had a relationship that was not right in God's sight, you can still hope for a bright tomorrow despite your despair today. God sees your hurt and feels compassion for you—even if your painful circumstances are a result of your bad choices. Learning from your mistakes and allowing God to change your life is still possible.

God has always been in the business of rescuing us after we have been drowning in destructive behavior...putting us on dry ground and then revealing to us His plan and purpose for our lives.

—*Acknowledge* to God the wrong behavior that led to your being rejected.

> *"If we confess our sins, he is faithful and just and will*
> *forgive us our sins and purify us from all unrighteousness"*
> (1 JOHN 1:9).

—*Ask* God to bring you to the point of seeing your sin as He sees it.

> *"Search me, O God, and know my heart; test me and*
> *know my anxious thoughts. See if there is any offensive*
> *way in me, and lead me in the way everlasting"*
> (PSALM 139:23-24).

—*Agree* with God that your behavior was egregious to Him and deserving of His disapproval and discipline.

> *"For I know my transgressions, and my sin is always*
> *before me. Against you, you only, have I sinned and*
> *done what is evil in your sight, so that you are proved*
> *right when you speak and justified when you judge"*
> (PSALM 51:3-4).

—*Assume* the responsibility of asking forgiveness from the person(s) you have wronged.

> *"If you are offering your gift at the altar and there*
> *remember that your brother has something against you,*

*leave your gift there in front of the altar. First go and be
reconciled to your brother; then come and offer your gift"*
(MATTHEW 5:23-24).

—*Ascertain* what need—love, significance, or security—you were seeking to meet through your wrong behavior.

*"Surely you desire truth in the inner parts; you
teach me wisdom in the inmost place"*
(PSALM 51:6).

—*Align* your thinking with God's thinking by engaging in daily Bible reading, scripture meditation, and scripture memorization.

*"Blessed is the man who does not walk in the counsel
of the wicked or stand in the way of sinners or sit in
the seat of mockers. But his delight is in the law of the
LORD, and on his law he meditates day and night"*
(PSALM 1:1-2).

—*Apply* the truths of God's Word to your life.

*"Show me your ways, O LORD, teach me your paths;
guide me in your truth and teach me, for you are God
my Savior, and my hope is in you all day long"*
(PSALM 25:4-5).

—*Act* out your identity in Christ.

*"I have been crucified with Christ and I no longer live, but
Christ lives in me. The life I live in the body, I live by faith
in the Son of God, who loved me and gave himself for me"*
(GALATIANS 2:20).

—*Associate* with others who are seeking to live lives pleasing to God.

*"He who walks with the wise grows wise,
but a companion of fools suffers harm"*
(PROVERBS 13:20).

K. How Did Jesus Respond to Rejection...
and How Are You to Respond?

Some people present a wrong picture of what it means to become a Christian, saying, "Come to Christ, and all your problems will be solved." Jesus never suggested such! In fact, the Bible makes it crystal clear that we are *called to suffer.*

Clearly, Jesus suffered very real rejection by the religious leaders of His day. But He was also rejected by dear friends and family...yet He was not emotionally devastated, neither was He derailed from His mission. Why? He knew the secret of being an overcomer: He "entrusted himself to him who judges justly" (1 Peter 2:23).

Jesus entrusted His very being into the hands of His heavenly Father, whom He knew would judge justly. When you experience rejection, you too will be an overcomer by following in the footsteps of Jesus.

> *"If you suffer for doing good and you endure it,*
> *this is commendable before God. To this you were*
> *called, because Christ suffered for you, leaving you an*
> *example, that you should follow in his steps...When*
> *they hurled their insults at him, he did not retaliate;*
> *when he suffered, he made no threats. Instead, he*
> *entrusted himself to him who judges justly"*
> (1 Peter 2:20-21,23).

—Jesus knew to expect unjust hatred, and He tells you to expect unjust hatred.

> *"They hated me without reason"*
> (John 15:25).

> *"I have chosen you out of the world.*
> *That is why the world hates you"*
> (John 15:19).

—Jesus knew to expect persecution, and He tells you to expect persecution.

> *"Blessed are those who are persecuted because of*
> *righteousness, for theirs is the kingdom of heaven"*
> (Matthew 5:10).

"If they persecuted me, they will persecute you also"
(JOHN 15:20).

—Jesus had enemies, yet He loved them; and He tells you to love your enemies and do good to them.

"Love your enemies"
(MATTHEW 5:44).

"Love your enemies, do good to them"
(LUKE 6:35).

—Jesus prayed for those who persecuted Him, and He tells you to pray for your persecutors.

*"Father, forgive them, for they do not
know what they are doing"*
(LUKE 23:34).

"Pray for those who persecute you"
(MATTHEW 5:44).

—Jesus modeled forgiveness toward those who sinned against Him, and He tells you to forgive those who sin against you.

"Forgive, and you will be forgiven"
(LUKE 6:37).

*"If you forgive men when they sin against you,
your heavenly Father will also forgive you"*
(MATTHEW 6:14).

—Jesus understood that those rejecting Him were really rejecting His Father, and He tells you that those who reject you are really rejecting Him.

"He who rejects me rejects him who sent me"
(LUKE 10:16).

—Jesus, when rejected, was dependent on His Father for every word He spoke. And He tells you, when you are rejected, to be dependent on the Holy Spirit for every word you speak.

"There is a judge for the one who rejects me and does

not accept my words; that very word which I spoke
will condemn him at the last day. For I did not
speak of my own accord, but the Father who sent me
commanded me what to say and how to say it"
(JOHN 12:48-49).

"Whenever you are arrested and brought to trial,
do not worry beforehand about what to say.
Just say whatever is given you at the time, for it
is not you speaking, but the Holy Spirit"
(MARK 13:11).

—Jesus knew that Herod wanted to kill Him (Luke 13:31), but love—
not fear—was Jesus' focus. And He tells you not to let fear of people
be your focus.

"You who kill the prophets and stone those sent
to you, how often I have longed to gather your
children together, as a hen gathers her chicks
under her wings, but you were not willing!"
(LUKE 13:34).

"Do not be afraid of those who kill the body but
cannot kill the soul. Rather, be afraid of the One
who can destroy both soul and body in hell"
(MATTHEW 10:28).

—Jesus said He would be rejected, but in the end there would be blessing. And He tells you that you will be rejected, but in the end there
will be blessing.

"He then began to teach them that the Son of Man
must suffer many things and be rejected by the elders,
chief priests and teachers of the law, and that he
must be killed and after three days, rise again"
(MARK 8:31).

"Blessed are you when men hate you, when
they exclude you and insult you and reject your
name as evil, because of the Son of Man"
(LUKE 6:22).

—Jesus expected trouble as He submitted to the Father's purpose, yet Jesus was an overcomer! And He tells you to expect trouble, but when trouble comes, if you will submit to the Father's purpose, you'll be an overcomer!

> *"Now my heart is troubled, and what shall I*
> *say? 'Father, save me from this hour'? No, it was*
> *for this very reason I came to this hour"*
> (JOHN 12:27).

> *"In this world you will have trouble. But*
> *take heart! I have overcome the world"*
> (JOHN 16:33).

When your pain seems endless and your heart feels tender to the touch, put yourself into His strong hands. He will hold you securely until there is true healing.

My Prayer of Response to Rejection

Dear Lord Jesus,

When life looks hopeless—
I'll live with Your hope.

When my heart hurts—
I'll not harbor hate.

When I'm rejected—
I'll live with Your peace.

When I'm betrayed—
I'll love with Your love.

Your humble child,

Amen.

Lauren Chapin

Growing up, I knew the kind of family I wish could have been mine. It was Lauren's family.

Lauren's nickname was "Kitten," an endearing term that brings to mind a cute, cuddly ball of fur. She was a delightful part of the family—accepted, wanted, loved.

It seemed so real, but it was all make-believe, in more ways than one. The Andersons were a made-for-TV family on the popular 1950s series *Father Knows Best.* They were the kind of family everyone longed to have. But the warmth and acceptance bestowed week by week upon little Kathy (or Kitten) onscreen were woefully absent in her off-screen life.

In real life, Lauren Chapin's heart was ruptured by rejection. While she had a TV father who "knew best," her real-life father rejected his role as protector and instead sexually abused her from ages three to five, and then again from 14 to 16. Likewise, she felt powerless to withstand an uncle's abuse for five years beginning at the tender age of three.

Lauren's alcoholic mother was verbally and emotionally abusive—not only outwardly, but in other ways, through a lack of time, lack of attention, lack of love. Too busy living the socialite lifestyle and too busy with acting aspirations for her two older sons, she abandoned her four-year-old daughter at a convent not far from home. There, further rejection resided. The nuns wrapped dirty socks around Lauren's hands and tied her wrists to bedposts in an effort to end her thumb-sucking habit.

In the midst of all this rejection, glimmers of hope remained. One day, Lauren received a call that her mother was going to pick her up. She was thrilled! One by one, parents picked up all the others girls waiting to go home for the weekend. Meanwhile, Lauren waited and waited, expecting each car to be her mother's *Maybe that's Mama,* she would think. As day turned to night, a deep sense of rejection returned. Finally, a car pulled up...and in her excitement, Lauren grabbed her little bag and raced toward the door—right through a plate-glass window! The car outside continued on its way—it wasn't her mother after all.

A nun called Lauren's mother, "Mrs. Chapin, your daughter has been badly hurt. She needs to go to the hospital. You must pick her up right away. There is no one here to take her." Yet, Lauren's mother did not come—she *would not* come, for she was too busy. In disgust, the nun slammed the receiver down.

An hour later, a neighbor's teenager drove Lauren to the hospital, where she received 150 stitches and then was taken home. She noticed the street filled with parked cars, her house filled with people, cocktails, and laughter. Bloodied but bandaged, Lauren saw her mother and impulsively ran to her, hugged her, and began sobbing.

Though initially startled, Lauren's mother regained her composure, then dispassionately pushed Lauren away. "Go to your room...go to your room." No comfort, no compassion, no concern. Blinded by tears and whimpering in pain, Lauren wondered, *What have I done to make Mom hate me so?*

Though Lauren's wounds had not yet healed, that following Monday she was sent back to the convent, where the nuns paraded her from room to room, standing her on a chair and announcing, "This is what happens when little girls run through the halls."

On the show *Father Knows Best,* Lauren Chapin played the role of Kathy Anderson. The show was wildly successful for seven years straight. Yet the pain of her personal rejection was so great that at the age of 11 she tried to commit suicide.

When *Father Knows Best* ended, Lauren was 14.

One Monday morning she walked up to the studio lot expecting the guard to let her walk through, but her pass had been revoked. She couldn't enter the lot, and she didn't know why. No one had told her the show had been cancelled.

Why? The teenage son, "Billy," was on marijuana, which defied the family image offered in the show. "Father" Robert

Young was in a deep depression, and college student "Betty" was married and pregnant. The TV network felt that the program was in too precarious a position, so they cancelled it. Lauren felt shocked, stunned, rejected.

Several months later, a judge awarded custody of Lauren to her father, who began molesting her again. At the age of 16 she eloped with a man she barely knew, just to get out of the house.

From there, her life continued to spiral down, down, downward—into drugs, prostitution, forgery, jail time, and even a month in a psychiatric ward. After she was released, she wandered about aimlessly, feeling like "a reject."

Why shouldn't she? Lauren had been repeatedly rejected by her mother. As a child she was told, "You're not beautiful. You're not pretty." She was rejected as a teenager (and as the breadwinner of her family), yet she was sued for the money *she* earned! And she was rejected as a young adult. She was told, "I hope your baby dies—you'll be a terrible mother."

Added to all this was the physical abuse she endured—beatings at home and being locked up in a small closet for hours. She felt so much hopelessness that before her thirtieth birthday, she had already attempted suicide at least ten times. She had experienced almost every kind of abuse imaginable. How could she *not* feel like a reject?

Then one day Lauren learned some truths that changed her life: God loved her (John 3:16), He would never reject her (Deuteronomy 31:8), and He offered to adopt her (John 1:12).

When Lauren came into a life-changing relationship with the Lord Jesus Christ, she experienced a security she had never known before. Few have experienced this reality or could speak these words with more conviction than Lauren: "Though my father and mother forsake me, the LORD will receive me" (Psalm 27:10).

After experiencing the ravages of rejection, Lauren finally found the love and acceptance she had always longed for. And because she was adopted into the family of God, she not only could rest securely in her Savior, but also found that her heavenly Father truly *does* know best.

====== *Rejection—Answers in God's Word* ======

Question: "What will God do when I have fear or become dismayed?"

Answer: "So do not fear, for I am with you; do not be dismayed, for I am your God. I will strengthen you and help you; I will uphold you with my righteous right hand" (Isaiah 41:10).

Question: "How does the Lord respond to those who are brokenhearted and crushed in spirit?"

Answer: "The LORD is close to the brokenhearted and saves those who are crushed in spirit" (Psalm 34:18).

Question: "How can I know that when others reject me, they are actually rejecting Christ?"

Answer: "He who listens to you listens to me; he who rejects you rejects me; but he who rejects me rejects him who sent me" (Luke 10:16).

Question: "I've been forsaken by my father and mother. Is there anyone who will never reject me?"

Answer: "Though my father and mother forsake me, the LORD will receive me" (Psalm 27:10).

Question: "Is there anything that can separate us from the love of God?"

Answer: "Neither death nor life, neither angels nor demons, neither the present nor the future, nor any powers, neither height nor depth, nor anything else in all creation, will be able to separate us from the love of God that is in Christ Jesus our Lord" (Romans 8:38-39).

Question: "Why will the Lord not reject you?"

Answer: "For the sake of his great name the LORD will not reject his people, because the LORD was pleased to make you his own" (1 Samuel 12:22).

Question: "What will never fail on account of the Lord's great love for me?"

Answer: "Because of the LORD's great love we are not consumed, for his compassions never fail" (Lamentations 3:22)

Question: "Why am I called a child of God?"

Answer: "How great is the love the Father has lavished on us, that we should be called children of God! And that is what we are! The reason the world does not know us is that it did not know him" (1 John 3:1).

Question: "How should I respond to God, who has not rejected me or withheld His love from me?"

Answer: "The LORD himself goes before you and will be with you; he will never leave you nor forsake you. Do not be afraid; do not be discouraged" (Deuteronomy 31:8).

Question: "Is there an appropriate Scripture to read when I feel like my whole life was a mistake and I should never have been born?"

Answer: "Praise be to God, who has not rejected my prayer or withheld his love from me!" (Psalm 66:20).

SELF-WORTH

Discovering Your God-given Worth

What happens when you long to receive a gift, but only your sister is given a gift? What happens when you long to be held on your mother's lap, but only your sister is allowed on her lap? What happens when you long for your mother's love, but your sister is the only one given her love?

Ask Dorie Van Stone.[1] Dorie would tell you that repeated rejection is the breeding ground for low self-worth. Her own mother never even wanted her—her mother always called her ugly.

Dorie never received the love and affection her heart so deeply craved. However, what a comfort for Dorie (and for all the Dories in the world, both male and female) to come to know this truth from God's Word:

> *"The LORD does not look at the things man*
> *looks at. Man looks at the outward appearance,*
> *but the LORD looks at the heart"*
> (1 SAMUEL 16:7).

Why should Dorie feel any sense of worth? Even before she and her sister were discarded at an orphanage, life with their mother was filled with rejection. Her mother would leave Dorie in charge of her little sister Maria for hours—a six-year-old girl responsible for the total care of a five-year old!

Each time this happened, Dorie longed desperately for her mother to return, saying to herself, *I hope she'll be glad to see me.* But each time her mother returned, she brushed right past Dorie to gather Marie in her arms, giving her great big hug and sometimes bringing a gift—always showering attention on Marie and never on Dorie. No wonder Dorie was left reeling with low self-worth.[2] As the psalmist said,

> *"Scorn has broken my heart and has left me*
> *helpless; I looked for sympathy, but there was*
> *none, for comforters, but I found none"*
> (PSALM 69:20).

I. DEFINITIONS OF SELF-WORTH

A. What Is Self-worth?

As a child, Dorie didn't have any concept of self-worth. How could she? As a continually rejected child, how could she feel any sense of significance, of value, of worth? Even more basic than that, how do you determine the worth of something or someone? How do you know your own worth?

Do you look to yourself or others in order to grasp your value? If you look anywhere other than to God—the God who created you with a purpose and a plan—your view of your value is in grave danger of being distorted. Before you were born, God established your true worth by creating you, by choosing you, and ultimately, by dying for you!

> *"He chose us in him before the creation of the*
> *world to be holy and blameless in his sight"*
> (EPHESIANS 1:4).

- *Worth* signifies the value, merit, or significance of a person or thing.[3]
- *Self-worth* is the belief that your life has value and significance.[4]
- *Worth,* in the biblical Greek text, is *axios,* which means "of weight and worth."[5] In biblical times, gold and other precious metals were placed on a balancing scale upon which their worth was determined by their weight, leading to the expression, "worth their weight in gold" (Lamentations 4:2).

Question: "How can anyone's worth be determined?"

Answer: At an auction, the worth of an item is determined clearly and simply by one thing—the highest price paid. Each item goes to the highest bidder. You were bought from the auction block of sin over 2,000 years ago when the heavenly Father paid the highest price possible for you—the life of His Son, Jesus Christ. By that one act, your worth was forever established by God.

Jesus Christ paid the ultimate price for you, willingly dying on the cross to pay the penalty for your sins. He loves you that much!

Your true worth is based not on anything *you* have done or will do, but on what *Jesus* has *already done*. Without a doubt, He established your worth—you were worth His life, you were worth dying for.

> *"Greater love has no one than this, that*
> *he lay down his life for his friends"*
>
> (JOHN 15:13).

B. What Is Self-esteem?

In Dorie's younger years, no one person valued her, no one found pleasure in her. And because no one esteemed her, she had no sense of self-esteem. She could easily see which of the other children around her were treated with value and, as a result, felt valuable. Her sister was one of those highly favored ones.[6]

What makes you feel good about yourself? Do you consider your opinions worthy of consideration by others? Do you expect others to respect your boundaries, or do you hold yourself in such low esteem that you do not establish and maintain healthy boundaries—boundaries that line up with God's purpose for your life? The Bible says,

> *"By the grace given me I say to every one of you:*
> *Do not think of yourself more highly than you ought,*
> *but rather think of yourself with sober judgment,*
> *in accordance with the measure of faith God has given you"*
>
> (ROMANS 12:3).

- *To esteem* means "to set a high value on."[7]
- *To esteem,* in biblical Hebrew, is *nabat,* which means "to esteem, to look with favor or regard with pleasure."[8]
- *To have self-esteem* is to respect or to have high regard for yourself.[9]

> *"A good name is more desirable than great riches;*
> *to be esteemed is better than silver or gold"*
>
> (PROVERBS 22:1).

Question: "Why do some people prefer not to focus on self-esteem, but only on self-worth?"

Answer: The phrase *self-esteem* actually has two different meanings that are opposite to each other.

—The first kind of *self-esteem* is an *objective regard of your value,* which the Bible refers to as *humility.* This self-worth is rooted in the recognition of your sin and your need for the Savior. It recognizes your need to live dependently on Him and affirms the fact that Christ established your worth by dying for you.

> *"This is the one I esteem: he who is humble and*
> *contrite in spirit, and trembles at my word"*
> (ISAIAH 66:2).

—The second kind of self-esteem is an *exaggerated regard of your value,* which the Bible refers to as *pride.* This self-esteem is rooted in the idea that you are "good enough" within yourself to meet your own needs and therefore you do not need to live dependently on the Savior. Your worth is established by your "inherent goodness" and personal accomplishments.

> *"Do nothing out of selfish ambition or vain conceit, but*
> *in humility consider others better than yourselves"*
> (PHILIPPIANS 2:3).

In the Bible, God places these two types of self-esteem in sharp contrast to one another:

> *"God opposes the proud but gives grace to the humble"*
> (1 PETER 5:5).

C. What Is an Inferiority Complex?[10]

How could Dorie not feel inferior when, for years, she was continuously treated as inferior? Emblazoned in her memory are scenes of her mother tucking her sister into bed saying, "Marie is a pretty girl—she's not like you." Then after tenderly kissing Marie, her mother would callously walk past Dorie.[11] Repeated instances of rejection are the building blocks of an inferiority complex. Constant rejection can cause a person to feel he or she has little worth, and lead that person to think such thoughts as these:

> *"Because of all my enemies, I am the utter contempt of*
> *my neighbors; I am a dread to my friends—those who see*
> *me on the street flee from me. I am forgotten by them as*
> *though I were dead; I have become like broken pottery"*
> (Psalm 31:11-12).

An *inferiority complex* is a painful, debilitating feeling of being less valuable than others.

— *Inferior* means less valued than others.

— A *complex* is a group of beliefs based on the past that has a powerful influence on present behavior.

An *inferiority complex* is an acute sense of low self-worth, which can produce two very different results:

—*Fearfully timid* attitudes and actions that cause the person to easily cave in to others or feel rejected by others.

"I'm nothing...I know I don't matter."

—*Overly aggressive* attitudes and actions expressed in an attempt to compensate for feeling rejected.

"Since people hate me, I'll give them something to hate!"

When Dorie was placed in an orphanage, she became the bitter bully who punched and pinched the other children just to make them cry. Openly hostile, Dorie used fear tactics to get her way—and get her way she did![12] This psalm describes what she was like:

> *"When my heart was grieved and my spirit embittered, I*
> *was senseless and ignorant; I was a brute beast before you"*
> (Psalm 73:21-22).

Mephibosheth

Mephibosheth felt like the weakest link in the royal chain. Crippled in both feet at a young age, he never felt able to live up to the accomplishments of his family. His grandfather, King Saul, was a fierce warrior. His father, Jonathan, was an accomplished soldier.

But Mephibosheth was unable to stand on his own two feet, let alone to do battle. Following the deaths of both Saul and Jonathan, when David claimed the throne, Mephibosheth sank into financial and emotional quicksand. He lived in the land of Lo-Debar, which means "the House of No Bread." Though his family had ruled the nation and enjoyed substantial wealth, he ended up with nothing. He went from the palace to poverty. Because he could not even afford his own lodging, he lived in another man's home.

King David summoned Mephibosheth to appear before his throne. Mephibosheth was afraid not only because his life offered no "value" to David, but also because the custom of the day was for kings to execute those who might pose as a threat for the throne.

Mephibosheth felt helpless and hopeless. He shuffled on his lame feet, crawling into the new king's house to answer David's summons. He threw himself on the ground before David and declared himself to be nothing more than a "dead dog" (2 Samuel 9:8). David's response shocked the young cripple, who had known little kindness in his life: "Don't be afraid...for I will surely show you kindness for the sake of your father Jonathan. I will restore to you all the land that belonged to your grandfather Saul, and you will always eat at my table" (2 Samuel 9:7).

Imagine Mephibosheth's astonishment! David—the powerful warrior-king—demonstrated compassion to a cripple. But why? Why would he show kindness to a weak invalid who was, in his own words, a dead dog who could offer no service to the king, who was a reminder of his grandfather's murderous vengeance—all directed toward the newly crowned king David? Because long before, David had entered into a covenant relationship with his dear friend Jonathan—a covenant vow of loyalty that extended to the family of Jonathan. And as David promised, "Mephibosheth ate at David's table like one of the king's sons" (2 Samuel 9:11).

Picture David's sons and daughters gathering for an evening meal: the aristocratic, selfish Amnon, the proud...handsome

Absalom…the beautiful sister Tamar…and the scholarly, quiet Solomon. Then shuffling along behind—taking his place among the king's sons and daughters at the finest table in the land—is this "dead dog" Mephibosheth. He may have once felt worthless and utterly without value, but because of the king's grace, he is now a part of the family, and he discovers he has infinite worth.

If you suffer from feelings of inferiority or feeling like an emotional cripple, know that the King of kings, in His grace, has reached out to you with care and compassion to *adopt you into His family* and take you as His own. The Bible says, "In love he predestined us to be adopted as his sons through Jesus Christ, in accordance with his pleasure and will" (Ephesians 1:4-5).

As a member of the family of Christ, you have a place reserved at the King's table…forever. Make no mistake, you are no mistake. Not only are you wanted, but you also have immeasurable worth.

D. What Is the Self-love Controversy?

Given her mother's rejection, Dorie struggled over a lack of self-worth. Some people would say she *should* not have any sense of self-worth because that's prideful. Others would say she *should* have self-worth because it's healthy. Which is right—especially from a Christian standpoint?

Is there a place in the life of a Christian for self-respect, self-worth, and self-love, or does the Bible exhort us to disrespect, devalue, and even hate ourselves? The Bible appears to support both self-love and self-hate, a seeming contradiction that has resulted in some very real controversy. Because the Bible cannot contradict itself, we need discernment to know how to think accurately about ourselves.

> *"The wise in heart are called discerning, and*
> *pleasant words promote instruction"*
> (PROVERBS 16:21).

The Three Views

1. I SHOULD NOT LOVE MYSELF

"It's wrong for me to love my own life. Instead, I should hate myself."

Biblical support:

> *"The man who loves his life will lose it, while the man who*
> *hates his life in this world will keep it for eternal life"*
> (JOHN 12:25).

> *"If anyone comes to me and does not hate his father*
> *and mother, his wife and children, his brothers and*
> *sisters—yes, even his own life—he cannot be my disciple"*
> (LUKE 14:26).

2. I SHOULD LOVE MYSELF

"God tells me in His Word that it is appropriate for me to love myself."

Biblical support:

> *"Love your neighbor as yourself"*
> (LEVITICUS 19:18).

This commandment is found twice in Leviticus, and then repeated in six other books of the Bible...a total of ten times!

—Leviticus 19:18,34   —Romans 13:9

—Matthew 19:19 and 22:39   —Galatians 5:14

—Mark 12:31 and 12:33   —James 2:8

—Luke 10:27

3. I DON'T KNOW WHETHER I SHOULD LOVE MYSELF, BUT I DO KNOW I SHOULD LOVE OTHERS

"I am unsure of what Scripture says about self-love, but I know I should have sacrificial love for others."

Biblical support:

> *"This is how we know what love is: Jesus*
> *Christ laid down his life for us. And we ought*
> *to lay down our lives for our brothers"*
> (1 JOHN 3:16).

Two Major Questions

Question #1: "In Luke 14:26, does Jesus really mean for me to hate my family and myself?"

Answer: To interpret any literary work correctly, a major element of interpretation must be considered: context! That is, we need to look at how "hatred" is used in context of the whole counsel of God's Word.

—Moses wrote, "Do not hate your brother in your heart" (Leviticus 19:17).

—The Ten Commandments state, "Honor your father and your mother" (Exodus 20:12). That does not say you are to hate your father and mother!

—The apostle John said, "Anyone who claims to be in the light but hates his brother is still in darkness" (1 John 2:9).

—Astonishing His hearers, Jesus said, "You have heard that it was said, 'Love your neighbor and hate your enemy.' But I tell you: Love your enemies and pray for those who persecute you" (Matthew 5:43-44).

Conclusion #1: Based on the *whole counsel of God,* we are *not* to carry hatred in our hearts. When Jesus spoke of hating our father, mother, sister, brother—and even our own lives—He was not promoting a lifestyle of personal hatred. Such a message is completely inconsistent with the heart of the Bible and the heart of the Lord.

Jesus instead appealed to His followers to hate anything that stood in the way of their giving their relationship with Him absolute priority. If we want to be true disciples, Jesus must be preeminent—He must occupy the place of highest priority in our lives. We should not let anyone or anything take the place that He alone should have.

The apostle Paul builds a case for this in Colossians chapter 1:

> *"By him all things were created: things in heaven and on earth, visible and invisible, whether thrones or powers or rulers or authorities; all things were created by him and for him. He is before all things, and in him all things hold together. And he is the head of the body, the church; he is the beginning and the firstborn from among the dead, so that in everything he might have the supremacy"*
> (COLOSSIANS 1:16-18).

Question #2: "The Bible says, 'Love your neighbor as yourself.' But am I really supposed to love myself, or is that arrogance and pride?"

Answer: When we hear the word *love,* we usually assume it refers to affectionate love or passionate love, but *agape* is the Greek word used in this passage, and *agape* refers to a commitment to do what is best on behalf of others.[13] If you truly love your neighbor as yourself, you must comprehend the context of this love, as well as understand its roots.

— Jesus presents the two most important commandments: "'Love the Lord your God with all your heart and with all your soul and with all your mind and with all your strength.'...'Love your neighbor as yourself.' There is no commandment greater than these" (Mark 12:30-31).

— The apostle Paul states that love is the fulfillment of the law: "Love does no harm to its neighbor. Therefore love is the fulfillment of the law" (Romans 13:10).

— We are to live with *agape* love, which is based not on feeling, but on commitment: "If you love those who love you, what credit is that to you? Even 'sinners' love those who love them...But love your enemies, do good to them, and lend to them without expecting to get anything back. Then your reward will be great, and you will be sons of the Most High, because he is kind to the ungrateful and wicked" (Luke 6:32,35).

— We are to love what God loves, which means, in part, that we are to value the truth that God loves us: "We love because he first loved us" (1 John 4:19).

Conclusion #2: The Bible says, "God is love" (1 John 4:8). The essence of God is *agape*—a love that always seeks the highest and best on behalf of others. If we are truly godly, then we will value what God values and love what He loves. We should love the fact that God has a purpose for us, that He values us, and that He has given us worth.

— You have *agape* love for yourself when you do what God says is best for you, cooperating with His perfect plan for your life.

— And you have *agape* love for those around you when you seek God's very best for them.

> *"Love the Lord your God with all your heart and*
> *with all your soul and with all your mind.' This*

> *is the first and greatest commandment. And the*
> *second is like it: 'Love your neighbor as yourself'"*
> (MATTHEW 22:37-39).

II. CHARACTERISTICS OF LOW SELF-WORTH[14]

In the throes of threatening circumstances, people react in one of three ways: fight, flight, or freeze. Sometimes that means get even, get going, or get hurt. Dorie chose to get even, to fight. Those who fight can quickly become aggressive victimizers. Because Dorie was beaten and abused, she chose to become defiant—to clench her fists and dominate her peers by intimidation.

Dorie would bully other children into compliance, threatening to "get them in the yard" if they didn't drink her buttermilk for her or let her go to the front of the bathing line. She forced her will on them and terrorized them by pinching or hitting them without provocation. According to her own words, "I was mean, mean, mean!"

Dorie felt no one would ever love her, so she took the offensive and gave people no reason to love her. She cried alone at night and made others cry during the day. No one would get the best of her...no one! Not even the terrible Miss Gabriel, the cruel matron of the orphanage.

Dorie had no one, so she needed no one. That was her philosophy—at least until the day she met Jesus and opened her heart to His life-changing love. He gave her a new heart, which He makes available to anyone who receives Him. The Lord makes this offer to everyone...

> *"I will give you a new heart and put a new*
> *spirit in you; I will remove from you your heart*
> *of stone and give you a heart of flesh"*
> (EZEKIEL 36:26).

A. What Does Low Self-worth Look Like?

Dorie says that when she went to grade school, "Those of us from the orphanage could be easily identified by our shabby clothes and distinctive haircuts." Miss Gabriel would place a bowl on the children's heads and snip off their hair. When they were seen marching to school, they felt the stares of the other children and their parents. Dorie thought, *We're all oddballs and besides, I'm ugly.* It's as though she kept looking through distorted mirrors at herself.[15]

Think about going to a fair and walking through a "fun house" filled with warped mirrors. Everywhere you look, you see distorted images of yourself that make you laugh. One mirror may make your head look like a huge oval egg. Another may make your neck disappear. And yet another may make your arms look like wavy tentacles and your hips look the size of a blimp.

Unfortunately, people like Dorie walk around with distorted mental images of themselves that are as warped as the fun house mirrors. Over time, their view of themselves has become warped by criticism, disapproval, and pain. Thank God He does not look at us from a warped perspective, but through the eyes of purest love. The closer we are to Him, the more we will be able to see ourselves through God's eyes. The Bible says:

> *"Now we see but a poor reflection as in a mirror;*
> *then we shall see face to face. Now I know in part;*
> *then I shall know fully, even as I am fully known"*
> (1 CORINTHIANS 13:12).

Checklist for Low Self-worth

To determine whether you are suffering with low self-worth, place a checkmark (√) by the statements below that are true about you.

Inner Insecurities

- ☐ I am self-critical and have feelings of self-loathing.
- ☐ I am fearful of failure and avoid risk-taking.
- ☐ I am overly affected by the opinions of others and strive to meet their standards.
- ☐ I am undeserving of and yet desperate for the approval of others.
- ☐ I am unhappy with my appearance and achievements.
- ☐ I am negligent of my appearance.
- ☐ I am unable to set appropriate boundaries.
- ☐ I am ashamed of my background and I often struggle with depression.
- ☐ I am controlled by a victim mentality.

☐ I am inferior and incompetent when compared to others.

If you struggle with insecurity, you need to take to heart these words of encouragement from the Bible:

> *"Be strong and courageous. Do not be afraid...*
> *for the LORD your God goes with you;*
> *he will never leave you nor forsake you"*
> (DEUTERONOMY 31:6).

Relational Roadblocks

☐ I am overly critical and distrustful of others.

☐ I am demanding and unforgiving of others.

☐ I am defensive when confronted.

☐ I am argumentative and resistant to authority.

☐ I am undeserving of and unable to accept compliments.

☐ I am afraid to get close to people and establish intimacy.

☐ I am a peace-at-all-costs people pleaser.

☐ I am reluctant to express my true feelings.

☐ I am hesitant to accept responsibility for my wrongs.

☐ I am often afraid to defend myself.

If you struggle with establishing healthy relationships, you need to know that...

> *"fear of man will prove to be a snare, but*
> *whoever trusts in the LORD is kept safe"*
> (PROVERBS 29:25).

B. What Are Substitutes for Healthy Self-worth?

Although Dorie was powerless to prevent the unjustified beatings given at the orphanage, she learned how to get power by overpowering the other children. This gave her the feeling of significance, a sense of self-worth.

"If I can be tough," she reasoned, "I can survive...I bullied the other children. I was never subtle. I pushed and shoved. I hit. If another child wouldn't let me see his toy, I would grab it. The others didn't hit me, but I hit them and felt good about it."[16]

All of this false bravado merely served as a substitute for true self-worth—a quick fix that was not a fix at all.

If you are suffering from a sense of low self-worth, you may be seeking ways to deny, disguise, or diminish your emotional pain. People cope with their woundedness in different ways...and many of these ways do not offer a cure, but rather a counterfeit—an adhesive bandage that only covers up the wound without healing it.

The problem with "self-worth substitutes" is that they do not deal with the cause of the pain—the wrong beliefs that fester in the heart and mind. The only solution to low self-worth is to apply the healing balm of truth to the wound in the soul in order that your mind will be transformed and your life changed. Therefore, beware of worldly substitutes that ultimately do not satisfy.

> *"Do not love the world or anything in the world. If*
> *anyone loves the world, the love of the Father is not*
> *in him. For everything in the world—the cravings*
> *of sinful man, the lust of his eyes and the boasting of*
> *what he has and does—comes not from the Father but*
> *from the world. The world and its desires pass away,*
> *but the man who does the will of God lives forever"*
> (1 JOHN 2:15-17).

Self-worth Substitutes

If you are suffering from feelings of low self-worth, you may be pursuing a substitute to help make up for any emotional deficit you feel. Place a checkmark (√) by the statements below that are true about you.

- ☐ I am impressed with status symbols and often live beyond my income.
- ☐ I am overly competitive and view losing as a reflection of my value and worth.
- ☐ I am seeking approval and am envious of important people.
- ☐ I am constantly striving for recognition.

☐ I am perfectionistic in an attempt to earn approval.

☐ I am addicted to substances, sex, food, or _____.

☐ I am angry and intimidating at times in order to accomplish my goals.

☐ I am financially extravagant in an attempt to impress others.

☐ I am obsessed with having certain possessions.

☐ I am insistent on getting my way.

If you struggle with any of these substitutes, ask yourself this question:

> *"What good is it for a man to gain the*
> *whole world, yet forfeit his soul?"*
> (MARK 8:36).

C. What Sabotages True Spiritual Growth?

At the orphanage where Dorie lived, Miss Gabriel believed that sickness was always a result of sin. Therefore, whenever Dorie became ill, the stern matron would snap, "It's the Lord! He's punishing you. If you weren't so naughty, you wouldn't be sick."[17] A harsh, punishing God was the only kind of heavenly Father Dorie ever heard about. She heard nothing about His love.

Those who have a warped view of themselves often have a warped view of God. When people feel unworthy of love, respect, and approval from others, often they feel even more unworthy of God's love, respect, and approval. Their faulty beliefs lead them to draw faulty conclusions about God. These wrong beliefs about God serve only to sabotage their relationship with God and kill any hope of ever feeling valued or used by God.

> *"There is a way that seems right to a man,*
> *but in the end it leads to death"*
> (PROVERBS 14:12).

Samaritan Woman

"Will you give me a drink?" It's a simple question, yet it stuns the woman holding the water jar by the well. She understands *what* He wants, but doesn't understand *why* He's asking her. A man she doesn't know, and a Jewish man at that, is initiating a conversation with her. Certainly He is familiar with the Mishnah, which states, "Don't talk too much with women." This authoritative rulebook of the day continues, "So long as a man talks too much with a woman, he brings trouble on himself, wastes time better spent on studying Torah, and ends up an heir of Gehenna [hell]."[18]

This woman is accustomed to being ignored. It's the price she pays for simply being a woman.

Now, it has to be obvious to the Jewish stranger that she's one of "them." Jewish opinion concerning Samaritans fluctuated throughout history, but the bigotry and strife between Jews and Samaritans was at times so severe that violence erupted between the two groups.[19] Therefore, the fact this man would dare drink from the cup of a Samaritan…how could this happen!

The Samaritan woman had grown up under the stigma of social and religious prejudice. Because of past intermarriages—the Hebrews with the ungodly Assyrians—the Jews did not treat the Samaritans as equals. Considered "half-breeds," the detestable Samaritans were excluded from Jewish temple worship. They were, at best, considered ignorant,[20] and at worst, "excluded from eternal life."[21]

Furthermore, Samaritans were so loathed that many Jews in Israel would journey far to the east—adding days to their travels—to avoid setting foot inside Samaria. As the adage of the day went, "May I never set eyes on a Samaritan."[22] Imagine how this racial discrimination had been an assault on this woman's sense of self-worth. So why would this Jewish man—easily detectable by His beard, robe and dialect—deliberately travel through Samaria and address a woman deemed racially inferior? That this was happening was simply shocking.

And there is yet another reason a conversation between the two would be considered controversial. Her immoral lifestyle was legendary among the locals—prompting her to fetch water at the noon hour rather than in the morning when the towns-people gathered at the well to gossip and get their water for the day.

Perhaps the Samaritan woman feels a slight sense of relief that at least *He,* this Jewish traveler, wouldn't know about her five husbands—and current lover. (But Jesus does know, and has sought her out to offer her a *new* life—eternal life.)

So she finally responds, "You are a Jew and I am a Samaritan woman. How can you ask me for a drink?"

Jesus answers, "If you knew the gift of God and who it is that asks you for a drink, you would have asked him and he would have given you living water" (John 4:10).

Living water? The woman is confused. Her focus is on the water well just a step away, but Jesus is describing how she can quench her spiritual thirst. He tries again to shift her thinking to the spiritual realm: "Everyone who drinks this water will be thirsty again, but whoever drinks the water I give him will never thirst. Indeed, the water I give him will become in him a spring of water welling up to eternal life" (John 4:13-14).

Although the woman doesn't grasp the greater meaning, she wants what Jesus is offering because, to her, it means no more laborious trips to the well. Then Jesus proceeds with presenting her greatest need—not water, but the way of salvation, through the *Savior.* And He uses an unusual approach to help her see that need.

"Go, call your husband and come back," He says (verse 16). Her secret sins are about to surface! She honestly replies that she has no husband, then Jesus reveals He knows about the five she has already had, as well as her present lover.

All of a sudden, a spiritual awakening begins. The Samaritan woman realizes she's conversing with more than just a common stranger. She identifies Jesus as a prophet, and He identifies Himself as the Messiah. When she gets a taste of living water, she can't wait to share it with others!

Leaving her water jar—and her old life—behind, this changed woman heads back into town and tells everyone she can about her divine encounter, encouraging them to come to the well and "taste" for themselves. They do…and many Samaritans ultimately become believers through the testimony of one woman who had been written off as worthless.

Once shunned and shamed, this Samaritan woman now has a new sense of self-worth—*in her Savior.* Her primary identity is no longer an immoral, detestable Samaritan woman. She is now a child of God, forgiven, and free to live in her new life.

The Jews might have thought she was unworthy of eternal life, but not Jesus. He stepped into Samaritan territory and brought dignity to the despised—to the one, and to the many. Heaven indeed will include even those whom the Jews referred to as half-breeds.

The woman at the well is so powerfully used by God that other Samaritans were compelled to say, "We know that this man really is the Savior of the world" (John 4:42).

Spiritual Sabotages

To determine whether you suffer from a sense of low self-worth and lack confidence in your relationship with God, place a checkmark (√) by the statements below that are true of you.

- ☐ I have difficulty feeling acceptable to God.
- ☐ I have difficulty admitting my guilt to God.
- ☐ I have difficulty forgiving God.
- ☐ I have difficulty trusting God.
- ☐ I have difficulty accepting the forgiveness of God.
- ☐ I have difficulty living in the grace of God.
- ☐ I have difficulty feeling loved by God.
- ☐ I have difficulty feeling wanted by God.

☐ I have difficulty thinking God has designed a special plan for me.

☐ I have difficulty believing the promises of God are for me.

If you are struggling spiritually, wondering about the reality and role of God in your life, you need to know that...

> *"The LORD is close to the brokenhearted and*
> *saves those who are crushed in spirit"*
> (PSALM 34:18).

Question: "How could a loving God allow abuse?"

Answer: God did not create people to be puppets but to be free agents, able to make their own choices. In granting people that freedom, He knew people would choose to sin against Him and against one another. Make no mistakes, God is not the abuser. He hates the evil of abuse and will one day repay those who do evil.

> *"I will punish the world for its evil, the wicked for*
> *their sins. I will put an end to the arrogance of the*
> *haughty and will humble the pride of the ruthless"*
> (ISAIAH 13:11).

III. CAUSES OF LOW SELF-WORTH

There are many reasons people fail to perceive themselves as having value or worth to God, themselves, or others. Generally, negative self-perceptions develop in people when they are treated in ways that cause them to feel they are not valued by significant people in their lives. Unless these perceptions are changed, they will worsen over time.

Negative perceptions that begin in childhood are difficult to replace with positive perceptions in adulthood. The best time for a person to examine and evaluate his or her self-worth is before self-perceptions become strong and solidified.

As in the case of Dorie, the more she was rejected, the more she rejected herself and those around her. Her greatest need was to have someone accept her and value her as a person. This would help heal her emotional wounds and cause her to see her significance. That Someone turned out to be the true Healer of the brokenhearted:

> *"He heals the brokenhearted and binds up their wounds"*
> (PSALM 147:3).

A. What Is the Impact of Rejecting Parents?

When Dorie and her sister were left at the orphanage, her mother promised to visit them. And she did—twice over a span of seven years. At the first visit, Dorie, exuding immense excitement, immediately ran to her, calling out, "Mother! Mother!" In her exhilaration, Dorie had forgotten she was to call her mother Laura, never Mother.[23]

Repeating her past pattern, this rejecting parent pushed Dorie aside only to greet her sister with both a hug and a gift. Such harsh, heartless rejection of Dorie continued all throughout her mother's lifetime.

The roots of rejection are not always easily uncovered, especially when their tentacles reach deep into childhood. Those who are rejected from conception can be affected for the rest of their lives from never feeling loved and accepted, or from never knowing the comfort of a mother's warm, reassuring embrace or the security of a father's strong, protecting arms.

When rejection is all you have known, identifying its origins can feel overwhelming and frightening. But if rejection is to be removed from your life, it must be fearlessly faced and dug up by the roots and replaced with the loving acceptance of the Lord.

> *"This is what the LORD says—he who made*
> *you, who formed you in the womb, and*
> *who will help you: Do not be afraid"*
> (ISAIAH 44:2).

The actions and attitudes of parents toward their children send clear messages to them about their value and worth as human beings. These messages plant themselves deeply in a child's heart and carry lifelong implications.

Addicted Parents	The Message Children Receive
• Chemically dependent parents	• "Their alcohol/drugs are more important than I am."

• Workaholic parents	• "Their work is more important than I am."
• Compulsive-spending parents	• "Their money and things are more important than I am."
• Perfectionist parents	• "Their demand for perfection is more important than I am."

Abusive Parents	**The Message Children Receive**
• Emotionally abusive parents	• "I am a nobody."
• Verbally abusive parents	• "I am deserving of put-downs."
• Physically abusive parents	• "I am meant to be a punching bag."
• Sexually abusive parents	• "I am nothing more than a sex object."

Myth: "I will never overcome my painful past. It's impossible for me to become whole."

Truth: No matter what your past was like or the pain inflicted on you by others, healing and wholeness are possible through Christ.

"With God all things are possible"
(MATTHEW 19:26).

B. How Can Rejection from Others Rule You?

In her book *Dorie: The Girl Nobody Loved,* Dorie wrote about monthly visits to the orphanage by couples who wanted to adopt a child:

> My dread of those "special days" escalated month by month. No doubt I reflected the rejection I felt. My shoulders drooped with the agony of that lineup. I could not look up with smiling anticipation as the cute children did. I detested being inspected by people I knew would never accept me, so I would hide. I would be dragged into the room with a dirty, tear-stained face.[24]

Thankfully, Dorie's story does not end with her not being chosen...for she *was* chosen by Another—by God Himself: "Has not God chosen those who are poor in the eyes of the world to be rich in faith and to inherit the kingdom he promised those who love him?" (James 2:5).

Those who repeatedly experience significant rejection by others receive the message that they deserve rejection. They then internalize that message and begin to reject themselves. This is especially true when rejection comes from those who are in positions of authority and on whom the child depends.

Such children grow up replaying in their minds the messages of rejection they have received until the voices of others become their *own* voices. Children find it virtually impossible to replace the big, booming voices of adults or parents with their own small, inner voices.

Only the loving, accepting voice of God is powerful enough to override and eventually silence voices with messages of rejection, and thus salvage the self-worth of those who experience rejection as children. Only God can bring them to the point of saying,

> *"Though my father and mother forsake
> me, the LORD will receive me"*
> (PSALM 27:10).

Parents and Authority Figures

	The Message Children Receive
Overly critical	"I am unacceptable."
Overly protective	"I am inadequate."
Overly controlling	"I am incompetent."
Overly permissive	"I am not valuable."

Siblings and Peers

Overly critical	"I am inferior."
Discouraging	"I am hopeless."
Pushy	"I am weak."
Overly competitive	"I am inept."

Society

Overly competitive attitudes	"I am insecure."
Materialistic	"I am unimportant."
Academic or physical limitations	"I am insignificant."
Racial or sexual discrimination	"I am rejected."

Have you let negative circumstances shape your thinking and self-perceptions? If so, allow God to search your heart and reveal any perceptions or messages that are inconsistent with His Word. The more you allow God's probing light to illumine the faulty thoughts and perceptions in your heart, the more you will be able to see your God-given worth and walk victoriously according to His Word. Let this be your commitment:

> *"We demolish arguments and every pretension that sets*
> *itself up against the knowledge of God, and we take*
> *captive every thought to make it obedient to Christ"*
> (2 CORINTHIANS 10:5).

Myth: "Because of the way I've been treated, I will never feel competent."

Truth: People fail people, and God never intended for your sense of competence to come from others. As you continue to yield your life to the Lord, your sense of competence will come from Him.

> *"Not that we are competent in ourselves to claim anything*
> *for ourselves, but our competence comes from God"*
> (2 CORINTHIANS 3:5).

C. Why Is Comparing Yourself to Others Costly?

Dorie's life was a perfect setup for comparing herself to others. Her mother constantly compared Dorie to her sister, Marie, resulting in her little sister receiving lavish affection and gifts and Dorie being pointedly ignored. Dorie's mother let Dorie know *she did not measure up.*

Everywhere Dorie turned, Marie was the favored one. Thus Marie was everything Dorie wanted to be. Both had brown eyes, but Marie's were beautiful. Both had dark hair, but Marie's lay in place. Marie's skin was fairer, her face was thinner. Dorie said, "I was looking for a way to be like her, but there was no way."[25]

At the orphanage, in school, and in the various foster homes in which the sisters lived, other children were chosen or received decent treatment while Dorie was rejected and subjected to abuse. Dorie described the couples who came to the orphanage considering which child they would choose—which child they would cherish—as "well-dressed and carefully manicured. We could hear their muffled conversations, 'She's cute, isn't she?' or, 'There's one we might want to talk about.' My heart beat faster. *Try me,* I screamed within, hoping that someone would look at me and want me. But my day never came. I soon got the message—only cute children are chosen."[26] Dorie lost out every

time she was compared to the other children. She was never chosen—*ever.*
How could she *not* compare herself to others under those circumstances?

However, God had a plan for Dorie, and He would work out His purpose, His will for her life. The Bible makes this clear:

> *"In him we were also chosen, having been predestined*
> *according to the plan of him who works out everything*
> *in conformity with the purpose of his will"*
> (EPHESIANS 1:11).

D. How Do We Compare Ourselves to Others?

Has comparing yourself to others become so automatic that you hardly notice you're doing it? People often compare themselves to others in appearance, abilities, affluence, and accomplishments. Read the statements below to see if they have become part of your self-talk.

Appearance

Physical features—"I am not as attractive as _____."
Clothes—"I cannot dress as nicely as _____."
Mannerisms—"I am not as graceful or suave as _____."

Abilities

Physical abilities—"I am not as athletic as _____."
Mental abilities—"I am not as smart as _____."
Social abilities—"I am not as popular as _____."

Affluence

Financial/job status—"I am not as financially secure as _____."
Family status—"I don't have a home as nice as _____."
Social status—"I am not as influential as _____."

Accomplishments

Education—"I don't have as many degrees as _____."
Talent—"I am not as gifted as _____."
Recognition—"I am not as accomplished as _____."

Myth: "I'll never be able to stop comparing myself to others."

Truth: Life is a series of choices, and while you may feel that you cannot change, God would not instruct you to do something without giving you the power to do it. God says if you compare yourself to others, you are not wise.

> *"When they measure themselves by themselves and*
> *compare themselves with themselves, they are not wise"*
> (2 CORINTHIANS 10:12).

E. Why Is Wrong Thinking So Wrong?

Dorie had every reason to develop wrong thinking and form faulty perceptions of herself. From her earliest memories, all she was told was that she didn't do anything right, that everything was her fault, that she wasn't good enough, that no one loved her or found value in her. She was convinced she was ugly. She thought, "I must be the ugliest child that ever walked. I felt so ugly on the inside that I believed I was ugly on the outside...maybe it's my curly hair or my nose!"[27]

In Hans Christian Andersen's fairy tale *The Ugly Duckling*,[28] the main character felt rejected by all the barnyard birds because they didn't like his looks or his awkward waddle. He didn't see the beautiful swan inside him, although the beauty was there all along. Many people are like this young swan, and look only at their outer image to determine their inner worth. If they could see what God sees, what a difference that would make!

Do you go through life fearing what others think? Some people look in the mirror and see only an ugly duckling—a sad little bird with no self-worth. In her early years, Dorie considered herself an ugly duckling—ugly, unadoptable Dorie. Not only was she called ugly, but she also felt ugly because of the repeated rejection she faced.

> *"Man looks at the outward appearance,*
> *but the LORD looks at the heart"*
> (1 SAMUEL 16:7).

A low sense of self-worth can result from how you perceive yourself and how you think others see/perceive you. *Faulty perceptions lead to faulty conclusions.*

Faulty Perception	Faulty Conclusion
Perfectionism	"I didn't do it right—I can't do anything right."

Overgeneralization	"I failed, so I must be a failure."
Overreacting	"I am horrible for having failed."
False guilt	"I am the reason my dad left/died."
Unforgiveness	"I can't forgive myself."
Projection	"My mother didn't love me; therefore, no one will ever love me."
Condemnation	"God could never forgive me."
Unrealistic expectations	"I'll never measure up to what people expect of me."
Fatalism	"No one believes I will ever amount to anything."
Hopelessness	"No one holds out any hope for my life."

Myth: "I will never be able to change the way I see myself or the way I think others see me."

Truth: Your faulty self-perception will automatically change as you fix your thoughts on the truth, and on Jesus.

> *"Therefore, holy brothers, who share in the*
> *heavenly calling, fix your thoughts on Jesus, the*
> *apostle and high priest whom we confess"*
> (Hebrews 3:1).

F. What Is the Root Cause of Low Self-worth?

Although Dorie never had a close friend at school, she tried. But even when she was out of the orphanage and in a foster home, she knew she looked different. One student pointed to her torn dress and jabbed, "Did that come out of the ark?" She forced a smile while the others laughed. Kids can be so cruel! Dorie confided, "How often I wished I could have spent the day in the restroom."[29] She just wanted to hide. Dorie found it difficult to survive the impact of a callous, cruel world without taking on the cynicism and bitterness of the world.

Whatever the contributing factors to your low estimation of your worth, they are held in place by wrong beliefs that you have come to embrace over the years. But a low opinion of yourself can be overcome by replacing your wrong beliefs with right beliefs.

> *"Do not conform any longer to the pattern of this*

> *world, but be transformed by the renewing of your*
> *mind. Then you will be able to test and approve what*
> *God's will is—his good, pleasing and perfect will"*
> (ROMANS 12:2).

Wrong Belief:

"My self-worth is based on how I see myself in comparison to others and how others view me."

Right Belief:

"My self-worth is not based on how I or others see me, but on how God sees me because I was created by Him in His image. Not only did Jesus pay the highest price for me by dying on the cross for my sins, but He also lives in me to fulfill His plan and purpose for me."

> *"We are God's workmanship, created in Christ Jesus to do*
> *good works, which God prepared in advance for us to do"*
> (EPHESIANS 2:10).

IV. STEPS TO SOLUTION

One day at the orphanage, Dorie sat riveted at the back of a room hearing words she had never heard before—words foreign to her heart—from a group of college students. But what Dorie heard couldn't be true. God didn't love her. God *couldn't* love her. *Nobody* loved her!

As the students prepared to leave, one of them turned around and spoke slowly with such sincerity that Dorie was stunned. The student said, "Even if you forget everything we have told you, remember: God loves you."

Though Dorie can't explain it, she *knew* this was true, and she spoke directly to God: "They said You love me. Nobody else does. If You want me, You can have me!" That very instant, an unexpected peace settled over Dorie. She thought, *This must be God.*

At that point, Dorie grabbed hold of that love and held on to God...and He never let her go. Nor will God ever let you go. He says His love is never-ending—for us all.[30]

> *"The LORD appeared to us in the past, saying:*
> *'I have loved you with an everlasting love; I*
> *have drawn you with loving-kindness'"*
> (JEREMIAH 31:3).

A. Key Verse to Memorize

There are some who say we should not think we have value, because doing so is prideful. But Scripture says this:

> *"Look at the birds of the air; they do not sow or reap or store away in barns, and yet your heavenly Father feeds them. Are you not much more valuable than they?"*
> (MATTHEW 6:26).

B. Key Passage to Read and Reread

Your real worth is stated clearly in Psalm 139:

Realize that God knows all about you . . . . verses 1-6

Remember that God is always with you . . . . verses 7-12

Respect the fact that God created you . . . . verses 13-14

Recognize that God uniquely designed you . . . . verses 15-16

Receive God's loving thoughts toward you . . . . verses 17-18

Renounce God's enemies as your enemies . . . . verses 19-22

Respond to God's life-changing work in you . . . . verses 23-24

If you feel as though you have little value, the Word of God has good news for you. The Bible speaks of God's own as being "worth their weight in gold" (Lamentations 4:2). Just think about how much *worth* that is! If gold were selling at $500 per ounce, one pound (16 ounces) of gold would be worth $8,000. A person who weighs 150 pounds would be worth $1.2 million—well over a million dollars.[31]

Interestingly, the Bible presents a Christian's worth as too great to be measured in mere monetary terms. Peter says that your faith alone is "of greater worth than gold" (1 Peter 1:7). Are you beginning to see how much *you,* combined with *your faith,* are worth in the eyes of God? You are indeed precious to God. You have God-given worth!

C. Seven Steps to Self-acceptance[35]

For years Dorie concealed a secret. She thought people would not believe her if she told the sordid truth. After Dorie left the orphanage at age 13, she went into the first of many foster homes in which she suffered merciless verbal and emotional abuse, as well as physical and sexual abuse. She was afraid to report those who violated her body because she was warned she would be killed if she said anything.

At one of the later homes, her rollaway bed was placed in a hallway where strange men passed by her in the night. Dorie's foster mother gave these men permission to perform immoral acts on Dorie, and she was repeatedly forced to participate in their perversions. As a result, she believed she could never be clean and whole again.

Dorie later said, "[God] gave the grace to bear my trials. It was He who chose me to belong to Him; He knew the first day of my life, as well as all the days in between. He knew that some day that dirty little girl would stand before thousands of people and tell them that God is faithful."

Although Dorie van Stone experienced the depths of degradation and disgrace at the hands of those with the hardest of hearts, the Lord raised His choice servant up to bring hope to multitudes around the world.

> *"Though you have made me see troubles, many*
> *and bitter, you will restore my life again; from the*
> *depths of the earth you will again bring me up"*
> (PSALM 71:20).

It *is* possible for you to acquire a positive self-image and to learn to value yourself as God values you. To do that, you need to accept the following seven truths about yourself:

1. *I accept* the truth that I was created in God's image.

> *"God created man in his own image, in the image of*
> *God he created him; male and female he created them"*
> (GENESIS 1:27).

2. *I accept* myself as acceptable to Christ.

> *"Accept one another, then, just as Christ accepted*
> *you, in order to bring praise to God"*
> (ROMANS 15:7).

3. *I accept* what I cannot change about myself.

> *"Who are you, O man, to talk back to God? 'Shall*
> *what is formed say to him who formed it, "Why did*
> *you make me like this?"'" Does not the potter have the*

> *right to make out of the same lump of clay some pottery
> for noble purposes and some for common use?"*
> (ROMANS 9:20-21).

4. *I accept* the fact that I will make mistakes.

> *"Not that I have already obtained all this, or have already
> been made perfect, but I press on to take hold of that for
> which Christ Jesus took hold of me. Brothers, I do not
> consider myself yet to have taken hold of it. But one thing I
> do: Forgetting what is behind and straining toward what
> is ahead, I press on toward the goal to win the prize for
> which God has called me heavenward in Christ Jesus"*
> (PHILIPPIANS 3:12-14).

5. *I accept* criticism and the responsibility for failure.

> *"I acknowledged my sin to you and did not cover up
> my iniquity. I said, 'I will confess my transgressions to
> the LORD'—and you forgave the guilt of my sin"*
> (PSALM 32:5).

6. *I accept* the fact that I will not be liked or loved by everyone.

> *"If the world hates you, keep in mind that it hated me
> first…If they persecuted me, they will persecute you also"*
> (JOHN 15:18,20).

7. *I accept* the unchangeable circumstances in my life.

> *"I have learned to be content whatever the circumstances"*
> (PHILIPPIANS 4:11).

D. How to Get Rid of Your Guilt

Dorie understands the waves of guilt with which countless victims struggle. Victims of childhood sexual abuse typically struggle with guilt even though they are not guilty of the abuse. A reason for the ongoing after-the-fact guilt is that they think or wonder whether they could have taken actions to lessen or stop the abuse. And because everyone experiences guilt from periodic instances of sin (not doing what is right in God's sight, whether in attitude or action), false guilt can get tangled together with true guilt.

Being pounded by prolonged guilt can strike a most damaging blow to your sense of worth, leaving you feeling dejected, discouraged, and demoralized. The problem with guilt is that it wears two faces: one is true, the other is false.

—*False guilt* is the enemy's way to shame you, condemn you, and produce disabling discouragement in you.

—*True guilt* is God's loving way to convict you, correct you, and conform you to the character of Christ.

Godly sorrow over true guilt moves you to repentance, forgiveness, and freedom. *Worldly sorrow*—produced by false guilt—moves you to depression, despair, and death. In order to know how to get rid of your guilt, you must first identify whether it is true or false guilt. Then you can respond accordingly.

> *"Godly sorrow brings repentance that leads to salvation*
> *and leaves no regret, but worldly sorrow brings death"*
> (2 CORINTHIANS 7:10).

—*False guilt* arises when you blame yourself even though you've committed no wrong, or when you continue to blame yourself long after you've confessed the wrong and turned from it.

—*False guilt* is not resolved by confession because it is not based on sin but on false accusations aimed at making you feel unforgiven and unaccepted by God.

> *"The accuser of our brothers, who accuses them before*
> *our God day and night, has been hurled down"*
> (REVELATION 12:10).

—*False guilt* can be resolved by conferring with wise, objective persons— mature Christians—who can help you determine whether the guilt you are feeling is false. If it is false guilt, remind yourself and your adversary, Satan, that (1) you are not guilty, or (2) you were guilty but have been forgiven by God. The Bible gives this assurance:

> *"There is now no condemnation for*
> *those who are in Christ Jesus"*
> (ROMANS 8:1).

—*True guilt* refers to the fact you are at fault.

—*True guilt* requires payment of a penalty so that fellowship with God and others can be restored.

—*True guilt* can be forgiven by God as you admit you have sinned and turn free your sin to Him.

Take a moment to pray:

Heavenly Father,

I confess my sin of (_____) to You,
and I am willing to turn from it.
Thank You for Your forgiveness.
I will rely on the power of Christ
within me to overcome my times of temptation.

Thank You for Your grace and mercy toward me.
In Jesus' name, I pray. Amen.

When you deal with your guilt God's way, you have assurance that the following promise is true for you:

"As far as the east is from the west, so far has
he removed our transgressions from us"
(PSALM 103:12).

E. Do You Need a New Self-image?

The Key to a Changed Life

Dorie wrote, "Let me encourage you to begin with God. Christ is the Wonderful Counselor, who can be trusted."[33] Money, education, possessions, and beauty are all things our society uses to gauge a person's worth. But we make a major mistake when we try to live by this value system. Why? Because it's hopelessly flawed. The world's value system is faulty because it's not the one God designed for us. It's not the one He intended humans to live by when He created us *in His very own image.* If you try to make it according to the world's system, you will never measure up, and you will never have total security. However, you can find complete security by learning to adopt God's value system.

If you trust God, He will begin to transform you from the inside out. Through His power, He will make you more like Him and make you the person you were always intended to be—*His precious child of infinite worth.*

═══════ *The Path to a Changed Life* ═══════

Are you ready to believe what God says about you? Are you willing to let Him change your heart and your life? The transformation begins by having a relationship with Jesus. God has provided you with four truths from His Word that will help you understand how to meet, trust, and intimately know Jesus.

1. GOD'S PURPOSE FOR YOU...IS *SALVATION*

—What was God's motive in sending Christ to earth? To express His love for you by making salvation available to you!

> *"God so loved the world that he gave his one and only Son,*
> *that whoever believes in him shall not perish but have*
> *eternal life. For God did not send his Son into the world to*
> *condemn the world, but to save the world through him"*
> (JOHN 3:16-17).

—What was Jesus' purpose in coming to earth? To forgive your sins, empower you to have victory over sin, and enable you to live a fulfilled life!

> *"I [Jesus] have come that they may have*
> *life and have it to the full"*
> (JOHN 10:10).

2. YOUR PROBLEM...IS *SIN*

—What exactly is sin? Sin is living *independently* of God's standard—knowing what is right, but choosing wrong.

> *"Anyone, then, who knows the good he*
> *ought to do and doesn't do it, sins"*
> (JAMES 4:17).

—What is the major consequence of sin? Spiritual death, spiritual separation from God.

> *"The wages of sin is death, but the gift of God*
> *is eternal life in Christ Jesus our Lord"*
> (ROMANS 6:23).

3. GOD'S PROVISION FOR YOU...IS THE *SAVIOR*

—Can anything remove the penalty for sin? Yes. Jesus died on the cross to personally pay the penalty for your sins.

> *"God demonstrates his own love for us in this:*
> *While we were still sinners, Christ died for us"*
> (ROMANS 5:8).

—What is the solution to being separated from God? Belief in Jesus Christ as the only way to God the Father.

> *"Jesus answered, 'I am the way, and the truth, and the*
> *life. No one comes to the Father except through me'"*
> (JOHN 14:6).

4. YOUR PART...IS *SURRENDER*

—Place your faith in (rely on) Jesus Christ as your personal Lord and Savior and reject your good works as a means of gaining God's approval.

> *"It is by grace you have been saved, through*
> *faith—and this not from yourselves, it is the gift of*
> *God—not by works, so that no one can boast"*
> (EPHESIANS 2:8-9).

—Give Christ control of your life, entrusting yourself to Him.

> *"Jesus said to his disciples, 'If anyone would come after*
> *me, he must deny himself and take up his cross and follow*
> *me. For whoever wants to save his life will lose it, but*
> *whoever loses his life for me will find it. What good will*
> *it be for a man if he gains the whole world, yet forfeits his*
> *soul? Or what can a man give in exchange for his soul?'"*
> (MATTHEW 16:24-26).

The moment you choose to believe in God—entrusting your life to Christ—He gives you His Holy Spirit to live inside you. Then the Holy Spirit enables you to live the fulfilled life God has planned for you. If you want to be fully forgiven by God and become the person He created you to be, you can tell this to Him in a simple, heartfelt prayer like this:

========= *Prayer of Salvation* =========

God,

I want a real relationship with You.
I admit that many times I've chosen
to go my own way instead of Your way.
Please forgive me for my sins.

Jesus, thank You for dying on the cross
to pay the penalty for my sins.
Come into my life to be my Lord and my Savior.
Show me my true value in Your eyes.
Through Your love and Your power,
make me the person You created me to be.

In Your holy name I pray. Amen.

If you sincerely prayed this prayer, you can know that you are forever a member of God's family...forever loved and forever accepted by Him!

"To all who received him, to those who believed in his
name, he gave the right to become children of God"
(JOHN 1:12).

F. Don't Be a Prisoner of Poor Parenting[34]

By the world's standards, Dorie had every right to hate her mother and harbor feelings of bitter unforgiveness. When her mother was charged with child neglect, Dorie had to appear in court. The judge asked her mother if Dorie was her child. After an agonizingly long pause, she answered, "Yes... but I'd have gotten rid of her before she was born if I could have!"

The judge ordered Dorie and her sister permanently taken from their mother, and as they left the courtroom, her mother muttered to Dorie, "If I ever see you again, I'll kill you!" Dorie later said that her mother's rejection was total and final and all hope of changing that was quenched. *Am I that awful?* she asked herself. Walking home alone, Dorie prayed aloud that God would help her to understand why her mother had abandoned her...and she prayed that she wouldn't hate her mother.

Dorie said, "In that moment God let me forgive her...I felt sorry for her. I had no hatred...That day God performed a healing work in my life and prevented a permanent scar." Dorie was able to

> *"get rid of all bitterness, rage and anger, brawling*
> *and slander, along with every form of malice"*
> (EPHESIANS 4:31).

Do you struggle with a sense of low self-worth today because of poor parenting from your past? Are you floundering now because you had faulty authority figures? If so, leave behind those feelings of worthlessness, and experience your worth—the worth you have in the eyes of your heavenly Father. He wants you to...

> admit the past truth,
>> address the present truth,
>>> appropriate God's truth.

> *"Show me your ways, O LORD, teach me your paths;*
> *guide me in your truth and teach me, for you are God*
> *my Savior, and my hope is in you all day long"*
> (PSALM 25:4-5).

═══ *Don't Let the Past Determine Your Present Worth* ═══

Identify the parenting style under which you were raised, then take the three appropriate steps to getting rid of your feelings of worthlessness.

Overly critical parents/authority figures

—*Admit the past truth:* "My parents were impossible to please."

—*Address the present truth:* "My worth is not based on pleasing people."

—*Appropriate God's truth:* "I am fully accepted by God."

> *"God, who knows the heart, showed that he accepted them*
> *by giving the Holy Spirit to them, just as he did to us"*
> (ACTS 15:8).

Overly protective parents/authority figures

—*Admit the past truth:* "I was smothered by my parents."

—*Address the present truth:* "My worth is not based on my ability to protect myself."

—*Appropriate God's truth:* "The Lord is my help in times of trouble."

> *"God is our refuge and strength, an*
> *ever-present help in trouble"*
> (PSALM 46:1).

Overly controlling parents/authority figures

—*Admit the past truth:* "I was not allowed to make my own decisions."

—*Address the present truth:* "My worth is not based on my decision making."

—*Appropriate God's truth:* "The Lord is my guide."

> *"God is our God for ever and ever; he*
> *will be our guide even to the end"*
> (PSALM 48:14).

Overly permissive parents/authority figures

—*Admit the past truth:* "My parents did not set firm boundaries for me."

—*Address the present truth:* "My worth is not based on my ability to set boundaries in my life."

—*Appropriate God's truth:* "The Lord has established my boundaries."

> *"You hem me in—behind and before;*
> *you have laid your hand upon me"*
> (PSALM 139:5).

G. How to Have a Heart of Forgiveness

Forgive? Did God really expect Dorie to forgive all who mercilessly used and abused her, who treated her worse than a rabid animal, who withheld from her all the longings of her heart? Such a thing would be humanly impossible. Why would she even *want* to forgive the evil done to her? How *could* she ever forgive it? And why *should* she forgive it?

People with a sense of low self-worth often struggle to get past the circumstances that were the breeding grounds for their low self-esteem. However, Dorie knew that in order to put the pieces of her broken life back together, it was necessary for her to forgive those who had grievously wronged her. The Bible says,

> *"Bear with each other and forgive whatever*
> *grievances you may have against one another.*
> *Forgive as the Lord forgave you"*
> (COLOSSIANS 3:13).

Because the issue of forgiveness is such a stumbling block to so many people, let's make sure we understand what it is and isn't:

Forgiveness is not...

—circumventing God's justice. God will execute His justice in His time and in His way.

—letting the guilty off the hook. It is moving them from your emotional hook onto God's hook.

—excusing sinful behavior. God says the offense is without excuse.

—stuffing your anger. It is resolving your anger by releasing it to God.

—being a doormat. It is being like Christ, and He is certainly not a doormat!

—forgetting. It is essential to remember in order to forgive.

—a feeling. It is an act of the will.

> *"You need to persevere so that when you have done the*
> *will of God, you will receive what he has promised"*
> (HEBREWS 10:36).

Forgiveness is...

—dismissing a debt owed to you. It is releasing the offender from the obligation to repay you.

—giving up the option of holding on to the offense. It is giving the offense to God.

—possible without reconciliation. It requires the action of only one person.

—extended even if it is never requested or earned. It is in no way dependent on any action by the offender.

—extending mercy. It is not giving the offender what is deserved.

—setting the offender free from you. It is to also set you free from the offender and free from bondage to bitterness.

—changing your thinking about the offender. It is seeing the offender as someone in need of forgiveness, just as you are in need of forgiveness.

> *"The Lord our God is merciful and forgiving,*
> *even though we have rebelled against him"*
> (DANIEL 9:9).

Make a list of the people you need to forgive

—Write down all offenses committed by each person.

—In prayer, one by one, release each offense to God.

—Take each offense off of your emotional hook and put it onto God's hook.

—Then take the offender off of your emotional hook and put that person onto God's hook.

=== *A Prayer of Forgiveness* ===

Lord Jesus,

Thank You for caring about
how much I have been hurt.
You know the pain I have
felt because of (list each offense).
Right now I release all that pain into Your hands.

Thank You, Lord, for dying on the cross
for me and extending Your forgiveness to me.
As an act of my will,
I choose to forgive (name).
Right now, I take (name)
off of my emotional hook,
and I place (name) on Your hook.
I refuse all thoughts of revenge.

I trust that in Your time and Your way,
You will deal with (name)
as You see fit. And Lord,
thank You for giving me
Your power to forgive so that I can be set free.

In Your precious name I pray. Amen.

Question: "How do I sustain a forgiving spirit?"

Answer: Most often, forgiveness is not an instantaneous, onetime event. You may need to repeatedly make a conscious choice to demonstrate forgiveness in your fight against bitterness. This is just part of the process of forgiveness. But your willingness to confront your hurts and face your wounds will be worth the emotional bruises you will likely experience. As you release each recurring thought of revenge for an offense, eventually the thoughts will diminish and disappear altogether.

Through the years, Dorie has been asked one question repeatedly: "Aren't you bitter toward your mother?" And Dorie's consistent reply?

> No. I am not. As a child in the orphanage, and the difficult years that followed, I experienced periods of bitterness, but I chose to forgive my mother even though I knew she would never respond to me. Perhaps the most basic mistake made by those who are bitter is the belief that they cannot forgive because they don't feel like it. Forgiveness is not an emotion. One can choose to forgive whether one feels like it or not. Many of us have had to reject our emotions, saying "No" to our natural inclinations and firmly declare, "I forgive."[35]

Jesus emphasizes the again and again nature of forgiveness when He says,

> *"If he sins against you seven times in a day...forgive him"*
> (LUKE 17:4).

H. Grasp Your God-given Worth

When Dorie went to school, she had no lunch...and no money to buy lunch. So during lunchtime she would tell others, "I'm going for a walk." Dorie later confessed that if she had stayed in the lunchroom, "the sight of food would have been too much."[36] The only clothes she owned were three tattered dresses and her scuffed shoes. To Dorie, the thought that she was valuable was beyond comprehension. But oh, how wrong she was!

If you struggle with a sense of low self-worth, realize just how *worthy* you are and embrace these words as your own, pursuing them as your goal:

> *"As a prisoner for the Lord, then, I urge you to live*
> *a life worthy of the calling you have received"*
> (EPHESIANS 4:1).

You Are Worthy

W Work on eliminating negative attitudes and beliefs.

"I will not hide my feelings or refuse to face them."

"I will not wallow in feelings of self-pity."

"I will not project my feelings onto others and become critical."

> *"Whatever is true, whatever is noble, whatever*
> *is right, whatever is pure, whatever is lovely,*
> *whatever is admirable—if anything is excellent*
> *or praiseworthy—think about such things"*
> (PHILIPPIANS 4:8).

O Obtain a scriptural understanding of the love you are to have for yourself.

"I am not to love myself with conceited love or pride."

"I am to love the truth that God loves me and has a purpose for me."

—*agape* love for myself: seeking God's highest purpose for me

—*agape* love for others: seeking the highest good of another

> *"The entire law is summed up in a single command:*
> *'Love your neighbor as yourself'"*
> (GALATIANS 5:14).

R Refuse to compare yourself with others.

"I will not measure myself by others."

"I will thank God for what He has given me and what He is making of me."

> *"We do not dare to classify or compare ourselves*
> *with some who commend themselves"*
> (2 CORINTHIANS 10:12).

T Thank God for His unconditional love for you.

"I will choose an attitude of thanksgiving even when I do not feel thankful."

"I will spend personal time with God, thanking Him for His unfailing love."

> *"We meditate on your unfailing love"*
> (PSALM 48:9).

H Hope in God's promise to mold you to be like Christ.

"I know that personal growth is a process."

"I know that God is committed to my growth."

> *"For those God foreknew he also predestined to*
> *be conformed to the likeness of his Son"*
> (ROMANS 8:29).

Y Yield your talents and abilities to helping others.

"I will be generous with my God-given gifts."

"I will realize my God-given worth as I focus on others."

> *"Carry each other's burdens, and in this*
> *way you will fulfill the law of Christ"*
> (GALATIANS 6:2).

I. How to Answer Seven Self-defeating Statements[37]

Dorie's image of herself was shaped in part by her father, whom she never met until after she became a young adult. Her time with him was very limited, yet he was still a major influence on her sense of self-worth.

Before they met, Dorie hoped she would finally have the father she had longed for. When she met with him, he seemed to care about her, and for the first time, she felt parental love. Then later, she shared her conviction that the Lord had called her to go as a missionary to New Guinea. Her sense of loss was profound when he scoffed, "If that's what you plan to do, then don't unpack your suitcase. From this moment on, you are not my daughter! I never want to see you again!"

As Dorie traveled back home, she cried out to the Lord, "He was the only person in the world who ever loved me. How could he do this to me?" Dorie's father had not only rejected her one last, painful time, but he had rejected Christ during that visit as well.

Soon, however, Dorie had the presence of mind to remember that God had not left her. She was not alone. She said, "When you have nothing left but God, you realize that God is enough. God has stood beside me when no one else wanted me; He was not going to abandon me now. God would have to heal the emotional pain that throbbed through my body."

From this time onward, Dorie began to allow the Lord to change her image of herself that had been perpetuated by her parents. She could choose to believe what the Lord said about her, not what her parents had said.

Here is how to answer seven self-defeating statements:

If you say, "I just can't do anything right,"

The Lord says, "I'll give you My strength to do what is right."

> *"I can do everything through him who gives me strength"*
> (PHILIPPIANS 4:13).

If you say, "I feel that I'm too weak,"

The Lord says, "My power is perfect when you are weak."

> *"My grace is sufficient for you, for my*
> *power is made perfect in weakness"*
> (2 CORINTHIANS 12:9).

If you say, "I feel I'm not able to measure up,"

The Lord says, "Rely on Me. I am able."

> *"God is able to make all grace abound to you, so*
> *that in all things at all times, having all that you*
> *need, you will abound in every good work"*
> (2 CORINTHIANS 9:8).

If you say, "I don't feel that anyone loves me,"

The Lord says, "I love you."

> *"I have loved you with an everlasting love; I*
> *have drawn you with loving-kindness"*
> (JEREMIAH 31:3).

If you say, "I can't forgive myself,"

The Lord says, "I can forgive you."

> *"I, even I, am he who blots out your transgressions, for*
> *my own sake, and remembers your sins no more"*
> (ISAIAH 43:25).

If you say, "I wish I'd never been born."

The Lord says, "Since before you were born, I've had plans for you."

> *"Before I formed you in the womb I knew you,*
> *before you were born I set you apart"*
> (JEREMIAH 1:5).

If you say, "I feel my future is hopeless,"

The Lord says, "I know the future I have for you."

> *"'I know the plans I have for you,' declares the*
> *LORD, 'plans to prosper you and not to harm*
> *you, plans to give you hope and a future'"*
> (JEREMIAH 29:11).

At times, do you feel inadequate, fearful, and insecure, even when you know you shouldn't? If so, you're not alone. When God first spoke to Moses, Moses was filled with insecurity and fear. At the burning bush, the Lord supernaturally appeared to Moses and instructed him to confront Pharaoh.

In response, Moses argued with God. He felt he was a nobody with no authority, no credentials, and no skills. He felt totally inadequate for the job and was terrified of failing. And on top of all that, he felt he couldn't speak well enough. So he told God to send someone else! But God wouldn't accept Moses' excuses. God said,

> *"Who gave man his mouth? Who makes him*
> *deaf or mute? Who gives him sight or makes him*
> *blind? Is it not I, the LORD? Now go; I will help*
> *you speak and will teach you what to say"*
> (EXODUS 4:11-12).

Take comfort in this: God knows your limitations better than you do, and those limitations cannot impede the work the Lord has laid out for you. Just as God used Moses to lead an entire nation to freedom, God will work in and through you to accomplish His purposes for you.

> *"Being confident of this, that he who began*
> *a good work in you will carry it on to*
> *completion until the day of Christ Jesus"*
> (PHILIPPIANS 1:6).

J. How to Improve Your "Sense of Self"[38]

The rejection Dorie endured as a child was a seemingly impossible obstacle to overcome, at least as most people would view her life. Even though she had overcome much of her childhood pain after she became a Christian, when her father died, some of the pain resurfaced.

When Dorie heard about her father's death, she and her husband drove to Oklahoma for the funeral. She signed the registry as his daughter and was stunned when the funeral director informed her that her father had no children! The director insisted that her presence would upset the family, and she was turned away from the funeral home. Later, Dorie's aunt called to ask that she not attend the funeral because the obituary had stated "no children" and there would be discomfort among the other family members if Dorie appeared. Dorie's father, even in death, had stung Dorie with yet another rejection—and this one delivered a great blow. She said, "My father's death ended all earthly ties with my relatives."[39]

However, Dorie did not lose her new sense of worth because of her father's rejection. She knew the Lord would always love her, have compassion on her, and be faithful to her. That was His promise of hope to her:

> *"I remember my affliction and my wandering, the*
> *bitterness and the gall. I well remember them, and my*
> *soul is downcast within me. Yet this I call to mind and*
> *therefore I have hope. Because of the LORD's great love*
> *we are not consumed, for his compassions never fail"*
> (LAMENTATIONS 3:19-22).

K. Line Up Your Self-image with God's Image of You

Your self-image has been shaped predominantly by the messages you have received and have internalized from others, from your experiences, and from your self-talk. When you were a child, you did not have control of those in authority over you, but that is no longer the case. You are now able to choose those with whom you associate, and you can certainly control your self-talk. Therefore, you can take an active part in changing any distortions you may have in your view of yourself.

Accept Yourself

—Stop striving for perfection or trying to be like someone else.

—Realize that the Lord made you for a purpose, and He designed your personality and gave you the gifts and abilities He wanted you to have in order to accomplish His purpose for you.

> *"Many are the plans in a man's heart, but*
> *it is the LORD's purpose that prevails"*
> (PROVERBS 19:21).

Thank God for Encouraging You

—Acknowledge and praise God for the abilities He has given you and the things He has accomplished through you.

—Engage in biblically based, encouraging self-talk and mute the condemning critics within and around you.

> *"May our Lord Jesus Christ himself and God our*
> *Father, who loved us and by his grace gave us eternal*
> *encouragement and good hope, encourage your hearts*
> *and strengthen you in every good deed and word"*
> (2 THESSALONIANS 2:16-17).

Accept the Compliments of Others

—To discount the positive comments of those who have heartfelt appreciation for you is to discount their opinions and their desire to express their gratitude to you.

—Practice graciously accepting compliments and turning them into praise to God for the affirmation that He is at work in you and producing good fruit through you.

> *"This is to my Father's glory, that you bear much*
> *fruit, showing yourselves to be my disciples"*
> (JOHN 15:8).

Release the Negative Past and Focus on a Positive Future

—Refuse to dwell on the negative things said or done to you in the past and release them to God.

—Embrace the work God is doing in your life now and cooperate with Him by focusing on Him and on His character. Trust in His promise to fulfill His purposes in you.

> *"It is God who works in you to will and to*
> *act according to his good purpose"*
> (PHILIPPIANS 2:13).

Live in God's Forgiveness

—God has extended forgiveness to you for all of your sins (past, present, and future). Confess and repent of anything offensive to God. Do not set yourself up as a higher judge than God by refusing to forgive yourself.

—Lay aside harsh judgment of yourself and accept that you will not be made fully perfect and totally without sin until you stand in the presence of Christ and are fully conformed to His image.

> *"We are children of God, and what we will be has not yet*
> *been made known. But we know that when he appears,*
> *we shall be like him, for we shall see him as he is. Everyone*
> *who has this hope in him purifies himself, just as he is pure"*
> (1 JOHN 3:2-3).

Benefit from Your Mistakes

—Realize that you can learn from your mistakes, as well as from the mistakes of others, and decide to view your mistakes as opportunities to learn needed lessons.

—Ask God what He wants to teach you from your mistakes. Listen to Him and learn from Him. Then move forward with a positive attitude and put into practice the insights you have gained.

"We know that in all things God works for
the good of those who love him, who have
been called according to his purpose"
(ROMANS 8:28).

Form Supportive, Positive Relationships

—Realize that critical people are hurt people who project their feelings of inadequacy onto others in an attempt to ease their own emotional pain.

—Minimize the time you spend with negative, critical people, whether family, friends, or coworkers, and seek out those who encourage and support you both emotionally and spiritually.

"He who walks with the wise grows wise,
but a companion of fools suffers harm"
(PROVERBS 13:20).

Formulate Realistic Goals and Plans

—Elicit the help of others to identify your strengths and weaknesses and the gifts God has given you. Consider also the things you are persuaded God has called you to do.

—Prayerfully set some reasonable, achievable goals that capitalize on your strengths and make a plan for how you will accomplish those goals.

"Do you not know that in a race all the
runners run, but only one gets the prize?
Run in such a way as to get the prize"
(1 CORINTHIANS 9:24).

Identify Your Heart's Desires

—Make a list of the things you have dreamed of doing but have never attempted because of a fear of failure or a lack of self-assurance.

—Share each desire with the Lord and ask Him to confirm to you which ones are from Him. Then lay out the steps you need to take in order to accomplish them.

> *"Delight yourself in the LORD and he will*
> *give you the desires of your heart"*
> (PSALM 37:4).

Plan for Success

—Anticipate any obstacles to accomplishing your goals and desires, and plan strategies for overcoming them.

—Think of yourself achieving each of your goals and doing the things God has put on your heart to do.

> *"May he give you the desire of your heart*
> *and make all your plans succeed"*
> (PSALM 20:4).

Celebrate Each Accomplishment

—Your feelings of self-worth and self-confidence will grow with the acknowledgement of each accomplishment.

—Rejoice with the Lord and other significant people over the things God and you have done together. Affirm and celebrate your success.

> *"There, in the presence of the LORD your God,*
> *you and your families shall eat and shall rejoice*
> *in everything you have put your hand to, because*
> *the LORD your God has blessed you"*
> (DEUTERONOMY 12:7).

L. How to Capture a Vision for Your Ministry

Dorie wrote, "I heard the voice of God—the voice that had whispered to me during those many years of loneliness, sorrow, and heartache; 'Dorie,

your end is going to be so much better than your beginning.'"⁴⁰ And how
true! Not only did Christ accept Dorie just as she was, but He also elevated
her to be His representative, His voice, His ambassador. To her amazement,
Dorie experienced firsthand these precious words from the Psalms:

> *"He raises the poor from the dust and lifts the*
> *needy from the ash heap; he seats them with*
> *princes, with the princes of their people"*
> (PSALM 113:7-8).

Mistreatment is no stranger to any of us. Why then, in the face of mis-
fortune, do some victims see themselves as having little value, while others
live victoriously in light of their true value? What makes the difference? The
victorious Christian learns priceless lessons through mistreatment.

—Allow your mistreatment to be the making of your ministry.

> *"The Father of compassion and the God of all*
> *comfort…comforts us in all our troubles, so that*
> *we can comfort those in any trouble with the*
> *comfort we ourselves have received from God"*
> (2 CORINTHIANS 1:3-4).

—Don't be consumed by the negatives you have received from others.

> *"Forget the former things; do not dwell on the*
> *past. See, I am doing a new thing! Now it springs*
> *up; do you not perceive it? I am making a way*
> *in the desert and streams in the wasteland"*
> (ISAIAH 43:18-19).

—Be consumed with the positives that you have received from God and
   that He leads you to pass on to others.

The blessing comes when you focus not on what you are *getting*, but on
what you are *giving*. Jesus suffered immense mistreatment, yet He was not
burdened with low self-worth. His ministry of compassion models for us
the fact that truly

> *"it is more blessed to give than to receive"*
> (ACTS 20:35).

"God wanted to prove that He can take care of a dirty, unwanted child. He could help me endure the beatings, the sexual abuse, and the rejection from my father as well as from my mother. God wanted to prove a point, and He did. Now I have the privilege of telling thousands of people that God can take 'nobodys' and make them into 'somebodys' for His name's sake." [41]

—DORIE VAN STONE

A Personal Note from June Hunt

Dear friend,

I know what it's like to struggle with feelings of low self-worth. In my heart of hearts, I believed I had little value—especially when compared to others.

My view of myself was based not on just one incident, but on continuous nonaffirming treatment by someone who had a powerful impact in my life.

As I look back on my childhood, I can see how my father's lack of affirmation and affection shaped my "reality"—the view that I had little value. I never sat on my father's lap, never felt special to him, never heard him say, "I love you." In truth, we never just talked. He simply wasn't interested.

At dinnertime my father enforced the old adage "Children are to be seen and not heard." He announced that we four children couldn't speak unless we had something of interest to say to the whole family. Of course he wasn't interested in anything we had to say, so we couldn't speak.

Then one day, after coming home from high school, I thought to myself, *I'm not showing any interest in him. I'm just focusing on myself and how he hurts us. Instead of being bitter, I'm going to be kind, and focus attention on him.*

Dad always arrived home at 5:50 p.m. and expected to

have dinner at 6:00 sharp. That day, when he arrived, I heard him walk into the house and close the door. I was ready; I was primed for my positive greeting. Although Dad had never asked about my day, I was going to break the ice and ask about his day.

Inside the narrow hallway, I approached him with confidence and a sincere smile. "Hi Dad, how was your day?"

He exploded, "Don't ever ask me that question! That's a stupid question! Never ask me that again!"

Blown away, I felt plastered against the wall...like a raw egg thrown full force, with the hurt and the humiliation oozing down the wall.

Even though this demoralizing encounter is "nothing" in light of truly severe traumatic hurts, even now, decades later, I still remember his yelling, his insensitivity, his harshness as though it were yesterday. (And, never again did I ask Dad about his day.)

It's painful to feel like a nonperson...insignificant...invisible. But God saw it all—including the skewed view of myself. How comforting to know that "the LORD is close to the brokenhearted and saves those who are crushed in spirit" (Psalm 34:18).

It helps me to know that the Lord draws close in times of trouble, when my heart is broken, when my spirit is crushed. He sees, and He cares.

Even if I periodically have difficulty *feeling* God's love (because my emotions can get stuck), *I know* He loves me. Even if I sometimes struggle with feeling insignificant, *I know* that I have worth, just as every person on earth does.

A major key to overcoming my struggle with self-worth has been this:

   —*Changing the focus* from my painful experiences with
      my earthly father to experience the perfect love of my
      heavenly Father

> —*Changing the focus* from my insecure family background to the security that I'm in the family of God
>
> —*Changing the focus* from my painful failures to the One who looks beyond my faults and calls me Friend
>
> We don't have to wonder about our self-worth when we see our God-given worth…when we see our God-given value… when we *see ourselves through God's eyes!*

Self-worth—Answers in God's Word

Question: "How can I know that I have value?"

Answer: "Look at the birds of the air; they do not sow or reap or store away in barns, and yet your heavenly Father feeds them. Are you not much more valuable than they?" (Matthew 6:26).

Question: "Do I have to change before God will love me?"

Answer: "But God demonstrates his own love for us in this: While we were still sinners, Christ died for us" (Romans 5:8).

Question: "Why do other people's accomplishments seem to be so much better when compared to mine?"

Answer: "We do not dare to classify or compare ourselves with some who commend themselves. When they measure themselves by themselves and compare themselves with themselves, they are not wise" (2 Corinthians 10:12).

Question: "How could God forgive me for the stupid things I've done?"

Answer: "If we confess our sins, he is faithful and just and will forgive us our sins and purify us from all unrighteousness" (1 John 1:9).

Question: "How can I overcome the feeling that I was not created to do anything good?"

Answer: "We are God's workmanship, created in Christ Jesus to do good works, which God prepared in advance for us to do" (Ephesians 2:10).

Question: "What should I remember when I feel like no one loves me?"

Answer: "How great is the love the Father has lavished on us, that we should be called children of God! And that is what we are! The reason the world does not know us is that it did not know him" (1 John 3:1).

Question: "Could I do something so bad that God would stop loving me?"

Answer: "The LORD appeared to us in the past, saying: 'I have loved you with an everlasting love; I have drawn you with loving-kindness'" (Jeremiah 31:3).

Question: "How do I overcome my feelings of incompetence?"

Answer: "Not that we are competent in ourselves to claim anything for ourselves, but our competence comes from God" (2 Corinthians 3:5).

Question: "If I am in Christ, why do I feel condemned?"

Answer: "Therefore, there is now no condemnation for those who are in Christ Jesus" (Romans 8:1).

Question: "Is there a Scripture truth to claim when I feel like my whole life was a mistake and I should never have been born?"

Answer: "My frame was not hidden from you when I was made in the secret place. When I was woven together in the depths of the earth, your eyes saw my unformed body. All the days ordained for me were written in your book before one of them came to be" (Psalm 139:15-16).

Anger: Facing the Fire Within

1. Ray Burwick, *The Menace Within: Hurt or Anger?* (Birmingham, AL: Ray Burwick, 1985), 18; Gary D. Chapman, *The Other Side of Love: Handling Anger in a Godly Way* (Chicago: Moody, 1999), 17-18.

2. W.E. Vine, Merrill F. Unger, and William White, *Vine's Complete Expository Dictionary of Biblical Words,* electronic ed. (Nashville: Thomas Nelson, 1996).

3. Vine, Unger, and White, *Vine's Complete Expository Dictionary of Biblical Words.*

4. David R. Mace, *Love & Anger in Marriage* (Grand Rapids: Zondervan, 1982), 42-45.

5. Adapted from Joseph P. Fried, "Following Up," *The New York Times,* June 9, 2002, http://query.nytimes.com/gst/fullpage.html?res=9400E3DA133DF93AA35755C0A9649C8B63; Jaxon Van Derbeken, "Fear of vigilantism blamed for convict's gun; Lawyer defends man who set son on fire in 1983," *San Francisco Chronicle,* January 28, 2005, http://www.sfgate.com/cgi-bin/article.cgi?f=/c/a/2005/01/28/BAG08B1T7J1.DTL; "Around the Nation; Father Who Burned Son Gets 13 Years in Prison," *The New York Times,* July 30, 1983, http://query.nytimes.com/gst/fullpage.html?res=9405E5D61039F933A05754C0A965948260&scp=15&sq=Charles+Rothenberg.

6. Gary Jackson Oliver and H. Norman Wright, *When Anger Hits Home* (Chicago: Moody, 1992), 84.

7. Chapman, *The Other Side of Love,* 19-22.

8. James Mahoney, *Dealing with Anger* (Dallas: Rapha, n.d.), audiocassette; H. Norman Wright, *Anger* (Waco, TX: Word, 1980), audiocassette.

9. Adapted from Mike Barber, "Crotchety Harry Truman remains an icon of the eruption," *Seattle Post-Intelligencer Reporter,* May 11, 2000, http://seattlepi.nwsource.com/mountsthelens/hary11.shtml; Donna duBeth, "Give 'em hell, Harry," *The Daily News,* March 26, 1980, http://www.tdn.com/helens/flash/mainpage.php?p=1113365891&w=D.

10. Christine Ammer, *The American Heritage Book of Idioms* (New York: Houghton Mifflin, 1997), 316.

11. Donna duBeth, "Give 'em hell, Harry," *The Daily News,* March 26, 1980, http://www.tdn.com/helens/flash/mainpage.php?p=1113365891&w=D.

12. For information on the Mt. St. Helen's eruption see, "Mt. St. Helen's Eruption, 1980," http://www.geology.sdsu.edu/how_volcanoes_work/Sthelens.html.

13. For this section see Les Carter, *Getting the Best of Your Anger* (Dallas: Rapha, n.d.), audiocassette; Wright, *Anger.*

14. For this section see Burwick, *The Menace Within,* 33-50.

15. Wright, *Anger.*

16. For this section see Wright, *Anger.*

17. For the three God-given inner needs, see Lawrence J. Crabb, Jr., *Understanding People: Deep Longings for Relationship* (Grand Rapids: Zondervan, 1987), 15-16; Robert S. McGee, *The Search for Significance,* 2d ed. (Houston, TX: Rapha, 1990), 27-30.

18. For this section see Oliver and Wright, *When Anger Hits Home,* 97.

19. For this section see: Wright, *Anger.*

20. McGee, *The Search for Significance,* 27; Crabb, *Understanding People,* 15-16.

21. For this section see: Wright, *Anger.*

22. McGee, *The Search for Significance,* 27; Crabb, *Understanding People,* 15-16.

23. For this section see: Wright, *Anger.*

24. Chapman, *The Other Side of Love,* 21; Russell Kelfer, *Tough Choices: Secrets to Bringing Self Under Control from the Book of Proverbs* (San Antonio, TX: Into His Likeness, 1991), 59-73.

25. See also Ronald T. Potter-Efron, *Angry All the Time: An Emergency Guide to Anger Control,* 2d ed. (Oakland, CA: New Harbinger, 2005).

26. For this section see David Powlison, "Anger Part 2: Three Lies About Anger and the Transforming Truth," *The Journal of Biblical Counseling* 14, no. 2 (Winter 1996): 18-21.

27. For this section see Kelfer, *Tough Choices,* 65-73; Oliver and Wright, *When Anger Hits Home,* 97.

28. For this section see S. Anthony Baron, *Violence in the Workplace: A Prevention and Management Guide for Business,* 2d ed. (n.p.: Pathfinder, 2001).

29. Oliver and Wright, *When Anger Hits Home,* 75-87.

Depression: Walking from Darkness into the Dawn

1. Merriam-Webster, *Merriam-Webster Online Dictionary* (Springfield, MA: Merriam-Webster, 2005), Merriam-webster.com, s.v. "Depression."

2. *Merriam-Webster Online Dictionary,* s.v. "Depression."

3. James Strong, *Strong's Greek Lexicon,* electronic ed. Online Bible Millennium Ed. V. 1.13 (Timnathserah Inc., July 6, 2002), s.v. "Bareo."

4. American Psychiatric Association, *Diagnostic and Statistical Manual of Mental Disorders,* 4th ed. (Washington, DC: American Psychiatric Association, 2000), 345.

5. For this section, see H. Norman Wright, *Beating the Blues: Overcoming Depression and Stress* (Ventura, CA: Regal, 1988), 9.

6. *Merriam-Webster Online Dictionary,* s.v. "Melancholia."

7. *Merriam-Webster Online Dictionary,* s.v. "Psychology."

8. See Stephen A. Grunlan and Daniel H. Lambrides, *Healing Relationships: A Christian's Manual for Lay Counseling* (Camp Hill, PA: Christian Publications, 1984), 121.

9. See *DSM-IV TR,* 679-83.

10. See *DSM-IV TR,* 679-83.

11. See *DSM-IV TR,* 349-56.

12. See *DSM-IV TR,* 374-75.

13. See *DSM-IV TR,* 345.

14. For this section, see *DSM-IV TR,* 345-82.

15. For this section, see *DSM-IV TR,* 382-401.

16. For this section, see *DSM-IV TR,* 403-05.

17. *Merriam-Webster Online Dictionary,* s.v. "Etiology."

18. *DSM-IV TR,* 401-05.

19. University of Alberta, "Depression Often Untreated In Parkinson's Disease Patients," *Science-Daily,* July 12, 2007, http://www.sciencedaily.com/releases/2007/07/070709181334.htm.

20. For this section, see *DSM-IV TR,* 405-09.

21. For information on Vincent van Gogh see Cliff Edwards, *Van Gogh and God: A Creative Spiritual Quest* (Chicago: Loyola University Press, 1989), 1, 7, 12, 15, 35-36.

22. Edwards, *Van Gogh and God,* 15.

23. For quotations in this paragraph see Edwards, *Van Gogh and God,* 1.

24. Vincent Van Gogh Gallery, "Van Gogh Quotes," http://www.vangoghgallery.com/misc/quotes.html.

25. Vincent Van Gogh Gallery, "Letter from Vincent van Gogh to Theo van Gogh 005," http://www.vangoghgallery.com/letters/005.html.

26. Dietrich Blumer, "The Illness of Vincent van Gogh," *The American Journal of Psychiatry,* vol. 159, 519-526.

27. Blumer, "The Illness of Vincent van Gogh."

28. Julius Meier-Graefe, *Vincent Van Gogh: A Biography,* trans. John Holroyd-Reece (New York: Courier Dover, 1987), 145.

29. For this section see Frank Minirth, *In Pursuit of Happiness* (Grand Rapids: Fleming H. Revell, 2004), 25-26.

30. For this section, see Minirth, *In Pursuit of Happiness,* 25-26.

31. For characteristics of mania and depression see Melissa Spearing and Mary Lynn Hendrix, *Bipolar Disorder,* rev. and updated ed., eds. Clarissa K. Wittenberg, Margaret Strock, and Lisa D. Alberts (National Institute of Mental Health 2001), http://www.nimh.nih.gov/publicat/bipolar.cfm; David E. Larson, ed., *Mayo Clinic Family Health Book,* 2d ed. (New York: William Morrow and Company, 1996), 1125-26.

32. Robert S. McGee, *The Search for Significance,* 2d ed. (Houston, TX: Rapha, 1990), 27; Lawrence J. Crabb, *Understanding People* (Grand Rapids: Zondervan, 1987), 15-16.

33. CNN, "Texas mother charged with killing her 5 children," June 21, 2001. http://archives.cnn.com/2001/US/06/20/children.killed/index.html.

34. For information on postpartum depression see Archibald D. Hart, "The Psychopathology of Postpartum Disorders," *Christian Counseling Today* 10, no. 4 (2002): 16-17.

35. *DSM-IV TR,* 422.

36. For this section, see Archibald Hart and Catherine Hart Weber, *Unveiling Depression in Women* (Grand Rapids: Revell, 2002), 49-65.

37. See Michael Lyles, *Women and Depression,* Extraordinary Women, EW 301, videocassette (Forest, VA: American Association of Christian Counselors, n.d.).

38. Christy Oglesby, "Postpartum Depression: More than 'Baby Blues,'" CNN.com, June 27, 2001, http://www.cnn.com/2001/HEALTH/parenting/06/26/postpartum.depression/index.html; *DSVM-IV TR,* 422-23; Hart and Hart Weber, *Unveiling Depression in Women,* 126.

39. For this section see *DSVM-IV TR,* 422-23; Michael R. Lyles, "Psychiatric Aspects of Postpartum Mood Disorders," *Christian Counseling Today* 10, no. 4 (2002): 19.

40. For this section see Hart and Hart Weber, *Unveiling Depression in Women,* 55.

41. For this section see Bill Kurtis, *The Andrea Yates Story,* videocassette (A&E Television Networks, 2003).

42. Minirth, *In Pursuit of Happiness,* 27.

43. Minirth, *In Pursuit of Happiness,* 43-45.

44. Minirth, *In Pursuit of Happiness,* 189-90.
45. *Merriam-Webster Online Dictionary,* s.v. "Repression."
46. Timothy Roche, "Andrea Yates: More to the Story," *Time,* March 18, 2002, http://www.time .com/time/nation/article/0,8599,218445,00.html.
47. Roche, "Andrea Yates: More to the Story," *Time.*
48. W.E. Vine, *Vine's Complete Expository Dictionary of Biblical Words,* electronic ed. (Nashville: Thomas Nelson, 1996), s.v. "Kyrios."
49. Minirth, *In Pursuit of Happiness,* 208.
50. See also W. Ian Thomas, *The Mystery of Godliness* (Grand Rapids: Zondervan, 1964), 54-69.
51. On the three God-given inner needs, see Lawrence J. Crabb, Jr., *Understanding People: Deep Longings for Relationship* (Grand Rapids: Zondervan, 1987), 15-16; Robert S. McGee, *The Search for Significance,* 2d ed. (Houston, TX: Rapha, 1990), 27-30.
52. A.J. Richardson, "The Importance of Omega-3 fatty acids for behavior, cognition, and mood," *Scandinavian Journal of Nutrition,* vol. 47, no. 2 (Lund, Sweden: Taylor and Francis Health Sciences, 2003), 93.
53. Alan C. Logan, "Neurobehavioral aspects of omega-3 fatty acids: possible mechanisms and therapeutic value in major depressions," *Alternative Medicine Review,* November, 2003, http://findarticles.com/p/articles/mi_m0FDN/is_4_8/ai_111303983.
54. Richardson, "The Importance of Omega-3."
55. For this section see Hart and Hart Weber, *Unveiling Depression in Women,* 180-81; SAD Association, "Symptoms," http://www.sada.org.uk/symptoms.htm.
56. Minirth, *In Pursuit of Happiness,* 163.
57. Charles H. Spurgeon, *Lectures to My Students* (Grand Rapids, MI: Zondervan, 1980), 158-64 (emphasis added).
58. Roy W. Fairchild, *Dictionary of Pastoral Care and Counseling,* eds. Rodney J. Hunter, et al. (Nashville: Abingdon, 1990), s.v. "Sadness and Depression."
59. Joshua Wolf Shenk, *Lincoln's Melancholy* (New York: Houghton Mifflin, 2005), 19.
60. Shenk, *Lincoln's Melancholy,* 62.
61. Shenk, *Lincoln's Melancholy,* 93.
62. *The Collected Works of Abraham Lincoln,* volume 7, ed. Roy P. Basler, "Reply to Loyal Colored People of Baltimore upon Presentation of a Bible," September 7, 1864 (New Brunswick, NJ: Rutgers University Press, 1953), 542.
63. Shenk, *Lincoln's Melancholy,* 193.
64. Shenk, *Lincoln's Melancholy,* 193.
65. Shenk, *Lincoln's Melancholy,* 193.
66. Shenk, *Lincoln's Melancholy,* 200.
67. Shenk, *Lincoln's Melancholy,* 209.
68. Shenk, *Lincoln's Melancholy,* 208.

Fear: Moving from Panic to Peace

1. Judges 6:3-4.
2. *American Heritage Electronic Dictionary* (Houghton Mifflin, 1992), s.v. "Fear."
3. W.E. Vine, Merrill F. Unger, William White, *Vine's Expository Dictionary of Biblical Words,* (Nashville: Thomas Nelson, 1985), s.v. "Fear."
4. Judges 6:14.

5. Judges 6:16.

6. See Exodus 33:20.

7. Lawrence O. Richards, *The Bible Reader's Companion* (Wheaton, IL: Victor Books, 1991), 72.

8. Mary Lynn Hendrix, *Understanding Panic Disorders* (US Department of Health and Human Service, National Institutes of Health), 2.

9. Mary Lynn Hendrix, *Understanding Panic Disorders*, 2-3.

10. *New Oxford Dictionary of English,* electronic ed. (Oxford University Press, 1998).

11. Vine, Unger, White, *Vine's Expository Dictionary of Biblical Words,* s.v. "Fear."

12. Vine, Unger, White, *Vine's Expository Dictionary of Biblical Words,* s.v. "Fear."

13. Oaklawn Toward Health and Wholeness, *What Everyone Should Know About Anxiety Disorders* (South Deerfield, MA: Channing L. Bete, Co., 1994), 2-3.

14. Kevin R. Kracke, "Phobic Disorders," *Baker Encyclopedia of Psychology & Counseling,* 2d ed., eds. David G. Benner and Peter C. Hill (Grand Rapids: Baker, 1999), 871-72.

15. For this section, see Kracke, "Phobic Disorders." Kracke renames the simple phobia as specific phobia.

16. Adapted from Florence Littauer, *Lives on the Mend* (Waco, TX: Word Books, 1985), 46-51.

17. Littauer, *Lives on the Mend,* 47-48.

18. Littauer, *Lives on the Mend,* 48.

19. Littauer, *Lives on the Mend,* 48.

20. Littauer, *Lives on the Mend,* 50.

21. For examples of abnormal fear see American Psychiatric Association, *Diagnostic and Statistical Manual of Mental Disorders,* 4th ed. (Washington, DC: American Psychiatric Association, 2000), 432.

22. Phobia Center of the Southwest, "Agoraphobia," 1990.

23. Judges 7:12.

24. Judges 8:10.

25. Deuteronomy 20:1-4,8.

26. See Karen Randau, *Conquering Fear* (Dallas: Rapha, 1991), 41-56.

27. See Randau, *Conquering Fear,* 41-56.

28. Deuteronomy 6:13.

29. Judges 8:10.

30. Judges 6:36-40.

31. Judges 6:14.

32. See Leslie Parrott, III, "Systematic Desensitization," *Baker Encyclopedia of Psychology & Counseling,* 2d ed., eds. David G. Benner and Peter C. Hill (Grand Rapids: Baker, 1999), 1193.

33. Shirley Babior and Carol Goldman, *Overcoming Panic Attacks: Strategies to Free Yourself from the Anxiety Trap* (Minneapolis, MN: CompCare, 1990), 59-62.

Grief Recovery: Living at Peace with Loss

1. For this section, see John A. Larson, "Grief," *Baker Encyclopedia of Psychology & Counseling,* 2d ed., eds. David G. Benner and Peter C. Hill (Grand Rapids: Baker, 1999), 519.

2. See James Strong, *Strong's Exhaustive Concordance of the Bible* (Nashville: Abingdon, 1986), 45.

3. Strong, *Strong's Exhaustive Concordance of the Bible,* 7.

4. For further information see Gary R. Collins, *Christian Counseling: A Comprehensive Guide,* rev. ed. (Dallas: Word, 1988), 352-53; H. Norman Wright, *Crisis Counseling: What to Do*

and Say During the First 72 Hours, updated and expanded ed. (Ventura, CA: Regal, 1993), 154-56; H. Norman Wright, *Recovering from the Losses of Life* (Tarrytown, NY: Fleming H. Revell, 1991), 53-61.

5. For further information, see Collins, *Christian Counseling,* 352–53; Wright, *Crisis Counseling,* 154-56; Wright, *Recovering from the Losses of Life,* 53-61.

6. For further activities, see Charlotte A. Greeson, Mary Hollingsworth, and Michael Washburn, *The Grief Adjustment Guide: A Pathway Through Pain,* Faire & Hale Planner (Sisters, OR: Questar, 1990), 200-02.

7. For further information, see Wright, *Crisis Counseling,* 158-59.

8. Wright, *Crisis Counseling,* 159-61.

9. Greeson, Hollingsworth, and Washburn, *The Grief Adjustment Guide,* 73; Wright, *Crisis Counseling,* 165.

10. See Collins, *Christian Counseling,* 352-53; Wright, *Crisis Counseling,* 154-56; Wright, *Recovering from the Losses of Life,* 53-61.

11. See Haddon W. Robinson, *Grief: Comfort for Those Who Grieve and Those Who Want to Help* (Grand Rapids: Discovery House, 1996), 11-16.

12. On the three God-given inner needs, see Lawrence J. Crabb, Jr., *Understanding People: Deep Longings for Relationship* (Grand Rapids: Zondervan, 1987), 15-16; Robert S. McGee, *The Search for Significance,* 2d ed. (Houston, TX: Rapha, 1990), 27-30.

13. Adapted from Glen W. Davidson, *Understanding Mourning: A Guide for Those Who Grieve* (Minneapolis: Augsburg Publishing House, 1984), 15-19.

14. For the benefits of suffering, see Joel A. Freeman, *God Is Not Fair* (San Bernardino, CA: Here's Life, 1987), 130-34.

15. See Wright, *Crisis Counseling,* 159.

16. For this section, see Davidson, *Understanding Mourning,* 24.

17. For this section, see Davidson, *Understanding Mourning,* 24-27.

18. See Wright, *Recovering from the Losses of Life,* 91-110.

19. For further information, see Wright, *Recovering from the Losses of Life,* 179-204.

Rejection: Healing a Wounded Heart

1. Adapted from *Merriam-Webster Collegiate Dictionary,* s.v. "Reject."

2. James Strong, *Strong's Greek Lexicon,* electronic ed., Online Bible Millennium Ed. v. 1.13 (Timnathserah Inc., 2002).

3. Adapted from *Merriam-Webster Collegiate Dictionary,* s.v. "Rejection," http://www.m-w.com (2001).

4. Strong, *Strong's Greek Lexicon.*

5. Adapted from *Merriam-Webster Collegiate Dictionary,* s.v. "Reject."

6. James Strong, *Strong's Hebrew Lexicon,* electronic ed., Online Bible Millennium Ed. v. 1.13 (Timnathserah Inc., 2002).

7. Adapted from *Merriam-Webster Collegiate Dictionary,* s.v. "Accept."

8. Strong, *Strong's Greek Lexicon.*

9. For this section, see Robert S. McGee, *The Search for Significance: Book and Workbook,* rev. ed. (Houston, TX: Rapha, 1987), 219-20.

10. For this section see McGee, *The Search for Significance,* 54-60.

11. McGee, *The Search for Significance,* 54-55.

12. For this section, see Charles Solomon, *The Ins and Out of Rejection* (Littleton, CO: Heritage House, 1976), 42-47.

13. For this section, see Solomon, *The Ins and Out of Rejection*, 47-54.

14. Solomon, *The Ins and Out of Rejection*, 13-18.

15. Solomon, *The Ins and Out of Rejection*, 18-25, 40-42; Charles Solomon, *The Rejection Syndrome* (Wheaton, IL: Tyndale House, 1982), 29-52.

16. Adapted from Jeff VanVonderen, *Tired of Trying to Measure Up* (Minneapolis: Bethany House, 1989), 75.

17. On the three God-given inner needs, see Lawrence J. Crabb, Jr., *Understanding People: Deep Longings for Relationship* (Grand Rapids: Zondervan, 1987), 15-16; Robert S. McGee, *The Search for Significance*, 2d ed. (Houston, TX: Rapha, 1990), 27-30.

18. This chart adapted from McGee, *The Search for Significance*, 135.

19. This chart adapted from McGee, *The Search for Significance*, 136.

20. For this section see Marshall Bryant Hodge, *Your Fear of Love* (Garden City, NY: Doubleday, 1967), 26.

21. For this section, see McGee, *The Search for Significance*, 137-53.

Self-worth: Discovering Your God-given Worth

1. Doris Van Stone with Erwin Lutzer, *Dorie: The Girl Nobody Loved* (Chicago: Moody Press, 1979).

2. Van Stone and Lutzer, *Dorie*, 11-15.

3. *Merriam-Webster Online Dictionary;* http://www.m-w.com, s.v. "Worth."

4. See Naji Abi-Hashem, "Self-Esteem," in *Baker Encyclopedia of Psychology & Counseling*, 2d ed., eds. David G. Benner and Peter C. Hill (Grand Rapids: Baker, 1999), 1085.

5. W.E. Vine, Merrill F. Unger, and William White, *Vine's Expository Dictionary of Biblical Words* (Nashville: Thomas Nelson, 1985), s.v. "Worth."

6. Van Stone and Lutzer, *Dorie*, 28-29.

7. *Merriam-Webster Online Dictionary*, s.v. "Esteem."

8. James Strong, *Strong's Hebrew Lexicon*, electronic ed. Online Bible Millennium Edition v. 1.13 (Timnathserah Inc., July 6, 2002).

9. *Merriam-Webster Online Dictionary*, s.v. "Self-Esteem."

10. For this section see *Merriam-Webster Online Dictionary*, s.v. "Complex, Inferior, Inferiority Complex."

11. Van Stone and Lutzer, *Dorie*, 13.

12. Van Stone and Lutzer, *Dorie*, 19-20.

13. See Spiros Zodhiates, *The Complete Word Study Dictionary: New Testament*, electronic ed. (Chattanooga, TN: AMG Publishers, 2000), s.v. "Agape."

14. For quotations and biographical information in this section see Van Stone and Lutzer, *Dorie*, 17-26.

15. Van Stone and Lutzer, *Dorie*, 23.

16. Van Stone and Lutzer, *Dorie*, 20.

17. Van Stone and Lutzer, *Dorie*, 21.

18. *The Mishnah: A New Translation*, trans. Jacob Neusner (New Haven, CT: Yale University Press, 1988), Abot 1.5.

19. See Flavius Josephus, *The Works of Josephus, The Wars of the Jews,* trans. William Whiston (Peabody, MA: Hendrickson Publishers, 1987), 2.12.3.

20. Alfred Edersheim, *The Life and Times of Jesus the Messiah,* vol. 1 (Bellingham, WA: Logos Research Systems, Inc., 2003), 400.

21. Merrill Unger, *Unger's Bible Dictionary* (Chicago: Moody Press, 1974), 960.

22. Alfred Edersheim, *The Life and Times of Jesus the Messiah,* 401.

23. Van Stone and Lutzer, *Dorie,* 27.

24. Van Stone and Lutzer, *Dorie,* 29.

25. Van Stone and Lutzer, *Dorie,* 29.

26. Van Stone and Lutzer, *Dorie,* 27-30.

27. Van Stone and Lutzer, *Dorie,* 29.

28. See Hans Christian Andersen, *The Ugly Duckling,* adapted by Jerry Pinkney (New York: William Morrow, 1999).

29. Van Stone and Lutzer, *Dorie,* 44.

30. For quotations and biographical information in this section see Van Stone and Lutzer, *Dorie,* 30.

31. One pound equals .454 kilograms. One hundred and fifty pounds equals 68.1 kilograms.

32. For quotations and biographical information in this section see Doris Van Stone and Edwin W. Lutzer, *No Place to Cry: The Hurt and Healing of Sexual Abuse* (Chicago, Moody Press, 1990), 27-28.

33. Doris Van Stone, *Dorie: The Girl Nobody Loved,* VHS (Chattanooga, TN: Precept Ministries, 1990).

34. For quotations and biographical information in this section see Van Stone and Lutzer, *Dorie,* 48.

35. Van Stone and Lutzer, *Dorie,* 147-48.

36. Van Stone and Lutzer, *Dorie,* 44.

37. For quotations and biographical information in this section see Van Stone and Lutzer, *Dorie,* 79.

38. *Creating Self-Esteem and Self-Confidence,* VHS Educational Video Network, ISBN 1-58950-403-8.

39. Van Stone and Lutzer, *Dorie,* 91-93.

40. Van Stone, *Dorie,* VHS.

41. Van Stone and Lutzer, *No Place to Cry,* 119.

About the Author

June Hunt is an author, singer, speaker, and founder of Hope for the Heart, a worldwide biblical counseling ministry featuring the award-winning radio broadcast by the same name heard daily across America. In addition, *Hope in the Night* is June's live two-hour call-in counseling program that helps people untie their tangled problems with biblical hope and practical help. Hope for the Heart radio broadcasts currently air in 25 countries.

Early family pain was the catalyst that shaped June's compassionate heart. Later, as youth director for more than 600 teenagers, she became aware of the need for sound biblical counseling. Her work with young people and their parents led June to a life commitment of *providing God's truth for today's problems.*

After years of teaching and research, June began developing scripturally based counseling tools called *Biblical Counseling Keys,* which address definitions, characteristics, causes, and solutions for 100 topics (such as marriage and parenting, anger and abuse, guilt and grief). Recently these individual topics were compiled to create the landmark *Biblical Counseling Library,* from which this handbook was extracted.

The *Counseling Keys* have become the foundation for the Hope for the Heart Biblical Counseling Institute initiated by The Criswell College. Each monthly conference in the Dallas-based institute provides training to help spiritual leaders, counselors, and other caring Christians meet the very real needs of others.

June has served as a guest professor at colleges and seminaries, both nationally and internationally, teaching on topics such as crisis counseling, child abuse, wife abuse, homosexuality, forgiveness, singleness, and self-worth. Her works are currently available in more than 20 languages, including Russian, Romanian, Ukrainian, Spanish, Portuguese, German, Mandarin, Korean, Japanese, and Arabic.

She is the author of *How to Forgive…When You Don't Feel Like It, Seeing Yourself Through God's Eyes, Bonding with Your Teen Through Boundaries, Caring for a Loved One with Cancer,* and more than 30 topical HopeBooks. June is also a contributor to the *Soul Care Bible* and the *Women's Devotional Bible.*

As an accomplished musician, June has been a guest on numerous national television and radio programs, including the NBC *Today* show. She has toured overseas with the USO and been a guest soloist at Billy Graham crusades. Five recordings—*Songs of Surrender, Hymns of Hope, The Whisper of My Heart, The Shelter Under His Wings,* and *The Hope of Christmas*—all reflect her heart of hope.

Learn more about June and Hope for the Heart at…

Hope for the Heart, Inc.
P.O. Box 7
Dallas, TX 75221

1-800-488-HOPE (4673)
www.hopefortheheart.org

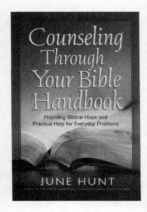

COUNSELING THROUGH YOUR BIBLE HANDBOOK

No matter what the problem, God doesn't leave us without hope or help. The Bible is richly relevant when it comes to the difficult dilemmas we all face. Here you will find 50 chapters of spiritual wisdom and compassionate counsel on even the hardest issues, such as...

- anger & adultery
- alcohol & drug abuse
- codependency & cults
- depression & divorce
- fear & phobias
- guilt & grief
- rejection & rape
- self-worth & suicide

The guidance in this handbook is grounded in Scripture which—when used properly—has the power to pull us out of life's ditches and put us on the road to inner freedom and fulfillment.

HOW TO FORGIVE... WHEN YOU DON'T FEEL LIKE IT

When someone hurts us, our natural response is to strike back. Rather than forgive, we want to return the pain and suffering. Rather than let go, we cling to our rocks of resentment, our boulders of bitterness. The result? We struggle under the weight of our grievances—all because we find it too hard to forgive.

Though we know God has called us to forgive, we find ourselves asking hard questions:

- What if it hurts too much to forgive?
- What if the other person isn't sorry?
- How can I let someone off the hook for doing something *so wrong*?

Biblical counselor June Hunt has been there herself, enabling her to speak from experience as she offers biblical help and hope with heartfelt compassion. If you've been pinned down under a landslide of pain, here's how to find true freedom through forgiveness.